"Written two thousand years ago, the Bible is actually ... ... source for the challenges of college students today. Who do I want amongst my peers and community? For which things and values do I want to stand? Do faith and intellect have to be in competition? . . . Dale Goldsmith's book is a primer on how to keep Jesus Christ front and center in our college years— and beyond."

—**Alison Boden**, Dean of the Chapel, Princeton University

"Goldsmith has written a fresh and engaging devotional guide for college students. He provides 365 lessons drawn from Colossians, Matthew, 1 Corinthians, and 1 Peter. These daily devotions walk through each New Testament book and connect them to students' life experiences. Along the way, Goldsmith gives guidance for reading the Bible. *Look, I Am With You* is a unique resource. If you are a college student or have one in your life, I highly recommend it!

—**Jeannine K. Brown**, Bethel Seminary, San Diego

"Goldsmith brings college students a useful and distinct devotional resource that invites them into the biblical narrative to equip them to examine many of the challenges that college presents [people] of faith. They gain help and encouragement to reflect on how they are following the living Lord and Teacher, as they develop their personal faith story. This is a beneficial tool in a time of considerable opposition and many alternatives to faith in Jesus Christ."

—**Scott Stewart**, Editor, The Quiet Hour

"Born from a lifetime of being a Christian in the University, these meditations are a gift that professors and students will cherish."

—**Stanley Hauerwas**, Gilbert T. Rowe Professor Emeritus of Divinity and Law, Duke University

"Without question, there is a dearth of thoughtful books about this period in a young adult's life we call the 'college years.' Once again, Dale Goldsmith seeks to fill that gap with his newest offering. In *I Am With You* you'll find sound biblical exegesis and time-honored wisdom infused into Goldsmith's delightful prose about how to navigate those often bewildering years. Delving deeply into four New Testament books, he rightly secures his place as one of the most significant theological voices writing to, rather than about, college students. I couldn't recommend a book more to college ministers (and their students) who are looking for a resource that applies biblical wisdom to the everyday life of young adults during their college careers."

—**Jason Brian Santos**, Coordinator for Youth, College and Young Adult Ministries (Presbyterian Church U.S.A.) and author of *A Community Called Taizé: A Story of Prayer, Worship, and Reconciliation*

LOOK–I AM WITH YOU

LOOK–I AM WITH YOU

DAILY DEVOTIONS FOR THE COLLEGE YEAR

An academic year of devotional readings based on
Colossians – Matthew – 1 Corinthians – 1 Peter
(In NRSV translation)

Dale Goldsmith

CASCADE *Books* • Eugene, Oregon

LOOK—I AM WITH YOU
Daily Devotions for the College Year

Cascade Books
An Imprint of Wipf and Stock Publishers
199 W. 8th Ave., Suite 3
Eugene, OR 97401

www.wipfandstock.com

ISBN 13: 978-1-4982-1973-0

Cataloguing-in-Publication Data:

Goldsmith, Dale.

    Look—I am with you : daily devotions for the college year / Dale Goldsmith.

    xvi + 270 p. ; 23 cm.

    ISBN 13: 978-1-4982-1973-0

    1. Devotional exercises. 2. Prayers. 3. College students. I. Title.

BV260 G56 2015

Manufactured in the U.S.A.   09/15/2015

Dedicated to those students
who want to follow

Jesus Christ

as Lord and Teacher in
their college experience.

So Jesus asked the twelve, "Do you also wish to go away?"
Simon Peter answered him, "Lord, to whom can we go?
You have the words of eternal life." John 6:67-68

And remember, I am with you always, to the end of the age.
Matthew 28:20b

CONTENTS

PREFACE

You are a Christian in college. College—public or private, state-supported or even church-related—can be a thoroughly secular, worldly place. That means that your Christian faith plays little role in most of what goes on at your school. It will mean that your college experience will present you with a lot of challenges to that faith. Some are challenges you would face anywhere—back at home, in the workplace, in the military. Others are unique to the college experience.

Some might think that their faith can take a vacation while they are in school. Christians know that the opposite is the case. In fact, considering what goes on in college, your faith needs more fuel in college than perhaps in any other environment. Why? Because you are constantly being confronted with new ideas, new facts, new theories to explain the new facts, new criticisms of all the theories. And new experiences. And new people. This is a busy time for your brain. And your thinking is connected closely to your faith and both are connected to how you live.

All of this comes at you pretty fast; and on a daily basis. And the new authorities—like teachers, books, and even roommates—are a constant presence. Which among all those authorities that clamor for your ear are you going to follow? Or will your primary authority figure be the Lord Jesus Christ? Will your primary authority source be Scripture?

As a Christian you expect to listen to Jesus and follow him in discipleship. Disciples need regular practice to develop their discipleship. Like an athlete or musician, you need regular practice that is rigorous, focuses on fundamentals, and constantly seeks improvement. Christian discipleship doesn't impose one strict pattern on everyone. Each one will nurture the unique gifts God has given—including what you are gaining from your college experience. So this is not the time to take a vacation from the Christian faith and wait to pick it up again . . . later.

Later? "Later" is when your intense exposure to all of the new college experiences will slow down. "Later" is when you will have already met that person with whom you hope to spend the rest of your life. "Later" is when you will have already picked a life's work and gotten prepared for it. "Later" happens after some of the biggest decisions of your life are already made. Can you afford to wait until "later" when some of your most decisive thinking is happening now?

So college is intense and will be challenging. The best resource for you as a Christian is Jesus Christ and you come closest to him through Scripture. But how does that work to help you in college? You probably don't envision yourself starting at the beginning of Genesis and reading until you find a passage that speaks to you about your roommate, time management, how old the universe is, or what to do on a date. But Scripture was written by and for Christians who were being challenged where they were, trying to live their faith in what was a relatively hostile external environment (the Roman Empire) and often a chaotic internal environment (disagreement among Christians about what the new faith meant).

While it is true that the New Testament writers did not attend college as you know it, they certainly did know a lot about the kinds of problems that occur on the college campus: intellectual challenges to the faith, conflict, pride, failure, questions of fairness and justice, getting along with others, sex, alcohol. What if you wanted to interact directly with those writers and could learn how they dealt with similar problems? What if some of those New Testament authors could be quizzed about their understanding of college-type problems and were asked for solutions to some of those issues? The results could be useful in terms of both analysis (of the college experience) and support (for you while you are experiencing it).

Each meditation in this book invites you to a conversation with the first-century Christian who authored the portion of Scripture printed at the top of each page. You have your story (who you are, what you are doing in college, where you are heading) and the biblical writers have their own faith story that informs what they write in their letters. Why were these four biblical texts used as the basis for the following meditations chosen and who is the Jesus you will encounter in each of them?

Colossians is a letter of St. Paul the Apostle to a church of Christians in what is today central Turkey. Those folks were honestly seeking to live their lives based on, and in accord with, Jesus Christ, and they wanted to make sure they had all their bases covered. The Paul-Colossian dialogue provides a positive, Christian understanding for someone with a vocation to be a theologically focused college student. It introduces a Jesus who is cosmic in creativity yet who still will make sense of things for you on a personal level.

The Gospel According to Matthew offers the complete picture of this Jesus who is so grandly described in Colossians. And it is the one of the four Gospels that particularly offers a Christology—a title or nickname or summary explaining some particularly important aspect of Jesus—that is most appropriate for your situation: Jesus the *Teacher.* Perfect!

Then First Corinthians. Things were not always sweetness and light in the early church. At Corinth they were particularly messy: conflicts, schisms, misbehavior, selfishness, pride, sexual deviance, overindulgence. (Almost begins to sound like life on some college campuses, doesn't it?) When Christians began to invent the church a lot of things needed attention. This letter can function for you as a kind of first-century preview of the academic life. But in this letter St. Paul offers a concrete and powerful focus to generate appropriate faithful responses to the various errors embraced by the Corinthians: the crucified Christ.

Finally, First Peter readjusts its readers' self-identity: they are "exiles"; and First Peter points out that Jesus provided both the model and the strength for you to follow in Jesus' "footsteps" as you finish your tenure as a student in the college experience and prepare to set out on the new phase of your vocation as a faithful Christian, seeking to be obedient and to find justice in following Christ who himself was an "exile."

May your story be strengthened by engagement with the stories and struggles these early texts offer. May your story be one that you write faithfully, nourished by those who have gone before and by the community of those to whom you are vitally connected through Christ in his body, the church. You've got messages; let's see what they're about.

Dale Goldsmith

Amarillo, Texas
August 1, 2015

Acknowledgements

EVERY BOOK HAS A story behind it. The story for this volume began long ago when, as an undergraduate far from my home church, regular (or at least intermittent) Bible study became a fruitful source of stability in the swirling chaos of an unexpectedly challenging college experience. As my time in college extended into a career as teacher and academic dean in college settings, the conviction grew that Scripture could be a source for making sense out of the American college experience—especially for helping individuals grow in faith, sort the "wheat from the chaff," and make sense out of the always new and often bewildering complexity of "going to college."

I am convinced that Scripture brings us as close to Jesus, the Lord and Teacher, as we are likely to get in this lifetime. My hope is that judicious, prayerful, and diligent openness to the Scripture and the meditations in this book will prove useful to students in navigating the sometimes-rough waters of academia.

Finally, no one has been a better teacher and practitioner of Scripture than my wife Katy, whose own engagement and application of Scripture began on the campuses where she studied and taught. There is no one to whom I owe more.

Tips for Getting the Most
from These Devotions

Devotional readings, or meditations on Scripture, need no special guidance; just jump in and start reading. But a few comments might be helpful.

First: Notice that each of the four biblical texts or "books" tells its own "story" of something that was important to the founding, the character, and the future viability of the earliest Christian church. So reading the devotions in order and noticing the underlying narrative framework will enhance the conversation that you have with the biblical authors.

Second: Remember that you are an important member of that grand community of Christians that stretches across time from Jesus up through today. Bring your personal story to the text's story—its portion of the great story of God's salvation history—and let the two stories meet, interact, conflict, merge, connect. The biblical text may seem unsettling at times, even impenetrable, and occasionally hard to apply to your situation. That's okay. Maybe the next reading will be just what you need. And maybe the one that didn't work for you today will be meaningful tomorrow. You don't have to "get it" every day. The meditation offered on the biblical text is certainly not the only way to reflect on this piece of Scripture. Be ready to follow your own insights.

Third: When reference is made to another biblical "book," that source is referred to in abbreviated form (example: Matt 1:5); when reference is to another verse in the same "book," only chapter and verse are used (example: 3:16).

Colossians

Academically Inclined Christians

THE FIRST READERS OF Colossians grappled with the nature of Christian faith in a setting where knowledge was a premier hallmark of religious life. These were folks who wanted to understand everything from science to philosophy. The letter deals with questions of an intensely personal nature as well as questions of cosmic proportions. The bonus is that both questions tie together in Jesus Christ.

The Colossians lived in a town—no longer extant—in what today is Turkey, and they had experienced the devastation of mass destruction by earthquake in 60–61 CE just prior to the writing and their reading of this letter. They had also experienced cultural and religious changes and the breakdown of old religious certainties. Perhaps in part to address the uncertainties of the times, they were experiencing a rise in the popularity of various religious cults and were even flirting with the possibilities of making up their religion as they went along. They were people trying to be religious and seriously thoughtful, piecing together a personally tailored mosaic of religious faith to address life's questions. Paul addresses the Colossians as fellow believers with whom he is eager to discuss issues of serious importance. His purpose was to encourage them to see that Jesus Christ could be at the center of their lives, hold things together for them, and make sense out of life.

1 – Warmest Greetings

Colossians 1:1–2 — (1) Paul, an apostle of Christ Jesus by the will of God, and Timothy our brother, (2) to the saints and faithful brothers and sisters in Christ in Colossae: Grace to you and peace from God our Father.

THIS IS SACRED SCRIPTURE. It is also a letter from one of the first Christians to several communities of new Christians. It is a positive letter, encouraging and uplifting, despite the fact that the author (Paul) has never seen these folks and that he is probably in jail for his activities as a missionary. Paul knows about these Colossians through Epaphras (1:7), and what he knows is positive. So the letter is a kind of conversation, picking up on what he knows and expanding on it.

In the years and centuries since this letter was written, sent, read, and then circulated to other nearby congregations, Christian churches have found it to be useful. That is why we begin this series of devotional readings with it. It is a letter that closely relates to the kind of situation you are experiencing in college, some 1,900-plus years later. Hopefully, you will feel welcome to participate in the conversation about the importance of Jesus Christ in the lives of people like you—people interested in learning about the world and in growing in the Christian faith.

Please listen to the description of what was going on in Colossae and to Paul's comments and suggestions. Listen to see if and how any of that might apply to you in your situation these many years later and many miles removed. Feel free to ask your own questions of the letter's text.

Remember that the Colossians were living their story, Paul was applying the gospel (the story of Jesus Christ), and that you are writing your own story as a college student and Christian. These written devotional paragraphs are merely "helps" that try to keep "on the same page" and point to relevant challenges in today's college experience that needs to be considered.

All of those sisters and brothers who have gone before you in the faith welcome you to the conversation.

Prayer: Thank you, Lord, for living, dying, and rising to embrace me among the saints. Amen.

2 – Thankful For Hope

Colossians 1:3–8 — (3) In our prayers for you we always thank God, the Father of our Lord Jesus Christ, (4) for we have heard of your faith in Christ Jesus and of the love that you have for all the saints, (5) because of the hope laid up for you in heaven. You have heard of this hope before in the word of the truth, the gospel (6) that has come to you. Just as it is bearing fruit and growing in the whole world, so it has been bearing fruit among yourselves from the day you heard it and truly comprehended the grace of God. (7) This you learned from Epaphras, our beloved fellow servant. He is a faithful minister of Christ on your behalf, (8) and he has made known to us your love in the Spirit.

GRIPE, GRIPE, GRIPE; GRUMBLE, complain, whine, criticize; carp, nitpick, moan and groan. Complaining is a common way to "communicate" since there is always something we can agree to complain about: the weather, politicians, the referee's latest decision, the food, the professor, the class schedule, the course requirements. And there is usually a sympathetic listener who will add his own verse to the lament. But isn't complaining usually an activity of the uninformed person? The complainer views the world from her own point of view and seldom truly understands the whole picture. College might be of some help at this point—offering perspectives from which to realize that life is complicated and that there may be good reasons why things are as they are.

Instead of complaining about whatever might be a problem in Colossae, Paul begins with thanksgiving. He takes his time to write to people he didn't know, in a place he had never visited, yet he is thankful. Here he is probably in jail, yet he is thankful. Why he is thankful? The Colossians have the three Christian virtues: faith, love and hope. He is especially thankful for their hope. Things might seem bad but there is a hope that is secure; it is a hope that does not depend upon humans; a hope that is established and guaranteed by God; a hope upon which faith is based and from which you can live out your life in love for others. Hope provides the grounding for your faith (ideas) and your love (actions). One author describes hope as "the adequacy of the power of Christ to overcome all other powers." You have that hope; and it's a sure thing—"laid up for you in heaven."

Prayer: Help me to be thankful—perhaps even for some of those things I gripe about. Amen.

3 – Filled with Knowledge

Colossians 1:9–12 — (9) For this reason, since the day we heard it, we have not ceased praying for you and asking that you may be filled with the knowledge of God's will in all spiritual wisdom and understanding, (10) so that you may lead lives worthy of the Lord, fully pleasing to him, as you bear fruit in every good work and as you grow in the knowledge of God. (11) May you be made strong with all the strength that comes from his glorious power, and may you be prepared to endure everything with patience, while joyfully (12) giving thanks to the Father, who has enabled you to share in the inheritance of the saints in the light.

TODAY'S COLLEGES GREW OUT of the church's long and patient efforts to provide education. So here you are, inheriting that gift. Can Paul's wish that the Colossians "endure everything with patience" be a reality for you as you move through your college career?

And don't skip that part where Paul tells these folks he hasn't met that he is praying that they be "filled with the knowledge of God's will." That can happen in college as a kind of value-added bonus as you study everything else—because everything you study will, at the same time, be about God's creation.

The fact that you have been admitted to college shows that the college is confident that you can complete the assignments, acquire the required knowledge, and get your degree. You will be expected to proceed step by step through your program, learning more and more. Then, at commencement, the speaker might even say, "This is only a beginning, a commencement, and you will go on learning the rest of your life." The real student never knows enough and never quits learning.

It is Paul's hope (and prayer) that his readers will grow in "knowledge of God's will." He prays that this increase in knowledge occurs with spiritual wisdom and understanding—"knowledge" being information; "wisdom," the practical application of that knowledge in your daily life; "understanding," a deep and sensitive comprehension that goes beyond mere information. The college setting is a great one for working seriously at the business of growing in "knowledge of God's will." The strength for all of this comes to you as God's gift. There is always a next step—more to know, more to love, more to learn. You won't need to ask what will be on the test. You will be ready.

Prayer: Thank you for the gifts of knowledge wisdom and understanding. I want more! Amen.

4 – Power of Darkness

Colossians 1:13–14 — (13) He has rescued us from the power of darkness and transferred us into the kingdom of his beloved Son, (14) in whom we have redemption, the forgiveness of sins.

WHAT DOES COLLEGE HAVE to do with politics? A lot. Will the state legislature allocate enough money to keep your school operating? Will it approve concealed or open carry of guns on campus? Do the local police have jurisdiction to enforce city or state laws on your campus? Paul is still in the thanksgiving mode as he expresses gratitude for God's liberation from the dominion of darkness to the kingdom of Christ. Is this only a figure of speech or is there some real change to which he refers? What it sounds like is a change of citizenship effected by God's executive decision to move Christians from living under the rule of one power (a bad one) to a new power (a good one).

Where is this power or kingdom of darkness? It seems to refer to any place in which God through Christ is not in charge. Isn't the expression "power of darkness" pretty harsh to use in describing a college? College is a power. Being in college is at least somewhat like living in any community. If God is not the top power and authority of the college (or community) what is the alternative? From a Christian perspective would such a community be okay? Sort of okay? Semi-okay? Almost okay? Or can we admit—at least while we read this New Testament letter—that the college would have to fall into the category of "darkness"—at least for the purpose of discussion?

The previous citizenship in which the pre-Christian Colossians had lived was characterized as sinful and wrong thinking—"the power of darkness." The new citizenship is characterized by forgiveness of sins—which is what redemption means here. We could not get away from the first power on our own. How can we live in the old place even though our commitment is to a new one? That is exactly one of the central questions addressed in this letter. In case you hadn't already guessed, this is not your old Sunday school religion. This is faith in the midst of the serious rough-and-tumble conflict between powers. There are two places—mutually distant regarding their nature, but paradoxically in the same place regarding geography. Here you are, right in the middle of those two "places"—God's kingdom and the American college experience. Knowing where you are is the first step in finding your way.

Prayer: God, equip me for my life on the margin between your kingdom and the world. Amen.

5 – First Things First

Colossians 1:15–17 — (15) He is the image of the invisible God, the first born of all creation; (16) for in him all things in heaven and on earth were created, things visible and invisible, whether thrones or dominions or rulers or powers—all things have been created through him and for him. (17) He himself is before all things, and in him all things hold together.

OCCASIONALLY I WORE A striped shirt to the university where I worked as an administrator. It reminded me of my role as referee, adjudicating the distribution of limited funds and perks among competing departments and professors. This happened because there was no single, unifying principle, goal, mission, or vision that bound us together. (If there had been, there would have been much less need for anyone to "administer.")

Today's passage is a song the early Christian church used—a chorus about Jesus Christ. It is a rave review of many of the great things about him that show him to be the greatest and most powerful thing there ever was (except for God). It is not unlike the praise songs popular today.

Often Christians look forward to a future when Christ will come and bring his kingdom into earthly reality. In fact, that temporal and chrono-logical view is probably the most frequent word picture the New Testament offers. However, here in Colossians we get a spatial orientation. Yesterday you read how God had moved you from one (evil, earthly, fleshly) kingdom into another better one. No waiting; it's a done deal. The great transformation and liberation has already occurred and you now can explore that new life with a Lord who is cosmic in scope yet makes sense out of everything for each individual person.

This hymn or chorus is full of spatial language. Actually, it's full of a lot of little words: prepositions. The creation of all things—especially all power—took place "in" Christ. The creation flowed "through" him as agent, so that he put his stamp on all of it. And it is "for" him—directed toward him as goal for use in accord with his purpose. He is "before" all things, in the lead, more important than all, and in the words of the poet T. S. Eliot he is "the still point of the turning world"—at the center. Jesus Christ is the glue that holds everything together.

Prayer: Help me to hold to the center, to Christ, and to know that he is at the heart of all my understanding. Amen.

6 – When Things Fall Apart

Colossians 1:15–17 — (15) He is the image of the invisible God, the first born of all creation; (16) for in him all things in heaven and on earth were created, things visible and invisible, whether thrones or dominions or rulers or powers—all things have been created through him and for him. (17) He himself is before all things, and in him all things hold together.

DIDN'T WE READ THIS yesterday? Yes; but in college repetition can really help.

Jonathan Edwards, an early American minister, missionary, and theologian, argued that it was only God's constant presence that kept the physical universe from collapsing back into the chaotic disorder from which God had ordered it. There is another way to read this idea that "in him all things hold together" that might mean a lot for a college student: that it is in Jesus Christ that things "hold together" in terms of making sense. It is only in Jesus Christ that you can truly and finally understand that things (at least eventually) make sense. Only by locating everything in Jesus Christ can life, death, joy, suffering, past, and future become acceptable.

In his poem "The Second Coming" the Christian poet W. B. Yeats wrote, "Things fall apart/the centre cannot hold." When there is no center, things do fall apart. In a wry criticism of the American college, Robert Hutchins, the then young and revolutionary president of the University of Chicago, observed that higher education lacked any centering vision or purpose; it went something like this:

Question: What holds the college together?

Answer: The heating system.

In such an environment, is it possible for Christians to know God in a center-less and secular college environment? Paul, writing to Christians who wonder about the relation of Christ to other claimants to your religious faith, quotes an early Christian hymn. The song hails Jesus Christ as primary ("image of the invisible God, first born of all creation") and as that which integrates everything, holds the entire cosmos together, and gives it all meaning. Everything connects and interrelates in Christ and Christ invites you to participate in that sense-making activity.

The tune of this early hymn may no longer be known, but the central message of a Christ who makes sense of everything is an incredible blessing—especially to anyone in the college experience.

Prayer: It is wonderful to know that Christ puts all the pieces together when things fall apart. Thank you. Amen.

7 – Getting It Together

Colossians 1:18–20 — (18) He is the head of the body, the church; he is the beginning, the first born from the dead, so that he might come to have first place in everything. (19) For in him all the fullness of God was pleased to dwell, (20) and through him God was pleased to reconcile to himself all things, whether on earth or in heaven, by making peace through the blood of his cross.

THE COACH, THE TEACHER, the president—these authority figures are important to the running of a college. If any of them leaves, there is a vacuum. And vacuums demand to be filled. Fast. A replacement is necessary for stability, for things to make sense and feel right. Of all the college employees whose leaving creates critical vacuums, athletic coaches are the best (or is it worst?). Particularly urgent to replace are the football and men's basketball coaches. Alumni want to know what will happen to the team for the next season. Student athletes need to have a new father figure . . . quickly. The press wants news.

Fortunately Christians will not be threatened by a vacancy at the top. Christ's tenure is secure because of his resurrection, and we are not vulnerable to any leadership change crisis. In this early Christian hymn, the focus has shifted from the cosmic Christ (verse 15) to a more personal level—God's desire that you and God be reconciled. The facts about Christ and his cosmos are now tied personally to you through a historical event (the cross) and the community of the church (body of Christ).

Opening this letter with such a positive affirmation of his readers and of the positive and absolutely cosmic scope of the work of Jesus Christ (from creation to reconciliation) is such good news. It is like a welcome sign just for you at the gate of your college. Studying this letter should produce a lot of strengthening to your faith and some specific answers to some of the many challenges to a Christian student in college.

Prayer: God, help me get my head around Jesus' cosmic creativity and his work on the cross. Amen.

8 – Lord, When Was I a Mad Scientist?

Colossians 1:21–23 — (21) And you who were once estranged and hostile in mind, doing evil deeds, (22) he has now reconciled in his fleshly body through death, so as to present you holy and blameless and irreproachable before him—(23) provided that you continue securely established and steadfast in the faith, without shifting from the hope promised by the gospel that you heard, which has been proclaimed to every creature under heaven. I, Paul, became a servant of this gospel.

THE MAD SCIENTIST IS (usually, thank goodness!) fictional and is often portrayed in bad movies where his diabolical plot to take over the world issues from a genius-level IQ gone berserk. By contrast, college folks tend to think of the mind as good. The Greek philosopher Plato (427–347 BCE) is an early advocate of the view that the mind is the essentially good core of humans. In college circles it is pretty much assumed that the mind has great potential.

You are the intellectual great-grandchild of the Western philosophical tradition (Plato and company), the grandchild of the Enlightenment (Kant and company) and the child of modernism. Part of the inheritance you share with your predecessors is an enormous confidence in human reason. The founders of those traditions all believed in the positive power of the mind. Well, perhaps not so much confidence in the reasoning of others, but plenty of confidence in their own.

You know that each of us has an individual bias, point of view, or perspective. But to what extent do you take seriously the possibility that one of the factors that may negatively affect your thinking is sin? It is hard to acknowledge that sin has what one writer calls the "epistemic impact of sin" or the impact of sin on your thinking. But if you take sin seriously—woe to us if we don't!—you can understand your self-centeredness and your estrangement from Christ. To the extent that Christ has not reconciled one's mind to God, there is a little of the mad scientist in everyone.

The good news is that Christ has put you in a new place. Once you are reconciled to God in Christ, there is no need to go about—as the Colossians apparently did—still looking for some additional truth to perfect Christ and fulfill the gospel. Now all there is left is for you to live out the faith you have been given.

Prayer: God, thank you that your reconciling love is more powerful than my hostile ideas. Amen.

9 – Vocation with a Vision

Colossians 1:24–26 — (24) I am now rejoicing in my suffering for your sake, and in my flesh I am completing what is lacking in Christ's afflictions for the sake of his body, that is, the church. (25) I became its servant according to God's commission that was given to me for you, to make the word of God fully known, (26) the mystery that has been hidden throughout the ages and generations but has now been revealed to his saints.

YOU PLAN FOR A career. That is part of what you will do in college. It could be a job, like it was for the father of a student of mine who had decided on his major by looking at a list of the best-paying jobs; he chose the top-income career . . . and hated it. Paul seems pretty happy about his "job" ("I am now rejoicing"—while suffering, and in jail!), which had to do with spreading God's word about Jesus Christ.

Do you know the story of the two workers who were asked what they were doing? The first, a bricklayer, said he was laying bricks. The second, also a bricklayer, responded that he was building a cathedral. They had the same skills, but radically contrasting frames of reference. They employed the same techniques, but saw themselves functioning in radically differing vocations. The one was locked in the tedium of doing the same task repeatedly; the second saw the worth of that mundane labor as part of a grander panorama.

Jobs can have their tedium and their pains. Jobs can be a drag or they can grab you as a vocation. They can give you identity and purpose, or they can be hated and feared. College is overwhelmingly about selecting and preparing for the working part of your life.

Have you decided what your career path is? How does that fit in "the big picture" as you view it? What kind of a person will that career make of you? Do you know the requirements and do you have a plan, the resources, and the will to carve it out for yourself?

Some people are claimed by a career. They have a *vocation*, a calling. They are part of something greater, called by something outside of themselves to build something grand. Paul tells the Colossians about his *vocation*. How are you coming along in choosing and preparing for yours?

Prayer: Thank you for those I name and those I cannot name who have prepared the way for me. Amen.

10 – Good Advice: If You Can Get It, Take It

Colossians 1:27–29 — (27) To them God chose to make known how great among the Gentiles are the riches of the glory of this mystery, which is Christ in you, the hope of glory. (28) It is he whom we proclaim, warning everyone and teaching everyone in all wisdom, so that we may present everyone mature in Christ. (29) For this I toil and struggle with all the energy that he powerfully inspires within me.

ONE OF MY PET peeves is that conversation you often overhear at church before morning worship—the conversation that focuses on the weather or the latest football game. The atmosphere is more "good 'ole boy" than an encounter of members of the body of Christ who are concerned to "present everyone mature in Christ."

In college, the role of your adviser can range from . . . well, one extreme to the other. Some faculty bridle at the role of *en loco parentis*—being in the position of parent—and avoid involvement in the nonacademic side of their advisees' lives. They see their role with their students as confined to the matter of academic requirements and signing forms.

Other faculty feel comfortable playing a more involved role in the lives of students. Theirs can even be an "in your face" approach to their students, confronting them with big issues and major decisions, tracking them down when they miss class, conversing with them about any and all issues in their advisees' lives.

If Paul had been an academic adviser, his commitment to "warning everyone" and "teaching everyone" clearly would place him at the intrusive end of the spectrum. You may be fortunate and get a good advisor and mentor. Accept it and listen. You may even get good advice and some tender loving care.

Paul's mission is not only to touch every one with the gospel but to equip and strengthen the Colossians in their Christian maturation. This letter was preserved in Scripture because it continued to be useful in doing the same thing for later generations of believers. As a young, and perhaps not as wise or as mature a Christian as you hope to be, you can be open simply to receive (at least some of) the advice that comes to you.

Prayer: Thank you, Lord, for those who work to get us matured— in school and in Christ. Amen.

11 – Mysteries—Academic and Spiritual

Colossians 2:1-3 — (1) For I want you to know how much I am struggling for you, and for those in Laodicea, and for all who have not seen me face to face. (2) I want their hearts to be encouraged and united in love, so that they may have all the riches of assured understanding and have the knowledge of God's mystery, that is, Christ himself, (3) in whom are hidden all the treasures of wisdom and knowledge.

MYSTERIOUS, IMPENETRABLE. IT COULD be a poem, how a muscle functions; there are many things that are hard to understand. Some of these "mysteries" can be resolved by more work, a remark by a professor, or a serendipitous inspiration; others may never be answered. But when the mystery is penetrated, you have new information. The real student is always seeking and finding more illumination.

You can have those deep and moving mysteries of faith as did John Wesley in his conversion experience. As the preacher described "the change which God works in the heart through faith in Christ," Wesley reported that, "I felt my heart strangely warmed. I felt I did trust in Christ." In this case, faith was a warm heart. Being forgiven, reconciled, accepted by Christ is a marvelous feeling.

But it is also describable. The instructor was asking the student about her faith. She was not shy; it was clear to the class that she was serious about and unashamed of her faith. But she was struggling to find the words with which to articulate her belief. The instructor, sensing a "teaching moment," pressed for her definition of faith. Her frustration mounted. Finally after the next push by the teacher, she tearfully blurted out, "I know what I believe; I just can't say it!" Yes, there is the indescribable and impenetrable, but the mystery of Christ *does* submit to language, to thought, to analysis, if only little by little.

Paul speaks of a mystery revealed; truth, not deception. Getting "assured understanding" and "the knowledge of God's mystery" is there, in "Christ himself." But it is a mystery that need not remain permanently and entirely impenetrable. It is an accessible mystery. It enables you to understand the will of God little by little. Faith is not private knowledge or opinion; it works out through the uniting in love of God's creatures. You can contribute. Your faithful response to the gospel is certainly your own and personal, but it is neither private nor inaccessible to others.

Prayer: Lord, help my faith to be passionate yet well thought through, comfortingly warm yet substantial. Amen.

12 – The Plausibility Argument

Colossians 2:4 — (4) I am saying this so that no one may deceive you with plausible arguments.

How EMBARRASSING IT IS to be fooled. It is also humiliating and maddening! I can still feel the anger over having my wallet stolen while I was driving an apparently nice young hitchhiker through his home town; and that was over thirty years ago. Or how I was fooled by the other Boy Scouts in Troop 881 about snipe hunting. There are many other arenas in which we can be fooled—with bad information, subtle omissions, faulty opinions, ill-based expectations, and outright lies. So one of the things they (your well-meaning professors) may tell you at your college is that they will prepare you to assess and evaluate information that you acquire so that your conclusions are solid and likely to be valid. Even so, you will be the recipient of dozens of "plausible arguments" during the course of your college career. In some classes you will be presented with a really powerful argument from a significant thinker only to see that argument rejected in the next class session by another even more plausible argument presented by another famous thinker. It can be really difficult to make decisions because plausible arguments are, well, really plausible.

You are on your own now. Your parents are probably worried about what you will think. But they are still confident—or at least pretending to be confident—that all is okay. If your college is typical, there will be little interest in religious faith and the truly deep questions in most of your classes. But there likely will be individuals and groups that will be urging one or another approach to really important issues. Some will argue (plausibly, of course) against any religious faith; others will urge an explicit kind of commitment or involvement. How do you decide?

What has Paul said so that no one will deceive you? He just reminded his readers that "all the treasures of wisdom and knowledge" are found in Christ. That is your resource. Keep Christ at the center at all times. Then you will have assured understanding because it is based on the most plausible argument ever—Jesus Christ.

Prayer: O Lord, do protect me from the deceit of dangerous arguments. Amen.

13 – To Be "In," or Not To Be

Colossians 2:5-7 — (5) For though I am absent in body, yet I am with you in spirit, and I rejoice to see your morale and the firmness of your faith in Christ. (6) As you therefore have received Christ Jesus the Lord, continue to live your lives in him, (7) rooted and built up in him and established in the faith, just as you were taught, abounding in thanksgiving.

MY WIFE SPENT FOUR wonderful years at a college that sadly closed its doors some years ago. She is a graduate of a school that no longer exists. She continues to attend the occasional alumni reunions—each time with fewer participants. Like alumni of other, still-existing schools, she and her fellow grads are bound together in spirit, but the numbers dwindle. There is no longer a place to be "in," where "roots" are put down and you are "built up" and "established." Rather than "abounding," diminishing seems the more operative term. (Note that *in* occurs eight times in this passage—especially "in spirit . . . in Christ . . . in him . . . in the faith . . . in thanksgiving.") How important it is that there be something to be "in." Without something to be "in," it is hard to be.)

In contrast, beginning in the 1980s, Duke University enjoyed the prestige that an outstanding basketball program brought—winning national and conference titles. In this day of freedom and of student suspicion of discipline, members of the Duke team had to be "rooted" in the coach's discipline and vision. He "built up" his team and "established" it as a great team by ensuring that each player did it his way. The result? The team "abounded" in success.

One group shrinks toward inevitable death; the other increases in morale and strength. In many ways, those are the options. Moments of rest, when nothing happens, are rare. You are always diminishing or growing.

The biblical passage for today represents one of those rare moments of pause. Paul applauds the Colossians for coming so far in Christ. Good work, he tells them. Relax for a moment. Remember that you have sent down roots into the Christ who has nourished you. You learned well. Relax. Enjoy.

But note the subtle warning: "Continue to live your lives in him." This "time out" is only the briefest rest. There is serious work ahead. The cosmic Christ is being challenged on all sides. You have done well so far; it's soon time to push ahead.

Prayer: Thank you for the promise and the equipment for growing strong and rich in the faith. Amen.

14 – Warning: Intellectual Hijackers

Colossians 2:8–10 — (8) See to it that no one takes you captive through philosophy and empty deceit, according to human tradition, according to the elemental spirits of the universe, and not according to Christ. (9) For in him the whole fullness of deity dwells bodily, (10) and you have come to fullness in him, who is the head of every ruler and authority.

ONCE I SAW A large banner suspended from windows above a pedestrian walkway on the campus of a major university. It read: "Jesus Christ, Lord of the Universe." I wondered if those who had hung the banner could make the less audacious claim: "Jesus Christ, Lord of the university"? Has it occurred to you that he is the Lord of the university? Have you questioned how he might be Lord of the university? Or even if he might be Lord over a department, or even over some individual teacher or just even a student . . . like you?

Or is the university so powerful that Jesus Christ cannot be its Lord? If that is the case, it sounds like the university may be one of those "powers" that Scripture mentions. God has ordained the "powers" for our benefit. For instance, government is an institution that provides services, protection, assistance. But we know that government occasionally gets off track and fails to provide for the people. It can lose its vocation and do really bad things—the execution of Jesus, the Holocaust, apartheid.

The problem with philosophy is that it is limited by the ability and perspective of the people who do it. That is the problem with human tradition—it is, well, human.

There is no doubt that philosophy is a powerful tool, useful in thinking about deep matters. Justin Martyr, a second-century Christian, argued that Christianity was in fact the best philosophy. St. Thomas Aquinas in the 1300s used the philosophical system of Aristotle to organize and express what Christians believed they knew about God. For such serious and thoughtful Christians philosophy was an excellent tool. For Justin it was of great help in defending the faith in the face of hostile and powerful foes. For Aquinas it was of help in organizing the faith, always provided that the center and the supreme authority was God. So, philosophy? Just be sure that Christ is at the center of what you do with it.

Prayer: Free me from loving my own thoughts and let me love you so passionately that I can think clearly. Amen.

15 – When in Trouble, Check the Cross

*Colossians 2:11–14 — (11) In him also you were circumcised with
a spiritual circumcision, by putting off the body of the flesh in
the circumcision of Christ; (12) when you were buried with him
in baptism, you were also raised with him through faith in the
power of God, who raised him from the dead. (13) And when you
were dead in trespasses and the uncircumcision of your flesh, God
made you alive together with him, when he forgave us all our trespasses, (14) erasing the record that stood against us with its legal
demands. He set this aside, nailing it to the cross.*

HAVE YOU EVER BEEN in trouble? Really BIG trouble? Do you remember
how it feels to be "on the carpet" in front of your parents for a really big boo-
boo? Or in front of the school principal? Or when you got a traffic ticket?
Take all those scared, guilty, embarrassed feelings, multiply by a gazillion,
and imagine yourself really guilty of every bad thing you ever did and imagine having done them to God who has called you into court on the charges.

Paul uses a legal metaphor to describe your pre-faith and post-belief
situations. Then you were doomed—in huge trouble with little hope of escape. Now, after the baptism of faith in Christ, you are alive. The charges—
whatever they were—are taken care of in Jesus' death on the cross.

Another way to describe the same transformation of your life is to use
another package of terminology and narrative. Before you were a member
of the kingdom of darkness. Then you were cut off from the dominion of
darkness, from untruth. This is in the Jewish language of "circumcision,"
using the term metaphorically, with reference to the cutting off of Jesus' life
in his death on the cross. Your "baptism" follows the model of death and
burial in Christ. The result of either way of describing things (circumcision
or baptism) was that you had been in one condition (sin, or "estranged and
hostile in mind") and are now forgiven and no longer considered guilty of
sin. All of that happened because of the critical event of Jesus' crucifixion.

*Prayer: Give me the gift of understanding Christian language and
of speaking clearly about your grace. Amen.*

16 – And the Winner Is . . .

Colossians 2:15 — (15) He disarmed the rulers and authorities and made a public example of them, triumphing over them in it [the cross].

THE MESSAGE OF THE cross is not simply that Jesus is alive; he is also *not* guilty as charged by the government and by the religious authorities. Oh yes, and he is the supreme ruler of every power anywhere in this or any other galaxy. And the cross has become a symbol of all that—even if it is often debauched as jewelry. (One writer sarcastically refers to this casual attitude as "Jesus on a bracelet.") Minimally, what was dismantled by the resurrection was the power of Rome (which finally fell in 410 CE) and the reliability of the popular religious prejudices that supported the politicians' actions against Jesus.

But there are still powers that oppose God. While God can take care of herself, those powers are sometimes effective in trapping you in seductive webs. It has been said that the task of the church is to be able to identify the principalities and powers that attempt to govern humans. In college there is a glut of claimants to the thrones of power. Some of these claimants—science, career, technology, history—derive much of their power from the fact that they are well presented, well argued, dressed in the finery of cultural or academic or financial acceptability. Then there are also those extracurricular claimants—sports, sex, alcohol, gambling . . . and the list goes on.

But above every principle, tradition, argument, system, ideology, religion, government, principality, and power is Christ who had been attacked by a coalition of the principalities of his day only to have his "sentence" reversed by God in the resurrection. You have been truly favored by a God who not only provides you with a forgiver and redeemer but also with the final and superior power over all other claimants. In a world of many competing powers it is comforting to know that there is one truly good power and that he is the most powerful one and he invites you to find your safety in him.

Prayer: Help me to recognize the principalities and powers and not be seduced by them. Amen.

17 – Don't Be Ashamed!

Colossians 2:16–19 — (16) Therefore do not let anyone condemn you in matters of food and drink or of observing festivals, new moons, or sabbaths. (17) These are only a shadow of what is to come, but the substance belongs to Christ. (18) Do not let anyone disqualify you, insisting on self-abasement and worship of angels, dwelling on visions, puffed up without cause by a human way of thinking, (19) and not holding fast to the head, from whom the whole body, nourished and held together by its ligaments and sinews, grows with a growth that is from God.

THERE IS NOTHING AS entertaining as the sight of politicians caught out in some embarrassment and scrambling for cover—or at least for a cover story. For example Watergate, Monica Lewinski, vicuna coats, Iran Contra, Teapot Dome—you never know what the source of shame and embarrassment will be, even for a United States president. Victims try to minimize the shame, opponents gleefully attempt to maximize it. In America today, however, where virtually anything goes, shame is almost never fatal to a career.

In the time of Jesus, shame was much more powerful in its effects than it is in our day. A prime example of shame was a sentence to death on a cross. Persons whom the powers that be wanted to publicly humiliate in the most horrible public exposure of physical nakedness and lack of control of bodily functions, were sentenced to crucifixion. This was a means of execution applied to a broad spectrum of people the government wanted to punish and hold up as warning examples. Jesus—as a public threat to Rome and a religious annoyance to the Jews who wanted to keep on good terms with Rome—was only one of the cross's innumerable victims.

Among the powers of the world are religious observances that have become absolutized in our lives. If we don't do them, shame! Shame! Paul points out that religious practices are only shadow—not the real thing. They are not what God has given you for nourishment and growth: Jesus Christ is. So don't get hung up on stuff like what to eat or pay undue attention to; what to avoid or with whom not to associate. Those are not deal-breakers. Only what has Jesus at the core is for real. His is the creation and he has sanctified it so that you can live fully in it.

Prayer: Help me to see in the light of Christ—what is substance and what is only shadow. Amen.

18 – Dogma–Tied by the World

Colossians 2:20–23 — (20) If with Christ you died to the elemental spirits of the universe, why do you live as if you still belonged to the world? Why do you submit to regulations, (21) "Do not handle, Do not taste, Do not touch"? (22) All these regulations refer to things that perish with use; they are simply human commands and teachings. (23) These have indeed an appearance of wisdom in promoting self-imposed piety, humility, and severe treatment of the body, but they are of no value in checking self-indulgence.

WHAT ARE THE BASIC constituents of the universe? People have been asking that question for centuries, first with religious answers and then "scientifically" by observation beginning with the Greek philosopher Thales (640–546 BCE) who proposed water (!) as the basic building block of matter. As advances in instrumentation enabled closer looks at the material world, scientists developed better theories, and the answer to the "basic elements" question has changed and we now know that it is . . . well, at this writing, the scientific answer is still a work in progress.

But there is also a less scientific version of the question. It's more like: "What is the basic driving force of human affairs?" For the answer, it seems that all you need to do is look at the misguided and selfishly used power under which Jesus was "legally" executed. How can Christians, reborn and reformed in our baptism into Christ, still think and act under the control of the basic operating principles of the "world" that killed him? Especially after Jesus' "conviction" had been so dramatically reversed by God's raising him from an unjust death?

Or what about this personally directed-at-you version of the question: "If with Christ you died to the elemental spirits of the universe" (or university?), how come you "submit to" (in the Greek, *dogmatizesthe*, or "let yourself be dictated to by the dogmas) "regulations" of the world?

Among the fundamental values or "dogmas" of the university are self-improvement, freedom, toleration, competition, concern for job preparation. Paul might dismiss them as "simply human commands and teachings" that only have the "appearance of wisdom." You and Christ "died to the elemental spirits of the universe" and you both are free to replace them with other loftier, more important things like love, compassion, hospitality, and service of others.

Prayer: Lord give me the insight to what those elemental principals are so I can live according to your will. Amen.

19 – Witness Protection Program

Colossians 3:1–4 — (1) So if you have been raised with Christ, seek the things that are above, where Christ is, seated at the right hand of God. (2) Set your minds on things that are above, not on things that are on earth, (3) for you have died, and your life is hidden with Christ in God. (4) When Christ who is your life is revealed, then you also will be revealed with him in glory.

REMEMBER ON THE TV program *Sesame Street* when they were teaching the concepts of "near" and "far"? Now you know that near and far, up and down, are not all that clear. You could theoretically move toward the "edge" of the universe, but since we now know that space curves, you would ultimately find yourself back more or less where you started. Reading the up/down language of Colossians as metaphorical is better than reading it literally. Our hope is in heaven (1:5a) means, importantly, that it is not here in the world of human beings and faulty human institutions.

God has delivered you from the "dominion of darkness" to the "kingdom of his beloved son" (1:13). In today's reading, that change is described in terms of your move from "down" on earth, among earthly things, to "up" in heaven and the things of Christ. The importance here is the change in who you are. You are changed; your behavior is changed.

Now, in college, you are studying to change into a lawyer, accountant, teacher. When you become one of them you must behave like one of them. In joining the group (becoming a lawyer, etc.) you "die" to your previous life, and assume a role of privilege and responsibility dictated and expected of you in your new life.

In Christ, you have experienced a radical change of identity. You have been liberated to become what God intended you to be when he created you. It is like being in a government witness protection program and being given a new identity; you don't want to let on to anybody what you were before you got into the program.

Prayer: Help me to think and act like I am really in a new place and that I am really a new person. Amen.

20 – Dump the Garbage

Colossians 3:5–8 — (5) Put to death, therefore, whatever in you is earthly: fornication, impurity, passion, evil desire, and greed (which is idolatry). (6) On account of these the wrath of God is coming on those who are disobedient. (7) These are the ways you also once followed, when you were living that life. (8) But now you must get rid of all such things—anger, wrath, malice, slander, and abusive language from your mouth.

SUCCESS IN COLLEGE MEANS adapting to college demands: less TV, less sleep, a willingness to reserve judgment on complex questions, polishing those reading and writing skills. Yes, there does come a time when the fateful words must be spoken: Don't do this; don't do that. A lot of folks think that the Christian faith is basically a series of variations on the "Don't" theme. Today's reading is the kind of passage that the biblically illiterate are sure dominates Scripture and the whole of the Christian faith: Don'ts. Read it carefully because—surprise!—it is almost the only "don't" in the whole letter. So little is spent on commands in this letter because the new nature of anyone in Christ spells out a picture that you will pick up on it in a flash.

Being in college as a Christian puts you on the margin where earthly habits battle heavenly ones. If you keep on living with the habits of the world, it is a denial of what you have learned in Christ and a rejection of the transformation going on in your life. It leads you in the direction of becoming what could be called a "Frankenstein's monster"—a little of this and a little of that. You definitely do not want a diabolically split personality.

If you think sex organs are the only organs that put you in danger you may not have been listening to your tongue lately. Words can be the most powerful tool in your toolbox, for good or for hurt. As a Christian you have a Christian language so that you can speak truths that go unnoticed or denied by society in general. Not only do you have the "use of Christian language," but you also need to develop the "Christian use of language." As you become disciplined to a helpful, precise, truthful use of language, you necessarily eliminate "anger, wrath, malice, slander and abusive language." As a person undergoing God's makeover, dumping the trash is part of the process. How can you tell what is garbage? For starters, anything that hurts others must go.

Prayer: Let me not resist the transformation going on in the new person Christ is making of me. Amen.

21 – Ultimate Makeover

Colossians 3:9–10 — (9) Do not lie to one another, seeing that you have stripped off the old self with its practices (10) and have clothed yourselves with the new self, which is being renewed in knowledge according to the image of its creator.

A BETTER MOVIE (MORE draw at the box office) than the "sex and say whatever you want to say" kind of movie might be one we could call *College Lies*. It might feature a university president who sexually harassed women; a researcher who not only invented her data but also the very subjects from whom she got the data; a coach who falsified his resume and played players who weren't exactly students; a student who didn't tell his parents that he had flunked his first two years because he had been playing cards. Unfortunately, these "characters" are all real.

The point is that people connected with American colleges and universities are not necessarily any more honest than the rest of the world. The things suggested for inclusion in our imaginary movie are things that the perpetrators hide behind lies. Christians would call lying a sin because in various ways it is hurtful to others. Does higher education need a makeover?

The makeover. A recent fad on reality TV. First was the makeover of the backyard, then the house, then the body. Would the made-over-one be pleased? We all have been the targets of makeovers since arriving on this earth—from what God intended to what American culture demanded.

While we await further developments in the TV world of makeovers, back to Paul. In this passage he continues to develop the gospel's unfolding promise: the gift of a new life to the Colossians (and all believers) and the new and better behaviors that show it off. He points out that Christians ought not to lie. (Why bother lying since you already have the truth in Christ?) Your new nature in Christ has a particularly important aspect to it—you are being renewed in knowledge after the "image of [your] creator." No lie!

Prayer: Help me be so renewed that I know the truth and tell the truth. Amen.

22 – And the Walls Came Tumbling Down

Colossians 3:11 — (11) In that renewal there is no longer Greek and Jew, circumcised and uncircumcised, barbarian, Scythian, slave and free; but Christ is all and in all!

WHEN I STARTED COLLEGE, among the strongest walls that separated students from each other were these three:

The wall that separated collegiate "Greeks" (fraternity/sorority students) from "non-Greeks."

The wall between the preppies and the public school graduates. When I entered college, my school had had a tradition of accepting primarily the wealthy and socially gifted applicants. My class was the first class in which the number of us public school grads equaled the number of "preppies."

The gender wall: boys vs. girls. Some years after I graduated, my all-male *alma mater* accepted women! The gender wall fell and everyone was welcome to attend. (Well, maybe not welcomed by all. For some, that wall was only violated, not eliminated.)

But you are being "renewed in knowledge" (3:10). You are getting new information—a new understanding that calls for the use of new wisdom. One piece of new(ly received) knowledge is truly big: there are no cultural distinctions (Greek/Jew, Mexican, Iraqi), no physical ones (circumcised/uncircumcised, black/white), no ethnic ones (Irish/Jewish), no political/social/economic ones (slave/free, PhD/GED) that Christians ought to take seriously (cf. Gal 3:28). You may learn classifications in class, but you will also learn ways in which everyone is the same—in their chemistry, their social needs, their political aspirations. Christ loves everyone despite the "human" classifications that might be used to classify, separate, or denigrate anyone. He has eliminated the walls of division. There is no way to put barriers between you and others now that your mind has been renewed. This is not just about being tolerant of others. This is a reconstruction of your mind, a re-creation produced by God. This is a recognition that sinful humans have arbitrarily made up the idea that particular characteristics could legitimately be used to separate you from others. It was like a bad April Fool's joke—just made up.

Who are the "they" to your "we"? From now on it has to be "we." (It's easier than trying to remember who exactly is a "them" and monitoring all the "us's" to make sure they're just like you.)

Prayer: Help me act re-created so that I will no longer notice any differences between me and others. Amen.

23 – Here Is Your New Wardrobe

Colossians 3:12–15 — (12) As God's chosen ones, holy and beloved, clothe yourselves with compassion, kindness, humility, meekness, and patience. (13) Bear with one another and, if anyone has a complaint against another, forgive each other; just as the Lord has forgiven you, so you also must forgive. (14) Above all, clothe yourselves with love, which binds everything together in perfect harmony. (15) And let the peace of Christ rule in your hearts, to which indeed you were called in the one body. And be thankful.

WEARING BRAND NAME SNEAKERS, school colors, the number of a star athlete, or T-shirts with aggressive, in-your-face statements is common. Why do people do that? Maybe to give a hint to the world about who the wearer would like to be.

Paul has the same idea: wear the stuff that will show the world that you are a Christian: for pants, how about "compassion, kindness, humility"? For shirts, "meekness . . . patience," forgiveness, "love . . . peace" (one for every day of the week)? Shoes: thankfulness?

These sound like they could be "values." Colleges are keen on values. Values are the warm, fuzzy stuff about which people can feel good. One thing about values is that that few people take the time to define them, and even fewer want to check to see if their values are really lived out in concrete action. But we really haven't much of a clue about what values are actually being embodied and passed on by the great and not-so-great colleges and universities. So if you start with some values that sound good and about which you needn't be specific, and which no one is going to measure, you have an unbeatable combination—at least for public consumption. Like a brand name outfit.

But if you check the list in the passage for today's meditation, you will note that each item describes the quality of relationships between persons: "compassion, kindness, humility, meekness . . . patience," forbearance, forgiveness, "love," and thankfulness. The good news is that you need not select and commit to any set of values. You have been embraced by a concrete person—Jesus Christ—who will be your guide as you go.

Prayer: Let me wear my finest "clothes" every day and let them shine so they are visible. Amen.

24 – Gimme That Full-Time Religion

Colossians 3:16–17 — (16) Let the word of Christ dwell in you richly; teach and admonish one another in all wisdom; and with gratitude in your hearts sing psalms, hymns, and spiritual songs to God. (17) And whatever you do, in word or deed, do everything in the name of the Lord Jesus, giving thanks to God the Father through him.

YOU ARE IN A hurry, in every way: to get to class, to get a date, to finish college, to own a boat! So is everyone else. In a hurry. Your professors, classmates, everybody driving on Main St. There is so much to do. And you would like some time off, just to relax, just for yourself. The nostalgic view of a typical college prof's office is one in which the shelves are filled with books, the desk piled high with papers cascading off onto comfy chairs occupying what little floor space is not littered with more books. It suggests that learning is a leisurely enterprise. A more recent, up-tempo view might show a full-time student, hurrying to her full-time job with a quick stop to attend to her full-time family. The old-fashioned, Hollywood vision of college may be losing ground to a newer picture of learning as a hi-tech process in which a rich array of electronic devices operate under fingertip control by the instructor who arrives hurriedly just in time to throw the master switch from a sterile office cubicle shared with some graduate students.

Just if it weren't getting too crazy, here comes Paul exhorting (suggesting? commanding?) Christians to "teach and admonish one another." You've got to be kidding! Isn't there already too much work—getting ready for class especially—to have to think about helping other Christians improve their "wisdom"? (You may not have thought college would be a vacation, but nobody seriously promised you that added responsibility.) For Christians, college is a gift intended to keep on giving—and demanding even more! This is a call to a rigorous and mutually up-building free-for-all in the context of the Christian's life with no holds barred. There is no limit on the toughness of the intellectual wrestling. The program Paul proposes to the intellectually curious in Colossae is one that is tough in terms of intellectual discipline. Criticism within the context of friendship depends on active participation of all members of the community in mutual correction of one another—in love, of course. Are you up for it?

Prayer: Let me instruct others gently and let me receive admonishing thankfully. Amen.

26

25 – What about Those Family Values?

Colossians 3:18–21 — (18) Wives, be subject to your husbands, as is fitting in the Lord. (19) Husbands, love your wives and never treat them harshly. (20) Children, obey your parents in everything, for this is your acceptable duty in the Lord. (21) Fathers, do not provoke your children, or they may lose heart.

YOU HAVE A "JOB description" to follow. It is in your course syllabi and school catalogue. These "position descriptions" govern your place and are used to evaluate you and are always derived from secular (worldly) sources.

Paul's inclusion of what biblical scholars call "household orders" is instructive since it acknowledges that Christians have the same mutual relationships and obligations everyone else has. Christian freedom doesn't cancel worldly relationships and obligations. On the contrary, it gives you opportunity to let God transform your secular job description into one serviceable for a servant of Christ, applicable at work, study, and play.

The relationships given the most attention in Paul's list are the up-to-down ones—husband, father, master. These are the ones that require the most caution because they are the most powerful and therefore most likely to abuse. The lists of household arrangements incorporated into the New Testament (also found in 1 Peter and Ephesians) are taken from pagan and Jewish sources and are given a Christian "spin"; for example, Jesus Christ is to be present in every relationship. Even though Christians now see themselves in new, fictive families, the social and biological family is still a reality for them. Paul wanted you to know that despite the revolutionary character of the new faith, Christians were not primarily here to tear things down.

The practice of Christians loving one another while they find themselves on the bottom end of an unequal relationship is the issue here. Is it possible to live according to Christ at the down end of an up-down relationship as well as at the up end? Paul pushed the envelope in mentioning women first. And even children! They were almost never mentioned in the pagan lists. Paul, however, addresses children as moral agents in their own right. Each person in any relationship deserves an appropriate response from the other; each stands in need of God in Christ.

Prayer: Help me to see Jesus in every relationship and to do each task in Christ. Amen.

26 – Living on the Margin

Colossians 3:22—4:1 — (22) Slaves, obey your earthly masters in everything, not only while being watched and in order to please them, but wholeheartedly, fearing the Lord. (23) Whatever your task, put yourselves into it, as done for the Lord and not for your masters, (24) since you know that from the Lord you will receive the inheritance as your reward; you serve the Lord Christ. (25) For the wrongdoer will be paid back for whatever wrong has been done, and there is no partiality. (4:1) Masters, treat your slaves justly and fairly, for you know that you also have a Master in Heaven.

IT IS EASY TO get annoyed at Christianity in general and the Bible in particular for not having more of a social conscience and a clearer program of social reform. That annoyance is particularly present when you read this passage about slaves. But the goal of Christians in the New Testament was forgiveness and love, not social change. Paul recognized that regardless of one's legal status as slave or free, everyone answered to someone in more authority. We are all "slaves," serving and answering to one or more masters.

The question this passage raises for you is: how do you live in a setting defined by hierarchies and up/down responsibilities. You live "in" but not "by" or "of" the world. Your relationship to Jesus and your existence in a new kingdom may trump but does not eliminate your life in this world.

As a college student you are definitely in the "down" end of most of your defining relationships: subject to college rules and regulations and responsible to your professors to do your school work.

But the body of Christ (the church) is truly a new kind of community. While members may still live in their biological/legal families, your Christian commitment, your transfer to the fictive family of Christians (a newly invented and established family in Christ), and your "re-citizenization" into the kingdom of light combine to provide a powerful framework in which you will be able to meet the challenges of both those relationships in which you have responsibilities of obedience (the "slave" ones) and those in which you are in charge (the "master" ones).

Prayer: May I serve you in all things whether I'm the boss or the grunt worker. Amen.

27 – Alert!

Colossians 4:2 — (2) Devote yourselves to prayer, keeping alert in it with thanksgiving.

WHEN BOARDING AN AIRPLANE do you ever glance into the cockpit and hope that the captain knows about each dial and lever and will be alert to each during the flight? Even those of us who live in less technically demanding environments need to be alert: Are there batteries in the smoke detector? Money in the checking account? What chapters were assigned for the test? Why is there need to be alert as a Christian? Shouldn't you be able to relax in the knowledge that Christ has redeemed you and is taking care of everything?

There are a number of similarities between the Christians in Colossae in 65 CE and Christians today that makes "keeping alert" important. First, the Colossian Christians were expecting the impending return of Christ and the final moment of existence on earth. I remember Claudio, a dear teacher who took his faith very seriously. He expected Christ to return "on the clouds" (1 Thess 4:17). On clear days, he would move freely around the classroom, but on cloudy ones he hung out near the window, frequently glancing out, just in case Christ should come in on one of those clouds. Today, many Christians expect the imminent return of Christ; others, processing that expectation differently, see the existential arrival of Christ in one's life to be right now, this very moment. "Now" is always the moment to be alert (and prayerfully thankful). Second, now as then you need to be alert to false teaching. After all, that is what this letter is about (and you are in college where you are constantly exposed to teaching—some of which could be false). Third, now as then, you need to be ready for the opportunity to grow in the faith and to be kind to others. Fourth, you need to be alert to the kinds of danger that put Paul in jail. Granted, in Colossians there does not seem to be the critical peril for Christians spoken of in 1 Peter or the book of Revelation, but Paul wasn't in jail for failing to pay a parking ticket. There was much in the Christian message that was considered unpatriotic, antisocial, and irreligious. (Do you ever wonder whether Christianity shouldn't still be illegal?) Fifth, you need to be alert in walking the difficult line between life in Christ and life in the world. There's a lot going on. No wonder you need to be alert. Prayer can help you calm down and focus.

Prayer: I feel surrounded by threats and opportunities; keep me alert to which is which. Amen.

28 – When Opportunity Knocks

Colossians 4:3–4 — (3) At the same time pray for us as well that God will open to us a door for the word, that we may declare the mystery of Christ, for which I am in prison, (4) so that I may reveal it clearly, as I should.

OPPORTUNITY KNOCKS? WHAT AN interesting image. It pictures you behind a closed door, waiting. Like sitting in jail with an indeterminate sentence. There is no suggestion that you can do anything to bring about the arrival of the one who will knock. The implication is that you have the choice to be prepared to respond or not. If you are prepared, are you on the same page as Paul—prepared for some specific opportunity, some already-chosen commitment to which you have given yourself wholeheartedly? And are you really ready when that "knock" comes? Are your college studies focused on being ready?

Paul was in jail, probably because of his activities as a Christian travelling around the Mediterranean world tending to the new Christian groups that he had founded. What exactly does Paul want to knock on that door? Is it release from prison? You would think so, but he doesn't say that. Rather, his concern is to get that opportunity—that break—that will allow him to keep on doing what got him in jail in the first place! He wants to tell people—and tell them as clearly as possible—about the total sufficiency of Christ in providing all that they need.

The mystery of Christ is an amazing gift that you can take into your college experience. One way to look at it is in terms of the powerful promise that Christ can finally explain all the mysteries that there are. Another way to look at it is to experience Christ's immense reconciling power personally in your own life and relationships. Remember, the "mystery" here is the total sufficiency of Christ alone.

In the face of what you learn in college you can wind up feeling rather insignificant; yet in Christ you are given significance, importance and uniqueness. Perhaps you are not the audacious bring-everyone-to-perfection go-getter that Paul was. But you have many wonderful opportunities to explore how "the mystery of Christ" meets you in your studies and experiences in college.

Prayer: Let me hear the prayers of others if they are prayers that I can answer. Amen.

29 – Carpe Diem

Colossians 4:5–6 — (5) Conduct yourselves wisely toward outsiders, making the most of the time. (6) Let your speech always be gracious, seasoned with salt, so that you may know how you ought to answer everyone.

WE DESIRE EFFICIENCY. EFFICIENCY is the maximizing of some input while other inputs are allowed to (relatively speaking) diminish. And here you are, a student, involved in one of the most inefficient enterprises one could imagine: education. Your course of study and your individual classes involve you in a lot of effort that seems unnecessary. Art survey courses are taught to future accountants, algebra to future nutritionists, physics to future English teachers. Students often wonder why they need a literature class when they are destined for a business career or a first aid class when their interests are in computer science. It all seems so inefficient. We waste the sophisticated knowledge of the art historian trying to get an accountant to grasp the difference between Manet and Monet; the art specialist spends forty-five hours a semester with those who are not artists. The student and teacher are "outsiders" to one another. You are called to efficiency—that is, to "making the most of the time." Okay, you say, you're all for efficiency.

Then Paul unpacks it for you. You are to be helpful to . . . "outsiders," those beyond your comfort zone. And you are to "conduct yourself wisely toward" them and "let your speech always be gracious." That is beginning to sound not only inefficient and time-consuming, but downright demanding with all of those qualifications. But after all, isn't one purpose of college to bring a whole lot of "outsiders" together, and communicating, and learning from each other? And in the end, isn't the family of Christians a bit like that also?

A really good college experience will cause interruption after interruption in your otherwise-settled life. Jesus was constantly interrupted by "outsiders." Indeed, his "thing" was precisely to be available to "outsiders." To the extent that you live as a Christian, you live for others. Working and studying at the boundaries where Christians live, you have great opportunities to interact with "outsiders" and to use your time well. Time is God's gift. What are you hoarding it for? Remember—sometimes you feel like an "outsider." Jesus was definitely an "outsider." He came to embrace the "outsiders." Is there an "outsider" you need to embrace today?

Prayer: Please let me use the time well and say and do the right thing, remembering I was once an outsider. Amen.

30 – With a Little Help from My Friends

Colossians 4:7–15 — (7) Tychicus will tell you all the news about me; he is a beloved brother, a faithful minister, and a fellow servant in the Lord. (8) I have sent him to you for this very purpose, so that you may know how we are and that he may encourage your hearts; (9) he is coming with Onesimus, the faithful and beloved brother, who is one of you. They will tell you about everything here. (10) Aristarchus my fellow prisoner greets you, as does Mark the cousin of Barnabas, concerning whom you have received instructions—if he comes to you, welcome him. (11) And Jesus who is called Justus greets you. These are the only ones of the circumcision among my co-workers for the kingdom of God, and they have been a comfort to me. (12) Epaphras, who is one of you, a servant of Christ Jesus, greets you. He is always wrestling in his prayers on your behalf, so that you may stand mature and fully assured in everything that God wills. (13) For I testify for him that he has worked hard for you and for those in Laodicea and in Hierapolis. (14) Luke, the beloved physician, and Demas greet you. (15) Give my greetings to the brothers and sisters in Laodicea, and to Nympha and the church in her house.

ONE OF THE GREAT things about the college experience is meeting new people. Some can be extraordinarily weird—subjects of stories you will tell in years to come. Some can challenge with their ideas and lifestyles. Others become dear and lifelong friends.

Paul mentioned ten persons by name and each was recognized for their special gifts or character. The persons mentioned were a motley group, representing the full gamut of social, religious, ethnic, and gender possibilities: Jews and gentiles; free and prisoners; locals and foreigners; male and female; and (probably) educated and uneducated. The mention of all these persons shows the variety found in the early church. Paul expected them all to know the will of God, come to an orderly and firm faith (2:5), understand the grace of God (1:6), be filled with knowledge, wisdom, and understanding (1:9), embrace Christ as the epistemological center of the cosmos (1:17), set their minds on things above (3:2), put on a new nature (3:10) and in all things love and be thankful.

The community, the body of Christ, within which you live and love is characterized by a rich variety of individuals, connected in Christ. That's how it started and that's how it is now.

Prayer: Thanks to God for giving us the solid connections to others in Christ. Amen.

31 – . . . Ends with a Bang, Not a Whimper

Colossians 4:16–18 — (16) And when this letter has been read among you, have it read also in the church of the Laodiceans; and see that you read also the letter from Laodicea. (17) And say to Archippus, "See that you complete the task that you have received in the Lord." (18) I, Paul, write this greeting with my own hand. Remember my chains. Grace be with you.

PUTTING YOUR EDUCATION INTO practice; that is "where the rubber meets the road." In olden times, education or training for a vocation was often conducted in an apprenticeship. Then schooling went indoors, into the classroom and library. In the last few decades it has come out again and moved, in part, from College Hill to Main Street in the form of work-study, *practica*, and field experiences.

Paul ends this letter with a bang! Instead of winding down the letter with a "sincerely yours," he speak harshly to someone named Archippus: "Do your assigned job!" Normally that might not be problematic, especially if "the task that you have received in the Lord" was either an easy one (visit the sick, raise a collection) or one known only to Paul and Archippus. However, it is possible that this task was both difficult and controversial.

In trying to answer the question, "What task?," one scholar offers an intriguing possibility. It rests on the probability that there is a close connection between this letter and the briefest of all Paul's letters, Philemon. [Take a minute to read it. The gist of it is that Paul wants Philemon, another of Paul's good friends, who lived in Colossae and owned a slave named Onesimus, to free this slave so that the freed slave could help Paul in his missionary work.]

The suggestion is that Archippus's task was the freeing of Onesimus and that Paul did not spell it out in Colossians because Archippus knew well enough what it was already from reading the letter to Philemon (Phlm 1–2). Explicit mention of such an assignment in a letter to be read publicly would be unnecessary. Archippus knew the assignment. It was crunch time for him.

More to the point, what is "the task that you have received in the Lord"? Whatever it might be, you may be confident knowing that Christ is all in all and that you live in the hope that is solidly laid up as your inheritance with God.

Prayer: Lord, grant me wisdom and strength to know and to do the tasks you have assigned to me. Amen.

Matthew

Jesus the Teacher, Up Close and Personal

IT IS NO SURPRISE that Matthew is the first writing in the New Testament. Matthew provided what the early Christian church most needed—instruction for the church and its members as they formed themselves as Christians in the hostile environment of the Roman Empire. In that situation, the early believers needed resources to help them understand what it meant to be a Christian, how to live with Jesus as their Lord, and how to do all of that in a world that was run by people and institutions who had conspired to kill Jesus and did not like his followers.

Therefore, the Gospel According to Matthew is a document about Jesus, the one who teaches the church what it means to be people of faith. It is the story of help for the helpless and hope for the hopeless; a series of glimpses into a world that the creator intended it to be; and the assurance of salvation through the life, death, and resurrection of Jesus the Son of God.

From that brief introduction, it should not be difficult to see what the first Gospel offers to college students: a Lord and Savior who is also a Teacher! When you get to college you expect to meet many teachers. But here is a reminder that—as a Christian—you will have your very own Teacher, accessible and eager to help you understand what is going on and to accompany you in meeting the challenges of the college experience.

But you don't read Matthew just because Jesus was a great teacher. You read it because Jesus is the Lord, the Messiah, the Son of God, and the Son of Man, and you want to know what all of those dimensions of Jesus—the christological titles that pepper the biblical texts—have to do with you and how they can help you become the person God intended you to be. Not only will you see who this Teacher is, how he taught, and what he taught. In some important ways you will be just like the disciples whose stories you will also follow as you follow Jesus through this text.

And you will be reading a great story—the greatest story ever told—that you can embrace and be embraced by, day by day. College may even help you write your own story in a more faithful way.

1 – Introducing Jesus

Matthew 1:1–17 — (1) An account of the genealogy of Jesus the Messiah, the son of David, the son of Abraham. (2) Abraham was the father of Isaac, and Isaac the father of Jacob, and Jacob the father of Judah and his brothers, (3) and Judah the father of Perez and Zerah by Tamar, and Perez the father of Hezron, and Hezron the father of Aram, (4) and Aram the father of Aminadab, and Aminadab the father of Nahshon, and Nahshon the father of Salmon, (5) and Salmon the father of Boaz by Rahab, and Boaz the father of Obed by Ruth, and Obed the father of Jesse, (6) and Jesse the father of King David. And David was the father of Solomon by the wife of Uriah, (7) and Solomon the father of Rehoboam, and Rehoboam the father of Abijah, and Abijah the father of Asaph, (8) and Asaph the father of Jehoshaphat, and Jehoshaphat the father of Joram, and Joram the father of Uzziah, (9) and Uzziah the father of Jotham, and Jotham the father of Ahaz, and Ahaz the father of Hezekiah, (10) and Hezekiah the father of Manasseh, and Manasseh the father of Amos, and Amos the father of Josiah, (11) and Josiah the father of Jechoniah and his brothers, at the time of the deportation to Babylon. (12) And after the deportation to Babylon: Jechoniah was the father of Salathiel, and Salathiel the father of Zerubbabel, (13) and Zerubbabel the father of Abiud, and Abiud the father of Eliakim, and Eliakim the father of Azor, (14) and Azor the father of Zadok, and Zadok the father of Achim, and Achim the father of Eliud, (15) and Eliud the father of Eleazar, and Eleazar the father of Matthan, and Matthan the father of Jacob, (16) and Jacob the father of Joseph the husband of Mary, of whom Jesus was born, who is called the Messiah. (17) So all the generations from Abraham to David are fourteen generations; and from David to the deportation to Babylon, fourteen generations; and from the deportation to Babylon to the Messiah, fourteen generations.

JESUS MAY BE NEW on the scene, like you, but his "story" goes way back. We discover sorrows, "interesting" female relatives, and political catastrophes. You can see how Jesus is positively, but selectively, shaped by that past. Will you build on the positive in your past, and leave the other baggage behind? This is a new day, a fresh start, with new opportunities. Can you pick out someone in your past who might be an asset as you move on in your college career?

Prayer: Lord, help me to know Jesus Christ who is the best teacher in helping me know myself. Amen.

2 – The Best-Laid Plans

Matthew 1:18-25 — (18) Now the birth of Jesus the Messiah took place in this way. When his mother Mary had been engaged to Joseph, but before they lived together, she was found to be with child from the Holy Spirit. (19) Her husband Joseph, being a righteous man and unwilling to expose her to public disgrace, planned to dismiss her quietly. (20) But just when he had resolved to do this, an angel of the Lord appeared to him in a dream and said, "Joseph, son of David, do not be afraid to take Mary as your wife, for the child conceived in her is from the Holy Spirit. (21) She will bear a son, and you are to name him Jesus, for he will save his people from their sins." (22) All this took place to fulfill what had been spoken by the Lord through the prophet: (23) "Look, the virgin shall conceive and bear a son, and they shall name him Emmanuel," which means, "God is with us." (24) When Joseph awoke from sleep, he did as the angel of the Lord commanded him; he took her as his wife, (25) but had no marital relations with her until she had borne a son; and he named him Jesus.

JOSEPH HAS JUST FOUND out that his fianceé, Mary, is pregnant. That was not part of Joseph's original plan. So, he develops a new plan; Matthew says it was "to dismiss her quietly." Apparently, in those days, that would have been an appropriate plan. He knew, of course, that he had not gotten her pregnant, so his plan seems designed to provide the best outcome for them both.

But Joseph's own plan was changed—overruled by God. He was to go ahead and marry her and they would have the baby as a family. As they say, the rest is history.

As a student, you know that having a plan can be a good idea. But, they also say, life is what happens when you are doing something else. With four or five classes, different assignments and deadlines in each class, other activities, a job, unplanned and spontaneous bull sessions, family crises, or a flat tire, you never know when you will need to flex. Joseph's story teaches that God has a safety net for when your plans fail. You need to have your plans, but don't think that they are the last word.

Prayer: Thank you God for being my safety net—even under my best-laid plans. Amen.

3 – Where is the King?

Matthew 2:1–12 — (1) In the time of King Herod, after Jesus was born in Bethlehem of Judea, wise men from the East came to Jerusalem, (2) asking, "Where is the child who has been born king of the Jews? For we observed his star at its rising, and have come to pay him homage." (3) When King Herod heard this, he was frightened, and all Jerusalem with him; (4) and calling together all the chief priests and scribes of the people, he inquired of them where the Messiah was to be born. (5) They told him, "In Bethlehem of Judea; for so it has been written by the prophet: (6) 'And you, Bethlehem, in the land of Judah, are by no means least among the rulers of Judah; for from you shall come a ruler who is to shepherd my people Israel.'" (7) Then Herod secretly called for the wise men and learned from them the exact time the star had appeared. (8) Then he sent them to Bethlehem, saying, "Go and search diligently for the child; and when you have found him, bring me word so that I may also go and pay him homage." (9) When they had heard the king, they set out; and there, ahead of them, went the star that they had seen at its rising, until it stopped over the place where the child was. (10) When they saw that the star had stopped, they were overwhelmed with joy. (11) On entering the house, they saw the child with Mary his mother, and they knelt down and paid him homage. Then, opening their treasure chests, they offered him gifts of gold, frankincense, and myrrh. (12) And having been warned in a dream not to return to Herod, they left for their own country by another road.

BY NOW YOU KNOW that you will be confronted by many claimants for your allegiance. Virtually anything can create a claim—socialism, bagels, TV, work, other people. It will take wisdom and courage to sort out the bogus kings (Elvis, King Kong) from the ones worthy of your commitment. We know we are just kidding when we use such terminology as "king." We don't have kings; it's a thing of the past. Taking orders from others seems unacceptable. Or is it?

In this story, three wise men must choose to obey "King Herod" or worship the "king of the Jews." Herod had all the marks of a king; Jesus was a baby in a diaper. To make a long and tense story short, they chose Jesus. You will be faced with the same sort of choice as professors, -isms, peers, and God in Jesus Christ confront you with the dilemma of the "wise men." With Jesus' help, you can make the right choice.

Prayer: Lord God, help me to study wisdom and power and to choose wisdom. Amen.

4 – Burden of the Wise: Unintended Consequences

Matthew 2:13-23 — (13) Now after they had left, an angel of the Lord appeared to Joseph in a dream and said, "Get up, take the child and his mother, and flee to Egypt, and remain there until I tell you; for Herod is about to search for the child, to destroy him." (14) Then Joseph got up, took the child and his mother by night, and went to Egypt, (15) and remained there until the death of Herod. This was to fulfill what had been spoken by the Lord through the prophet, "Out of Egypt I have called my son." (16) When Herod saw that he had been tricked by the wise men, he was infuriated, and he sent and killed all the children in and around Bethlehem who were two years old or under, according to the time that he had learned from the wise men. (17) Then was fulfilled what had been spoken through the prophet Jeremiah: (18) "A voice was heard in Ramah, wailing and loud lamentation, Rachel weeping for her children; she refused to be consoled, because they are no more." (19) When Herod died, an angel of the Lord suddenly appeared in a dream to Joseph in Egypt and said, (2) "Get up, take the child and his mother, and go to the land of Israel, for those who were seeking the child's life are dead." (21) Then Joseph got up, took the child and his mother, and went to the land of Israel. (22) But when he heard that Archelaus was ruling over Judea in place of his father Herod, he was afraid to go there. And after being warned in a dream, he went away to the district of Galilee. (23) There he made his home in a town called Nazareth, so that what had been spoken through the prophets might be fulfilled, "He will be called a Nazorean."

SNEAKING OUT OF TOWN at night is suspicious behavior. It needs looking into. But then you discover that baby Jesus would be killed if they stayed. Herod was acting on what the military calls "actionable intelligence"—information that calls for a response. Herod's "intelligence" was that his challenger for the throne could be found among the babies in a certain area. His response was totally and disgustingly gross.

As you go through college you will confront moments when you will have a variety of responses available to you—most pretty mundane, but some hard. Your decisions will call for wisdom. College doesn't teach wisdom. Art history? Yes. American lit? Yes. But wisdom? It's a good thing that Christ can be your Wisdom (1 Cor 1:30).

Prayer: Lord, teach me wisdom so that—like the wise men—I may travel by another way, your way. Amen.

5 – The "Tan Man"

Matthew 3:1–12 — (1) In those days John the Baptist appeared in the wilderness of Judea, proclaiming (2) "Repent, for the kingdom of heaven has come near." (3) This is the one of whom the prophet Isaiah spoke when he said, "The voice of one crying out in the wilderness: 'Prepare the way of the Lord, make his paths straight.'" (4) Now John wore clothing of camel's hair with a leather belt around his waist, and his food was locusts and wild honey. (5) Then the people of Jerusalem and all Judea were going out to him, and all the region along the Jordan, (6) and they were baptized by him in the river Jordan, confessing their sins. (7) But when he saw many Pharisees and Sadducees coming for baptism, he said to them, "You brood of vipers! Who warned you to flee from the wrath to come? (8) Bear fruit worthy of repentance. (9) Do not presume to say to yourselves, 'We have Abraham as our ancestor'; for I tell you, God is able from these stones to raise up children to Abraham. (10) Even now the ax is lying at the root of the trees; every tree therefore that does not bear good fruit is cut down and thrown into the fire. (11) I baptize you with water for repentance, but one who is more powerful than I is coming after me; I am not worthy to carry his sandals. He will baptize you with the Holy Spirit and fire. (12) His winnowing fork is in his hand, and he will clear his threshing floor and will gather his wheat into the granary; but the chaff he will burn with unquenchable fire."

EVERYONE CALLED HIM THE "Tan Man." It was winter but he rode his bike shirtless and silent around the University of Kansas campus. He looked disheveled, like the cartoon figure with the sandwich board that read, "Repent" and something about the end of the world. The rumor was that he was a veteran of the Vietnam War.

In the Gospel, the message of repentance is delivered by a strange-looking character who dresses in animal skins and lives out in the desert on a diet of bugs and honey. Unlike the Tan Man or the cartoon figure, John's message of repentance was clear: "change [your] mind." (That is what "repent" means in Greek.) Why? With Jesus, there is good reason to change your mind. There is a new world coming. You need to get with the new situation.

Once you were not a college person; now you are and that means thinking about things differently, particularly since Jesus is in your vicinity and installing a new kingdom.

Prayer: God of wisdom, keep my mind always turned in your direction. Amen.

6 – Do I Have to Do That?

Matthew 3:13–17 — (13) Then Jesus came from Galilee to John at the Jordan, to be baptized by him. (14) John would have prevented him, saying, "I need to be baptized by you, and do you come to me?" (15) But Jesus answered him, "Let it be so now; for it is proper for us in this way to fulfill all righteousness." Then he consented. (16) And when Jesus had been baptized, just as he came up from the water, suddenly the heavens were opened to him and he saw the Spirit of God descending like a dove and alighting on him. (17) And a voice from heaven said, "This is my Son, the Beloved, with whom I am well pleased."

BEFORE COLLEGE, WHEN YOU lived at home, there were probably a lot of things you had to do that you didn't think you needed to do—like be home by 10 PM week nights. Now you're in college and . . . you discover that college will make you do things you don't want to do—like fill out a form that you already filled out. Or maybe they want you to learn something that you absolutely know you will never need to know.

This is really where it gets interesting. Let's say you are going to be a brain surgeon or an orchestra conductor and your college says you must learn a foreign language. You think: I'll never need another language because everything I will need to know is already written in English. And then you wind up in the Army fighting in Afghanistan or stranded as a tourist in Argentina. Surprise! It would really have helped to know the local language.

Or you say you are going into sales and advertising and your college says you also need to have math. You think, I'll need to know about interpersonal relationships and TV because that's where supply meets demand; but who needs math? And then your boss sends you to accounting to figure out if the company is really making money.

John the Baptist called people to repent—literally, "change their minds"—and make that "change" (repentance) public by being baptized. While Jesus did not need to repent or be baptized he went to John and was baptized. Here was an example—one of the first of many—of Jesus' doing what he really didn't need to do but did anyway. Usually, doing what college wants you to do won't hurt. And who knows, it might turn out that you really did need it.

Prayer: Lord, can you give me the grace to do what I have to do even though I don't want to? Amen.

7 – Don't Mess with My Resume

Matthew 4:1–11 — (1) Then Jesus was led up by the Spirit into the wilderness to be tempted by the devil. (2) And he fasted forty days and forty nights, and afterward he was famished. (3) The tempter came and said to him, "If you are the Son of God, command these stones to become loaves of bread." (4) But he answered, "It is written, 'One does not live by bread alone, but by every word that comes from the mouth of God.'" (5) Then the devil took him to the holy city and placed him on the pinnacle of the temple, (6) saying to him, "If you are the Son of God, throw yourself down; for it is written, 'He will command his angels concerning you,' and 'On their hands they will bear you up, so that you will not dash your foot against a stone.'" (7) Jesus said to him, "Again it is written, 'Do not put the Lord your God to the test.'" (8) Again, the devil took him to a very high mountain and showed him all the kingdoms of the world and their splendor; (9) and he said to him, "All these I will give you, if you will fall down and worship me." (10) Jesus said to him, "Away with you, Satan! for it is written, 'Worship the Lord your God, and serve him only.'" (11) Then the devil left him, and suddenly angels came and waited on him.

Do you ever wonder if your parents would like you more if you changed in some way? Jesus is the Son of God. Okay, but what does that mean? The ability to leap tall buildings in a single bound? Having a chart-busting IQ? Being the nicest person of all time?

Here at the beginning of his public ministry, Jesus is questioned by the devil, and we get to eavesdrop on this conversation where the "job description" for Son of God is the topic. Satan tempts Jesus with options—all of which look good. He doesn't try to sidetrack Jesus from his role as Son of God as much as it is to get him to betray his "family." Satan wants Jesus to live out his Sonship in the service of another family.

The options presented by Satan are stunning: feed the hungry, use the power of God for personal gratification, take over the whole world. But the real temptation—the elephant in the room—was to deny God and accept the plan and the authority of Satan.

This story is about Jesus, not about you. But you might learn from it that you are part of a family and growing into who you are to become does not necessitate your leaving that family.

Prayer: Father of Jesus, I am thankful that Jesus' deepest loyalty is to you. Amen.

8 – The World's Shortest Sermon

Matthew 4:12–17 — (12) Now when Jesus heard that John had been arrested, he withdrew to Galilee. (13) He left Nazareth and made his home in Capernaum by the sea, in the territory of Zebulun and Naphtali, (14) so that what had been spoken through the prophet Isaiah might be fulfilled: (15) "Land of Zebulun, land of Naphtali, on the road by the sea, across the Jordan, Galilee of the Gentiles—(16) the people who sat in darkness have seen a great light, and for those who sat in the region and shadow of death light has dawned." (17) From that time Jesus began to proclaim, "Repent, for the kingdom of heaven has come near."

IN MANY OF YOUR classes, the main thing the instructor wants to accomplish is to shake up your thinking and open you to thinking in new ways. But even students can be hesitant about thinking in new ways. You can overestimate the probable (the sun will rise tomorrow) and underestimate the improbable (the events of 9/11).

An improbability that Christians have struggled with for centuries is that of the kingdom of God. (In the Gospel of Matthew, it is always called "the kingdom of heaven.") It is a shorthand expression for the effective rule of God over the world and for the commitment of all people to live as God intended us to live when he created us. This "kingdom of heaven" was described by Jesus in his numerous parables as he told story after story, comparison after comparison to try to suggest what it might be like if God were totally accepted as "in charge." If that happened, there truly would be a change of thinking.

Jesus came into the world at a time when a foreign nation ruled his people. That was about the fifth different foreign government that had ruled God's people since 587 BCE. They were getting pretty tired of it. But Jesus had a truly game-changing idea: that God should be acknowledged as ruler of all people and that people accept that as the motivating idea in their lives. And that was his message: "Repent, for the kingdom of heaven has come near." Indeed Jesus incarnated that kingdom, making it happen and making it near. It still is near because he still brings it.

Prayer: Help me to repent each and every day to look for the new ideas that you have for me. Amen.

44

9 – Disengagement

Matthew 4:18-22 — (18) As he walked by the Sea of Galilee, he saw two brothers, Simon, who is called Peter, and Andrew his brother, casting a net into the sea—for they were fishermen. (19) And he said to them, "Follow me, and I will make you fish for people." (20) Immediately they left their nets and followed him. (21) As he went from there, he saw two other brothers, James son of Zebedee and his brother John, in the boat with their father Zebedee, mending their nets, and he called them. (22) Immediately they left the boat and their father, and followed him.

THE TRANSITION TO COLLEGE can be hard. Part of it is the newness. New people. New places. New stuff.

But what about the old stuff. Do you leave it behind? Do you keep connected to it? How does that work?

You can't just up and leave it all behind; even if you wanted to. There are things that can't be changed: family relationships, deeply held convictions, some personal habits (good ones and bad ones).

Your encounter with Jesus has something of the same effect. That faith encounter forces you to reconsider how your new life as a disciple will look. How much of the old life is brought along and how to bring it along.

The experience of the first disciples—Peter, Andrew, James, and John—is instructive. It is not necessarily a model for you, but it could be helpful. There are things that they left behind and things that they kept.

What they left behind was the stuff, the technology. Peter and Andrew "left their nets." Without nets, no way could they catch fish. This is a definite break. James and John "left the[ir] boat." Again—no way could they catch fish without their boat.

But they also left "their father"! That was a major reorientation. You need to think about that one.

What they did not leave behind was their calling or vocation. Their vocation was to catch fish and feed people. Jesus took that call and elevated it: to catch people for the kingdom of heaven and to feed them what they really needed.

We all need to sort through what should be left behind and what can be taken with and transformed by Jesus.

Prayer: Help me to discern what I need to let go and what I need to keep. Amen.

10 – Here's the Plan

Matthew 4:23-25 — (23) Jesus went throughout Galilee, teaching in their synagogues and proclaiming the good news of the kingdom and curing every disease and every sickness among the people. (24) So his fame spread throughout all Syria, and they brought to him all the sick, those who were afflicted with various diseases and pains, demoniacs, epileptics, and paralytics, and he cured them. (25) And great crowds followed him from Galilee, the Decapolis, Jerusalem, Judea, and from beyond the Jordan.

DO YOU EVER WONDER what others really think of you? What is the word about you "on the street"? Do you think that what people say about you—your "fame" for want of a better term—could be based on your physical appearance, your family background, your character, some outrageous behavior you exhibit? Have you cultivated a *persona* designed to elicit some specific response from your public? Would your reputation involve your Christian faith and actions that grow out of that faith? Or would your reputation be built on something else?

Another question: What would you like people to think of you? In the extreme case, what would you like said at your funeral or inscribed on your tombstone?

We have learned that Jesus was the Son of God. So far in Matthew's gospel we have heard that from the author (with the genealogy), from God (at the baptism), and from Satan (in the temptation). Jesus was aware who he was and because of who he was, and his call, and his struggle with Satan, he had begun to work out what it was that he was to do: teach, proclaim God's kingdom, and heal all who came to him.

Based on what he was doing, "his fame" went out to all the inhabitants of the land. We learn a couple of things from this. Jesus' vocation to proclaim and push God's agenda to make life good for everyone was stunning enough to provide the basis for some serious and far reaching "fame." We also know that eventually Jesus would probably run into trouble with the legally constituted political and religious authorities who would value their own careers more than they would like to see the people under their care helped.

Maybe "fame" is not a desirable goal. Jesus was never out to blow his own horn and get "fame" and attention for himself. Perhaps the best thing is to focus on your own calling (vocation) and let the chips fall where they may.

Prayer: Keep me aware that my main concern is to be known by you. Amen.

11 – I'm Not on the List!

Matthew 5:1–12 — (1) When Jesus saw the crowds, he went up the mountain; and after he sat down, his disciples came to him. (2) Then he began to speak, and taught them, saying:

(3) "Blessed are the poor in spirit, for theirs is the kingdom of heaven.

(4) Blessed are those who mourn, for they will be comforted.

(5) Blessed are the meek, for they will inherit the earth.

(6) Blessed are those who hunger and thirst for righteousness, for they will be filled.

(7) Blessed are the merciful, for they will receive mercy.

(8) Blessed are the pure in heart, for they will see God.

(9) Blessed are the peacemakers, for they will be called children of God.

(10) Blessed are those who are persecuted for righteousness' sake, for theirs is the kingdom of heaven.

(11) Blessed are you when people revile you and persecute you and utter all kinds of evil against you falsely on my account. (12) Rejoice and be glad, for your reward is great in heaven, for in the same way they persecuted the prophets who were before you."

I WRITE THIS ON Christmas Eve when that icon of American consumerism, selfish individualism, and shallow moralism—a. k. a. Santa Claus—begins his trek from his shop at the North Pole to my house with my present because I think that I deserve it because I've been good (according to my own "naughty or nice" list [that I made up]).

But college students aren't on Jesus' list of the blessed! It doesn't say, "Blessed are those who study, for they shall succeed." It doesn't mention those who are poor because of educational loans or who hunger for fall break. So how do you get on the list? There are two options. One is to change yourself to fit his categories. That is the "do-it-yourself" option so prevalent in America. It's exactly what you are up to in college—self-improvement.

The other option is more realistic. It is to recognize who you are and what you are into. If you are not on Jesus' list, if you aren't ready for the kingdom of heaven, the first step is to admit it. If you don't know which way to change (repent), then acknowledging you are not on track is the first step in finding the right one.

Prayer: Help me to see myself through your eyes and not the world's. I want to be on your list. Amen.

47

12 – Irreplaceable

Matthew 5:13–16 — (13) "You are the salt of the earth; but if salt has lost its taste, how can its saltiness be restored? It is no longer good for anything, but is thrown out and trampled under foot. (14) You are the light of the world. A city built on a hill cannot be hid. (15) No one after lighting a lamp puts it under the bushel basket, but on the lampstand, and it gives light to all in the house. (16) In the same way, let your light shine before others, so that they may see your good works and give glory to you Father in heaven."

PARSONS, ST. MARY OF the Plains, Emporia. These are among the many American colleges that no longer exist. They were established to do something that their founders felt deeply about. Now they are gone—mostly due to lack of money. That doesn't mean that the vision that inspired them is not important.

The demise of a college is a wrenching experience. Employees lose jobs, buildings and resources go unused and unattended. Worst of all, the students and alumni are orphaned. It is as if a parent—the *alma mater*—has died. The "person" who gave them a unique training or fellowship is gone. There is no "home" to return to. The loss is the loss of something essential in the lives of the bereft alumni. When such a loss occurs, what exactly is lost? Is it irreplaceable? Today, if a college closes (dies), there are still more than 4,000 others to take its place. Or are there? Is there another one just like the one that disappeared?

In what respect would the world suffer loss if you were not here? Someday you won't be. How critical a loss will that be? Jesus addresses the disciples and calls them "salt" and "light." These labels are often reapplied to the church. If there were no Christian church, what would be lost? The Christian church is unique. Like "salt," it is irreplaceable; there is no substitute. Like "light," it is unique; there is nothing that can replace it. You belong to something unique and important. The world needs the church. And you are a unique and necessary part of that church. And the church is uniquely necessary—as "salt" and "light"—to you.

Prayer: Lord, you have made me unique—especially when I am salt and light to others. Amen.

13 –The World's Strongest Person

Matthew 5:17-20 — (17) Do not think that I have come to abolish the law or the prophets; I have come not to abolish but to fulfill. (18) For truly I tell you, until heaven and earth pass away, not one letter, not one stroke of a letter, will pass from the law until all is accomplished. (19) Therefore, whoever breaks one of the least of these commandments, and teaches others to do the same, will be called least in the kingdom of heaven; but whoever does them and teaches them will be called great in the kingdom of heaven. (20) For I tell you, unless your righteousness exceeds that of the scribes and Pharisees, you will never enter the kingdom of heaven.

DID YOU HAVE TO fill out an application for or meet any requirements to join your church? What are the expectations that you must meet to continue your membership? Are there any standards that need to be met for you to be generally accepted as Christian in America?

Someone was describing the standards and expectations for Christians in his hometown during his youth: Christians were people who were nice to the mail man. That suggests that to be considered a Christian you don't need to clear a very high bar. Or, to put it another way, everyone is a Christian. Is that really the kind of group to which you want to belong? The comedian Groucho Marx once told of a country club that had standards so low that it would even admit him; he wasn't sure that he really wanted to join an organization where standards were that low.

The disciples spent some time discussing which of them was the greatest (most important) in the kingdom of heaven (18:1). Jesus preempted any such discussion by issuing the criteria by which Christians would be evaluated. In addition to being a servant and facing the power of the Roman empire, the criteria for greatness had to do with teaching God's laws (all of them) and doing God's laws (again, all of them). This is not work for the fainthearted.

The German philosopher Nietzsche was scornful of Christianity because he saw it as producing wimps—people who would be subservient. He missed the point: Christians turned out to be the most powerful of all in the Roman Empire because they stood up to its power by loving and serving others and enduring persecution. Can Christians today pass this same standard?

Prayer: God of power, give me the strength to be a college student, and to be strong when necessary. Amen.

14 – It All Depends

Matthew 5:21-26 — (21) "You have heard that it was said to those of ancient times, 'You shall not murder'; and 'whoever murders shall be liable to judgment.' (22) But I say to you that if you are angry with a brother or sister, you will be liable to judgment; and if you insult a brother or sister, you will be liable to the council; and if you say, 'You fool,' you will be liable to the hell of fire. (23) So when you are offering your gift at the altar, if you remember that your brother or sister has something against you, (24) leave your gift there before the altar and go; first be reconciled to your brother or sister, and then come and offer your gift. (25) Come to terms quickly with your accuser while you are on the way to court with him, or your accuser may hand you over to the judge, and the judge to the guard, and you will be thrown into prison. (26) Truly I tell you, you will never get out until you have paid the last penny."

IN THESE "BUT I say to you" statements of Jesus he clearly was questioning the authority of the Jewish religious and cultural traditions of his day. He was proposing an entirely new way of thinking on the topic of killing. The real question had never been whether killing was wrong; it was only to define the circumstances that justified killing—to clarify when it would be right to kill. We were all aware that all sorts of "killings" occur every day: in war, in auto accidents, in capital punishment, in not sending food to starving refugees.

For Jesus, there were no "it all depends" moments. He laid down an entirely new paradigm: no killing, period. Don't even think about it.

Here you are, between the commonly accepted way of thinking (killing is okay under some circumstances) and a new paradigm (don't even think about it). In college you have some space to think about the two paradigms—their foundations, their implications. Moving from one to another is a huge deal.

In his important study of how paradigms change in science (from, say, the world is flat to the world is round), Thomas Kuhn (*Structure of Scientific Revolutions*) showed that such changes do not occur smoothly (or easily) but when the shift in paradigms from one to another occurs, the old one can't be understood through the framework of the new one (and vice versa).

Jesus' "But I say to you" challenges your faith with a similar change—to make the total leap of faith.

Prayer: Help me to know that it is you who calls me to a truly radical new understanding. Amen.

15 – Tinkering with the Rules

Matthew 5:27–32 — (27) "You have heard that it was said, 'You shall not commit adultery.' (28) But I say to you that everyone who looks at a woman with lust has already committed adultery with her in his heart. (29) If your right eye causes you to sin, tear it out and throw it away; it is better for you to lose one of your members than for your whole body to be thrown into hell. (30) And if your right hand causes you to sin, cut it off and throw it away; it is better for you to lose one of your members than for your whole body to go into hell. (31) It was also said, 'Whoever divorces his wife, let him give her a certificate of divorce.' (32) But I say to you that anyone who divorces his wife, except on the ground of unchastity, causes her to commit adultery; and whoever marries a divorced woman commits adultery."

ONE OF MY FAVORITE student-worn T-shirts said, "Question Authority." Indeed, that is pretty much what college ought to be about. But don't waste your time questioning all authority—speed limits, income tax law, gravity. You can't win most of your battles; so be selective about the battles you choose.

Do you need to read all of the assignment? Can you skim it? Skip it? What about challenging the dormitory rules? Should you sneak your pet snake into your room? Or a gun? If you are really that much smarter than the professor and the people who run the college, why are you paying them the big bucks instead of having them paying you? There are so many rules to break and so little time to do it. Maybe it is easier just to follow the rules and even try to understand them.

A news story reported the discovery of a young man in a motel room. The bathroom was splattered with blood. He was bleeding and in shock. A Bible lay on the bed, open to the Matthean passage you are reading today. Apparently the unfortunate young man had taken this portion literally, trying to cut off his hand. He should have tried to understand the rule first. Once you accept that Jesus is your true Teacher and offers the ultimate paradigm to guide you, you can work at refining your understanding of his truth.

Prayer: Give me the courage to take what you say seriously and the wisdom to understand it clearly. Amen.

16 – What You See is What You Get

Matthew 5:33–37 — (33) "Again, you have heard that it was said to those of ancient times, 'You shall not swear falsely, but carry out the vows you have made to the Lord.' (34) But I say to you, Do not swear at all, either by heaven, for it is the throne of God, (35) or by the earth, for it is his footstool, or by Jerusalem, for it is the city of the great King. (36) And do not swear by your head, for you cannot make one hair white or black. (37) Let your word be 'Yes, Yes' or 'No, No'; anything more than this comes from the evil one."

DID YOU EVER DISMANTLE a radio, a car, or a toy just to see how it worked? Then did you reassemble it and find that there were pieces left over that you couldn't fit back in?

One thing that you will encounter in college is the need to integrate facts, ideas, and theories. A theory or paradigm is an explanation. Its purpose is to explain things. If facts are left out of the explanation, then the explanation is inadequate, and a better, more inclusive theory is needed.

Take for example the explanation (paradigm) of how the planets move. The ancient Greek scientist Ptolemy (85–165 CE) theorized that the planets followed perfectly circular orbits around the earth. However, since each planet's actual path was different, he had to work in a lot of extra theoretical details. As additional factual observations added data, Ptolemy's theory became too cumbersome. Finally Copernicus (1473–1543) offered an apparently simpler solution: the planets circled the sun, not the earth. His theory was undercut by Newton (1642–1727) with an even simpler explanation based on more information. The newer theories worked better to integrate more facts into a simpler explanation. There was less left out that had to be explained by some other theory. There was more coherence and cohesiveness. More integrity.

"What you see is what you get" can be a high complement about a person. A person behaves one way to some people and the opposite toward others is what Scripture calls a "double-minded" person (Ps 119:113; 1 Tim 3:8; Jas 1:7, 4:8). Such people lack integrity. Integrity is defined in the dictionary as characterized by being undivided or complete. Integrity is not complicated. In fact, the simpler the better. Just as a good theory is simpler than a bad one, a person with true integrity is single—"yes" or "no." Anything messier and more complicated is suspect.

Prayer: Give me the purity of heart to be totally yours. Amen.

17 – Love Whom?

Matthew 5:38–48 — (38) "You have heard that it was said, 'An eye for an eye and a tooth for a tooth.' (39) But I say to you, Do not resist an evildoer. But if anyone strikes you on the right cheek, turn the other also, (40) and if anyone wants to sue you and take your coat, give your cloak as well; (41) and if anyone forces you to go one mile, go also the second mile. (42) Give to everyone who begs from you, and do not refuse anyone who wants to borrow from you. (43) You have heard that it was said, 'You shall love your neighbor and hate your enemy.' (44) But I say to you, Love your enemies and pray for those who persecute you, (45) so that you may be children of your Father in heaven; for he makes his sun rise on the evil and on the good, and sends rain on the righteous and on the unrighteous. (46) For if you love those who love you, what reward do you have? Do not even the tax collectors do the same? (47) And if you greet only your brothers and sisters, what more are you doing than others? Do not even the Gentiles do the same? (48) Be perfect, therefore, as your heavenly Father is perfect."

IF YOU COUNTED THE number of folks who have bumper stickers that read, "Don't get mad, get even" and compared that to the number whose bumper sticker is "Love your enemies," the "get even" folks would probably outnumber the "enemy lovers."

Jesus set the bar pretty high when he told his disciples to love their enemies. Who would want to do that? It is absolutely clear what is wrong with your enemy. (You fill in the list.) Any objective observer should agree: My enemy is a good-for-nothing blankety-blank you-know-what; his mother couldn't even love him.

Later, when asked about the greatest commandment, Jesus may seem to have backed off a bit when he said: "Love your neighbor." But we don't do well even with that limitation. Love is the kind of thing that takes it all out of you. And then calls for more. And it's so hard to quantify. Like, when have you loved enough? Or put differently: When have you received enough love? How do you know when you've had too much? Do you get a stomachache or a headache? Do you get a notice from the banker indicating you're overdrawn?

Jesus' whole deal cannot be quantified. Here in college, as in life, you want to quantify—get certain grades, get requirements "out of the way"—but Jesus is never in the counting game.

Prayer: God of love, may I love others as you have loved me. Amen.

18 – Shhhhh!

Matthew 6:1–8; 16–18 — (1) "Beware of practicing your piety before others in order to be seen by them; for then you have no reward from your Father in heaven. (2) So whenever you give alms, do not sound a trumpet before you, as the hypocrites do in the synagogues and in the streets, so that they may be praised by others. Truly, I tell you, they have received their reward. (3) But when you give alms, do not let your left hand know what your right hand is doing, (4) so that your alms may be done in secret; and your Father who sees in secret will reward you. (5) And whenever you pray, do not be like the hypocrites; for they love to stand and pray in the synagogues and at the street corners, so that they may be seen by others. Truly, I tell you, they have received their reward. (6) But when you pray, go into your room and shut the door and pray to your Father who is in secret; and your Father who sees in secret will reward you. (16) And whenever you fast, do not look dismal, like the hypocrites, for they disfigure their faces so as to show others that they are fasting. Truly, I tell you, they have received their reward. (17) But when you fast, put oil on your head and wash your face, (18) so that your fasting may be seen not by others but by your Father who is in secret; and your Father who sees in secret will reward you."

WILL THAT BE ON the test? (Do I need to study it? Or can I ignore it? Do not ask your professor this question. Ever.)

One of my favorite teachings of Jesus is when he tells us not to do something. That's cool. The less there is to do in the Christian life, the more time I have to do my own thing. So I shouldn't show off my piety. That will work; it will cut down on the time pretending to be holy. Don't give alms in public. A serious economy move; I'm on it already. Don't pray out loud. I always feel uneasy about public praying. Don't fast. Wait: don't fast means don't don't eat. Really? Okay; because I really like to eat.

Is there a common thread here? Anything that ties all these low-profile, "do not" commands together? What if we were to compare them to athletics? The athlete practices, exercises, trains, learns routines, watches her diet—all in private. In public, she performs. All the rest was preparation, disciplining (disciple-ing?) herself into what she believed she was.

In private you can concentrate on gearing yourself into the most appropriate response to God.

Prayer: God of power, control the temptation of pride that always lurks at my doorstep. Amen.

19 – The Prayer

Matthew 6:7–15 — (7) "When you are praying, do not heap up empty phrases as the Gentiles do; for they think that they will be heard because of their many words. (8) Do not be like them, for your Father knows what you need before you ask him. (9) Pray then in this way: Our Father in heaven, hallowed be your name. (10) Your kingdom come. Your will be done, on earth as it is in heaven. (11) Give us this day our daily bread. (12) And forgive us our debts, as we also have forgiven our debtors. (13) And do not bring us to the time of trial, but rescue us from the evil one. (14) For if you forgive others their trespasses, your heavenly Father will also forgive you; (15) but if you do not forgive others, neither will your Father forgive your trespasses."

ONE OF THE NEAT things about college is the creativity of some teachers. A really creative teacher helps you learn from things you'd never thought of: garbage, tree rings, or paintings that don't seem to look like anything.

Could you learn something from a prayer? We normally think of prayers as vehicles for asking God for something, or maybe expressing appreciation for something. But what about prayer as a teaching/learning exercise?

What was your last prayer about? Health for a sick relative? Success in a class? Healing in a personal relationship? Americans are good at knowing what they want. How about the run-up to Christmas when all the letters from kids to Santa appear in the newspaper? Each child tells exactly what they want: item after item. But almost never a thought about Santa giving something to someone else.

If we use the Lord's Prayer as a model for our prayers, we begin by praying for something pretty big: God's kingdom. Asking that God really take over the world is tantamount to relinquishing your own control over it. And then there is the part about asking for food. Didn't you already pay hard-earned cash for food service? And the worst part is the one asking for forgiveness—which is supposed to be God's favorite thing to do for us humans—and then making his forgiving you depend on your forgiving others.

Someone has written that we need to be taught what it is that we should want. Perhaps you could use this prayer regularly to shift your focus from what you want to what God wants you to want.

Prayer: Help me, O Lord, to listen to what you have taught me to pray for. And to truly want it. Amen.

20 – Heads or Tails?

Matthew 6:19–24 — (19) "Do not store up for yourselves treasures on earth, where moth and rust consume and where thieves break in and steal; (20) but store up for yourselves treasures in heaven, where neither moth nor rust consumes and where thieves do not break in and steal. (21) For where your treasure is, there your heart will be also. (22) The eye is the lamp of the body. So, if your eye is healthy, your whole body will be full of light; (23) but if your eye is unhealthy, your whole body will be full of darkness. If then the light in you is darkness, how great is the darkness! (24) No one can serve two masters; for a slave will either hate the one and love the other, or be devoted to the one and despise the other. You cannot serve God and wealth."

EVERY COIN FLIP IS absolutely decisive: heads or tail; no in-betweens. It may not seem so at this moment in your college career, but each decision you make can be decisive. At least, each decision excludes alternative possibilities. Sure, deciding between a banana split and a milk shake is not a big deal. But consider bigger decisions. You chose this college, not another one. That means that you will meet Bob and Ray, not Frank and Guido; you will date Peter or Mary, not Junior or Sara. It may mean that you will marry Billy or Martha, not Tom or Sissie.

And there are a lot of possibilities for a major. Of course, you may have decided on that already: science, taking you into medicine; accounting, taking you into business; English, taking you into teaching. Even within the major, there are choices: biology from Professor Smith or Professor Jones? Introduction to education from Mr. Wills or Ms. Peterson? Sociology from Dr. Green or Dr. White?

These can seem like easy choices but can have unforeseen but enormously decisive consequences. And we make a lot of these life-determining decisions on pretty flimsy (irrational, silly) grounds. I chose one school instead of another because of what I was told about taking music lessons. Then I never took music lessons, but I did wind up meeting the girl I would marry.

Sometimes it is not so much a matter of the choice you make but of making the best of those choices. Sometimes it is absolutely crucial which choice you make—God is the best choice then.

Prayer: I may not always make right choices but I thank you for choosing me. Amen.

56

21 – What, Me Worry?

Matthew 6:25–34 — (25) Therefore I tell you, do not worry about your life, what you will eat or what you will drink, or about your body, what you will wear. Is not life more than food, and the body more than clothing? (26) Look at the birds of the air; they neither sow nor reap nor gather into barns, and yet your heavenly Father feeds them. Are you not of more value than they? (27) And can any of you by worrying add a single hour to your span of life? (28) And why do you worry about clothing? Consider the lilies of the field, how they grow; they neither toil nor spin, (29) yet I tell you, even Solomon in all his glory was not clothed like one of these. (30) But if God so clothes the grass of the field, which is alive today and tomorrow is thrown into the oven, will he not much more clothe you—you of little faith? (31) Therefore do not worry, saying, 'What will we eat?' or 'What will we drink?' or 'What will we wear?' (32) For it is the Gentiles who strive for all these things; and indeed your heavenly father knows that you need all these things. (33) But strive first for the kingdom of God and his righteousness, and all these things will be given to you as well. (34) So do not worry about tomorrow, for tomorrow will bring worries of its own. Today's trouble is enough for today."

IT MUST HAVE BEEN easy for Jesus to go around telling people to "not worry about tomorrow." He didn't have bills, assignments, a job, a car, climate change, and a dozen other crises like you do. It is hard to keep a focus on God or any other single thing and not to worry about what might or might not happen.

In college the syllabus lets you know what's coming (papers, tests, etc.). But anxiety is about all that other stuff that might or might not happen. Talk about opening yourself up to problems, this is it. Søren Kierkegaard, the nineteenth-century Danish Christian existentialist, wrote a book titled *Purity of Heart Is to Will One Thing.* It was about our all-out commitment to find in God the assurance impossible to find elsewhere. We Americans are all over the map looking for meaning—and wind up with a lot of anxiety and worry.

Jesus' invitation not to worry reminds you that you can't do much about most stuff, and that he will care for you in whatever does happen.

Prayer: Thank you for caring about what I can't foresee or control. Amen.

22 – Golden Rule

Matthew 7:1–12 — (1) "Do not judge, so that you may not be judged. (2) For with the judgment you make you will be judged, and the measure you give will be the measure you get. (3) Why do you see the speck in your neighbor's eye, but do not notice the log in your own eye? (4) Or how can you say to your neighbor, 'Let me take the speck out of your eye,' while the log is in your own eye? (5) You hypocrite, first take the log out of your own eye, and then you will see clearly to take the speck out of your neighbor's eye. (6) Do not give what is holy to dogs; and do not throw your pearls before swine, or they will trample them under foot and turn and maul you. (7) Ask, and it will be given you; search, and you will find; knock, and the door will be opened for you. (8) For everyone who asks receives, and everyone who searches finds, and for everyone who knocks, the door will be opened. (9) Is there anyone among you who, if your child asks for bread, will give a stone? (10) Or if the child asks for a fish, will give a snake? (11) If you then, who are evil, know how to give good gifts to your children, how much more will your Father in heaven give good things to those who ask him! (12) In everything do to others as you would have them do to you; for this is the law and the prophets.

YOU ARE THE DECIDER of ethical behavior. The rules for what you do are up to you. You create them on the basis of how you would like to be treated by others. Would you like them to be polite? Would you like them to help you when you feel sad, depressed, in need? The answers constitute an ethical picture that is rich in possibilities for what others might do for you, but demanding in what you are called upon to do for others, and unimaginably rewarding in what others will experience as a result of your behavior.

But what if others don't respond well to you? What if, instead of doing to you as you would like them to, they are hurtful? Sorry, Jesus didn't say anything about that. In fact, of course, he knew that people wouldn't necessarily treat you well. He was teaching you how to act. He wasn't teaching others how to act; nor are you to tell others what to do. You are here to figure out what you are supposed to do. So, use your imagination. Think of what would you like others to do and do it!

Prayer: Keep me mindful of others. Amen.

23 – No Pain, No Gain

Matthew 7:13-14 — (13) Enter through the narrow gate; for the gate is wide and the road is easy that leads to destruction, and there are many who take it. (14) For the gate is narrow and the road is hard that leads to life, and there are few who find it.

"THE GATE IS NARROW and the road is hard." That's a good athletic metaphor. To squeeze through a narrow gate you must be lithe, slim. To make it on a hard way you need stamina, strength, energy, resilience, and focus. No place here for the weak, the wimpy, the faint of heart, or the out of shape. It is also a good metaphor for college success. Ultimately, success (A's, a degree, honors) depends on performance, which in turn depends on disciplined commitment. We Americans have it easier than everyone else precisely because our lives have more support—electricity, calories, housing, medical care—than anyone else enjoys. We are on Easy Street, the Yellow Brick Road, on our way to "happily ever after."

We are a secular culture in many ways. Most of us say we believe in God and if you have gone to many funerals, the dearly departed are generally guaranteed an honored position near God in heaven because of . . . well, because of whatever the presiding minister can pull out of the collection of anecdotes supplied by loved ones to show that the deceased had been a "good" person. We are Christians whether we like it or not. We are Christians no matter who we are. Dietrich Bonhoeffer, the famed pastor and theologian who was imprisoned and hanged by the Nazis in the closing days of WWII called this "cheap grace"—everybody is okay.

Is there anything wrong with this picture? Remember Groucho Marx's quip that he would not want to be a member of a group that had standards low enough to let him in? When we consider the time—sometimes even years!—and the demands to know about the faith required for church membership of converts in the days when Christianity was still illegal under the Roman Empire, we ought to be ashamed of how easy we have it.

If you want to do things right, the way Jesus is instructing, what would make it so hard to attain the life he promises? It must be that it is hard to keep your focus on Christ. But the thing is that when you focus on Jesus, the whole thing gets radically simplified.

Prayer: Don't let me focus on the narrow gate or the hard way, but only on you, O Christ. Amen.

24 – Jekyll or Hyde?

Matthew 7:15–23 — (15) Beware of false prophets, who come to you in sheep's clothing but inwardly are ravenous wolves. (16) You will know them by their fruits. Are grapes gathered from thorns, or figs from thistles? (17) In the same way, every good tree bears good fruit, but the bad tree bears bad fruit. (18) A good tree cannot bear bad fruit, nor can a bad tree bear good fruit. (19) Every tree that does not bear good fruit is cut down and thrown into the fire. (20) Thus you will know them by their fruits. (21) Not everyone who says to me, 'Lord, Lord,' will enter the kingdom of heaven, but only the one who does the will of my Father in heaven. (22) On that day many will say to me, 'Lord, Lord, did we not prophesy in your name, and cast out demons in your name, and do many deeds of power in your name?' (23) Then I will declare to them, 'I never knew you; go away from me, you evil-doers.'"

HOW MANY PERSONALITIES DO you have? Do you offer one *persona* to your grandparents and another to your roommate? Do you talk the same way to your parents as to your boy- or girlfriend? This is not to say that you have multiple personality disorder and need psychiatric attention. But it is to say that you might want to notice how you may differ as you relate to different audiences. The real test of who people are, says Jesus, is found in their "fruits"—what they actually do. They may talk the talk, but do they walk the walk?

Time for an inventory of your personalities. Check for several features: Is this particular *persona* consistent with your highest hopes for yourself? Is it the real you? Are there basic elements in it that are consistent with all your other *personae*? Are there elements in it that you don't use in other relationships? Are there gestures, words, or topics that you avoid or include? What is that telling the other person about you? The issue here is whether there is a fundamental consistency across all of the "you's" that you present to others.

Have the fragmenting possibilities of the college experience affected you in such a way as to encourage you to see your life in different parts, each needing a different you?

Prayer: Creator God, love all of the "me's"; bring them together into the one person you created me to be. Amen.

25 – The One Teacher

Matthew 7:24-29 — (24) "Everyone then who hears these words of mine and acts on them will be like a wise man who built his house on rock. (25) The rain fell, the floods came, and the winds blew and beat on that house, but it did not fall, because it had been founded on rock. (26) And everyone who hears these words of mine and does not act on them will be like a foolish man who built his house on sand. (27) The rain fell, and the floods came, and the winds blew and beat against that house, and it fell—and great was its fall!" (28) Now when Jesus had finished saying these things, the crowds were astounded at his teaching, (29) for he taught them as one having authority, and not as their scribes.

"OH YEAH? WHO SAYS?" You encounter a truth claim and want to know the source. As you become more sophisticated, you may become more skeptical. Does your uncle Herb really know that scientists who claim humans are affecting the global climate are on the payroll of the Weather Channel? Does the man you chatted with awaiting your dental appointment really know that your college's basketball players are on steroids? Does the candidate who spoke yesterday really know that her opponent is in the pocket of "special interests"?

One reason for your increasing skepticism about truth claims is the fact that in college you are daily sitting in the presence of people who have authority as opposed to people who only claim authority. Professors are people with authority because they know their stuff on the basis of personal, firsthand experience and study. Your college hired them because they are authorities and can communicate that knowledge comfortably and effectively to you.

This difference between those who are authorities because they just know the stuff, and those who always have to refer to some other source must have been what distinguished Jesus from others in his day. Is this to say that Jesus is just like your teachers? In some ways, perhaps, but there is one more thing that really distinguishes Jesus from all others. Each of your teachers is an authority in his (or her) own area: one is a math whiz, another seems to know every novel ever written, while a third has perfect pitch and can play every instrument in the band. Jesus is the authority for the most important subject you will every study: life.

Prayer: Help me to grow in my trust of you to lead me through life. Amen.

26 – Trifecta

Matthew 8:1–17 — (1) When Jesus had come down from the mountain, great crowds followed him; (2) and there was a leper who came to him and knelt before him, saying, "Lord, if you choose, you can make me clean." (3) He stretched out his hand and touched him, saying, "I do choose. Be made clean!" Immediately his leprosy was cleansed. (4) Then Jesus said to him, "See that you say nothing to anyone; but go, show yourself to the priest, and offer the gift that Moses commanded, as a testimony to them." (5) When he entered Capernaum, a centurion came to him, appealing to him (6) and saying, "Lord, my servant is lying at home paralyzed, in terrible distress." (7) And he said to him, "I will come and cure him. " (8) The centurion answered, "Lord, I am not worthy to have you come under my roof; but only speak the word, and my servant will be healed. (9) For I also am a man under authority, with soldiers under me; and I say to one, 'Go,' and he goes, and to another, 'Come,' and he comes, and to my slave, "Do this,' and the slave does it." (10) When Jesus heard him, he was amazed and said to those who followed him, "Truly I tell you, in no one in Israel have I found such faith. (11) I tell you, many will come from east and west and will eat with Abraham and Isaac and Jacob in the kingdom of heaven, (12) while the heirs of the kingdom will be thrown into the outer darkness, where there will be weeping and gnashing of teeth." (13) And to the centurion Jesus said, "Go; let it be done for you according to your faith." And the servant was healed in that hour. (14) When Jesus entered Peter's house, he saw his mother-in-law lying in bed with a fever; (15) he touched her hand, and the fever left her, and she got up and began to serve him. (16) That evening they brought to him many who were possessed with demons; and he cast out the spirits with a word, and cured all who were sick. (17) This was to fulfill what had been spoken through the prophet Isaiah, "He took our infirmities and bore our diseases."

THREE OF THE LEAST lovable folks around in Jesus' day—a leper, a foreigner, a mother-in-law—need help. Jesus cures them all. We don't know what his methods were. Fortunately, he still invites anyone with problems to ask him for help.

(And do we really agree that these three folks aren't lovable? God loves them. Jesus loves them. How can you not?)

Prayer: I don't care how, but take from me what would keep me from being who you want me to be. Amen.

27 – Discipled or Dismissed?

Matthew 8:18–27 — (18) Now when Jesus saw great crowds around him, he gave orders to go over to the other side. (19) A scribe then approached and said, "Teacher, I will follow you wherever you go." (20) And Jesus said to him, "Foxes have holes, and birds of the air have nests; but the Son of Man has nowhere to lay his head." (21) Another of his disciples said to him, "Lord, first let me go and bury my father." (22) But Jesus said to him, "Follow me, and let the dead bury their own dead." (23) And when he got into the boat, his disciples followed him. (24) A windstorm arose on the sea, so great that the boat was being swamped by the waves; but he was asleep. (25) And they went and woke him up, saying, "Lord, save us! We are perishing!" (26) And he said to them, "Why are you afraid, you of little faith?" Then he got up and rebuked the winds and the sea; and there was a dead calm. (27) They were amazed, saying "What sort of man is this, that even the winds and the sea obey him?"

SO FAR, THE STORY of Jesus is spectacular: a childhood escape from attempted murder; public recognition as a uniquely authoritative speaker; fame as a miracle worker. Jesus is someone people want to follow. The idea is that if you could hook up with him you would be safe from danger and positioned to be where the action is. People want to get on the Jesus bandwagon.

But it's hard to carry through. Look at the scribe—an important Jewish functionary. Jesus points out to him that he (Jesus) "has nowhere to lay his head." To follow him means that you will enter unexplored territory with no certainties or expectations. Another "disciple" wants to join, but Jesus' answer is "now or never." Don't even take the time to bury your father! Those who did follow Jesus—into a boat on a stormy sea—saw Jesus fall asleep. In a storm! They interpreted this as Jesus' disregard for them.

Discipleship is not a simple matter. It requires that aspirants count the cost and then cut themselves off completely from their former lives and the securities that had accompanied them. And trust Jesus completely.

Is discipleship possible in college? Aren't there too many distractions for such a focused commitment? Why follow Jesus anyway? To paraphrase Peter's response to Jesus found in the Gospel of John when Jesus asked if the disciples would fall away as many had done (John 6:68): Where else would we go if we don't go with you?

Prayer: Lord, if I am to be a disciple and follow you, I will need some help. Amen.

28 – Two Wild and Crazy Guys

Matthew 8:28—9:1 — (28) When he came to the other side, to the country of the Gadarenes, two demoniacs coming out of the tombs met him. They were so fierce that no one could pass that way. (29) Suddenly they shouted, "What have you to do with us, Son of God? Have you come here to torment us before the time?" (30) Now a large herd of swine was feeding at some distance from them. (31) The demons begged him, "If you cast us out, send us into the herd of swine." (32) And he said to them, "Go!" So they came out and entered the swine; and suddenly, the whole herd rushed down the steep bank into the sea and perished in the water. (33) The swineherds ran off, and on going into the town, they told the whole story about what had happened to the demoniacs. (34) Then the whole town came out to meet Jesus; and when they saw him, they begged him to leave their neighborhood. (9:1) And after getting into a boat he crossed the sea and came to his own town.

JESUS JUST KEEPS ON going, answering humans in need wherever he goes. His "story" is one of doing good; but the response is almost always mixed. We can see how he is getting into more trouble with people who have religious, cultural, political, and economic objections to his mission.

If these had been your pigs, you would have been pretty upset with Jesus for (i) "infecting" them with a demon, and (ii) sending them off of a cliff to drown in the Sea of Galilee.

On the other hand, if you were one of the demoniacs from whom Jesus had driven out "their demons" (as we might refer today to the nightmarish emotional horrors that the mentally ill can suffer), you would have been liberated.

But then on yet another hand, if you had been mentally incapacitated and suddenly found yourself sane, balanced, and in your right mind again, would you be excited about returning to your old life, old friends, old job? Would they all be happy to see you?

And then on the (last) other hand, you can understand the locals ("the whole town") who had learned of all the personal, social, and economic rearrangements for which Jesus was responsible: Wouldn't it just be better if he were to move on? We don't need more of the same.

Following Jesus—or even just being there, near him—can put you in a wild and crazy place. Especially in college where "on the one hand" is always answered with "on the other hand."

Prayer: Lord, if I am to be a disciple and follow you, I will need courage. Amen.

29 – Fix or Forgive?

Matthew 9:2–8 — (2) And just then some people were carrying a paralyzed man lying on a bed. When Jesus saw their faith, he said to the paralytic, "Take heart, son; your sins are forgiven." (3) Then some of the scribes said to themselves, "This man is blaspheming." (4) But Jesus, perceiving their thoughts, said, "Why do you think evil in your hearts? (5) For which is easier, to say, 'Your sins are forgiven,' or to say, 'Stand up and walk'? (6) But so that you may know that the Son of Man has authority on earth to forgive sins"— he then said to the paralytic—"Stand up, take your bed and go to your home." (7) And he stood up and went to his home. (8) When the crowds saw it, they were filled with awe, and they glorified God, who had given such authority to human beings

NO MATTER WHAT JESUS does, he draws criticism. In this case some scribes accuse Jesus of blaspheming—basically attacking God—when he forgives the paralytic. Jesus sees a person in need, and instead of addressing the physical problem he basically says, "Don't worry; I forgive your sins." And the poor fellow is still lying there wondering why he had been carried all the way for that. But if we can trust Jesus, he acts as if the main problem we all have is sin. He knew that only God forgives sin. So there is a kind of arrogant logic in Jesus' behavior. He takes care of first things first by forgiving the man's sins. And he does that as if he were God. No wonder the scribes are critical. Jesus has just implicitly declared himself God—or at least possessing a power and prerogative of God.

Knowing the scribes' thoughts, Jesus poses a tough dilemma: Which is easier, to forgive sins or heal disease? He doesn't wait for an answer but goes ahead and heals the man as a kind of proof that he also has the power to forgive sins.

Occasionally you will get a tough question like that from a professor— a question that seems impossible to answer. She knows you can't answer it. Maybe she knows that no one can answer it. But she is trying to get you to think. What has Jesus gotten you to think about? You probably already know that only God can forgive sins and that only God could perform a miracle. What you may really be brought up short on is the question buried here: What do you personally make of the fact that Jesus forgave sins and healed catastrophically damaged bodies?

Prayer: God almighty, I am filled with awe and I glorify you because of the authority you gave to Jesus. Amen.

30 – Misbehaving Teacher?

Matthew 9:9–13 — (9) As Jesus was walking along, he saw a man called Matthew sitting at the tax booth; and he said to him, "Follow me." And he got up and followed him. (10) And as he sat at dinner in the house, many tax collectors and sinners came and were sitting with him and his disciples. (11) When the Pharisees saw this, they said to his disciples, "Why does your teacher eat with tax collectors and sinners?" (12) But when he heard this, he said, "Those who are well have no need of a physician, but those who are sick. (13) Go and learn what this means, 'I desire mercy, not sacrifice,' For I have come to call not the righteous but sinners."

HAVE YOU HEARD ANY gossip lately about misbehavior on the part of teachers? About teachers dating students? About sexual misconduct? While this isn't common, it does happen, and when it does, all kinds of consequences result. Administrators freak out. Faculty get fired. People sue. Bad publicity explodes. Teachers are not supposed to be "pals" with students. They are supposed to be teachers.

So when Jesus (the teacher) recruits Matthew to be a disciple (student) and they go off to a party where disciples, (other) tax collectors, and sinners are all hanging out together, the Jewish Pharisees have a concern: What is the teacher doing hanging out with folks in a setting that is not the regular teacher/student setting?

Jesus changes the topic.

(Before following Jesus' detour in the conversation, please note: Taking care in your choice of friends—classmates, workmates, roommates, even professors—is very important. Be wise; be cautious; be prayerful. Okay—back to the passage.)

Speaking as a doctor rather than a teacher, Jesus says he has come to "heal the sick." In this instance, his diagnosis is quick and results in . . . a teaching: "Go and learn what this means, 'I desire mercy; not sacrifice.'" This "diagnosis/teaching" is that a sacrifice is selfish—under your control, limited (to a pigeon, or a dollar), and performed for your own benefit. Mercy is done for others and you can't measure it.

Prayer: Help me to seek the best from each of my teachers. Amen.

31 – Mystifying Multitasker

Matthew 9:14-26 — (14) Then the disciples of John came to him, saying, "Why do we and the Pharisees fast often, but your disciples do not fast?" (15) And Jesus said to them, "The wedding guests cannot mourn as long as the bridegroom is with them, can they? The days will come when the bridegroom is taken away from them, and then they will fast. (16) No one sews a piece of unshrunk cloth on an old cloak, for the patch pulls away from the cloak, and a worse tear is made. (17) Neither is new wine put into old wineskins; otherwise, the skins burst, and the wine is spilled, and the skins are destroyed; but new wine is put into fresh wineskins, and so both are preserved." (18) While he was saying these things to them, suddenly a leader of the synagogue came in and knelt before him, saying, "My daughter has just died; but come and lay your hand on her, and she will live." (19) And Jesus got up and followed him, with his disciples. (20) Then suddenly a woman who had been suffering from hemorrhages for twelve years came up behind him and touched the fringe of his cloak, (21) for she said to herself, "If I only touch his cloak, I will be made well." (22) Jesus turned, and seeing her he said, "Take heart, daughter; your faith has made you well." And instantly the woman was made well. (23) When Jesus came to the leader's house and saw the flute players and the crowd making a commotion, (24) he said, "Go away; for the girl is not dead but sleeping." And they laughed at him. (25) But when the crowd had been put outside, he went in and took her by the hand, and the girl got up. (26) And the report of this spread throughout that district.

ONE RESPONSE TO A confusing situation is to use laughter to hide your confusion. But be cautious about laughing at someone else who has a new idea—the earth is round, etc.; he might have the last laugh.

Perhaps the onlookers in this story could be forgiven for their confusion. Maybe the disciples don't "fast" (as in not eat) but Jesus certainly is "fast" (as in quick) as he races through a teaching and healing "schedule" that would weary a whole team of do-gooders. Perhaps the onlookers concluded that the poor fellow was too exhausted to notice that the girl was dead. At least those onlookers had a laugh in the midst of what was a sad time for the family and friends of the girl. But Jesus was focused—on caring for peoples' needs. No joke.

Prayer: Thank you, Jesus, for slowing down for me. Amen.

32 – Jesus' Best-Obeyed Command

Matthew 9:27–31 — (27) As Jesus went on from there, two blind men followed him, crying loudly, "Have mercy on us, Son of David!" (28) When he entered the house, the blind men came to him; and Jesus said to them, "Do you believe that I am able to do this? " They said to him, "Yes, Lord." (29) Then he touched their eyes and said, "According to your faith let it be done to you." (30) And their eyes were opened. Then Jesus sternly ordered them, "See that no one knows of this." (31) But they went away and spread the news about him throughout that district.

Isn't it great when the teacher says, "There is no assignment for tomorrow"? It doesn't happen often—it's like a miracle—but when it does happen, you pay attention to what the teacher tells you (not!) to do.

Did you ever wonder which of Jesus' commandments was the best-kept one? Of course we know which one (actually two) he considered most important: Love God and love your neighbor. In applying the second half of the command, the disciples got all tangled up determining just who the neighbor was that they were supposed to love (so they wouldn't love anyone else accidentally?). Then he gave them the "love your enemy" command. So it is a safe bet that these are not the commands that we Christians have hurried to obey.

You can probably guess the answer to the question about which is the best-kept command. It is the easiest one to keep. It is a command he often makes after performing a miracle for someone. He commands them not to tell what has happened to them! But wouldn't you know—more often than not, those people run off and blab it to everybody! Just because Jesus cured them from blindness or raised their loved one from the dead, they think it is worth spreading it all around the neighborhood. And in direct conflict with Jesus' command.

Has anything happened to you that is good enough to break Jesus' command not to tell anyone?

Prayer: Sorry that I told somebody what a wonderful gift you have given me. I hope I can do it again! Amen.

33 – Bitter Pills

Matthew 9:32–36 — (32) After they had gone away, a demoniac who was mute was brought to him. (33) And when the demon had been cast out, the one who had been mute spoke; and the crowds were amazed and said, "Never has anything like this been seen in Israel." (34) But the Pharisees said, "By the ruler of the demons he casts out the demons." (35) Then Jesus went about all the cities and villages, teaching in their synagogues, and proclaiming the good news of the kingdom, and curing every disease and every sickness. (36) When he saw the crowds, he had compassion for them, because they were harassed and helpless, like sheep without a shepherd.

ONE OF THE MAIN things that recommends Jesus to us human beings is that he not only became fully human (born as a real baby, died a painful physical death) but that he experienced life in many of the ways we all experience it. That includes that familiar experience of getting blamed for something you didn't do, or not getting credit for something you did do.

You could say that was "the story of Jesus' life." Today's selection is a thumbnail episode that could represent the entirety of his life. Jesus encounters a man who is unable to speak—a horrible debility, particularly without the technical aids now available to help someone communicate so many thoughts that could not otherwise find the wings to others' ears. Whatever response the mute man has is over-shouted by the crowd (Yeah!) and the Pharisees (Boo!). The latter not only are (i) not happy for the cured man and (ii) not impressed with Jesus' gift of healing; they mount a campaign against Jesus, accusing him of complicity with the very forces he has used his God-given powers to overcome.

The Pharisees are acting like jerks.

Jesus must be seeing the handwriting on the wall—that the establishment guys are out to blacken his name and reputation and possibly do worse. So he has a couple of choices: quit this teaching-healing ministry before it gets him in bad trouble; or, keep at it because that is what God has sent him to do.

Scripture tells us that he kept right on with his ministry, encouraged when he saw how needy the crowds were—"harassed and helpless." If that is how you feel sometimes, Jesus can be the one to help you.

Prayer: Thank you, Lord, for not abandoning your call to help the needy and to announce the kingdom. Amen.

34 – Reflections on Discipleship

Matthew 9:37—10:16 — (37) Then he said to his disciples, "The harvest is plentiful, but the laborers are few; (38) therefore ask the Lord of the harvest to send out laborers into his harvest." (10:1) Then Jesus summoned his twelve disciples and gave them authority over unclean spirits, to cast them out, and to cure every disease and every sickness. (2) These are the names of the twelve apostles: first, Simon, also known as Peter, and his brother Andrew; James son of Zebedee, and his brother John; (3) Philip and Bartholomew; Thomas and Matthew the tax collector; James son of Alphaeus, and Thaddaeus; (4) Simon the Cananaean, and Judas Iscariot, the one who betrayed him. (5) These twelve Jesus sent out with the following instructions: "Go nowhere among the Gentiles, and enter no town of the Samaritans, (6) but go rather to the lost sheep of the house of Israel. (7) As you go, proclaim the good news, 'The kingdom of heaven has come near.' (8) Cure the sick, raise the dead, cleanse the lepers, cast out demons. You received without payment; give without payment. (9) Take no gold, or silver, or copper in your belts, (10) no bag for your journey, or two tunics, or sandals, or a staff; for laborers deserve their food. (11) Whatever town or village you enter, find out who in it is worthy, and stay there until you leave. (12) As you enter the house, greet it. (13) If the house is worthy, let your peace come upon it; but if it is not worthy, let your peace return to you. (14) If anyone will not welcome you or listen to your words, shake off the dust from your feet as you leave that house or town. (15) Truly I tell you, it will be more tolerable for the land of Sodom and Gomorrah on the day of judgment than for that town. (16) See, I am sending you out like sheep into the midst of wolves. So be wise as serpents and innocent as doves."

JESUS HAD WORK TO do, including entrusting his ministry to his disciples—none of whom were qualified for that responsibility. How do you feel about being a disciple of Jesus when discipleship is spelled "teach" or "heal" or "preach" or at least "be helpful"? Inadequate? That's okay. You aren't loved by God and Jesus because you are prepared to conquer the world. Now that you're in college, can you list the gifts that college makes available to you so that you can develop some of your potential, skills, and interests to become a more effective disciple of Jesus?

Prayer: Make me humble and realistic about what I don't know and eager to learn what I need to know. Amen.

35 – Warning and Assurance

Matthew 10:17–25 — (17) "Beware of them, for they will hand you over to councils and flog you in their synagogues; (18) and you will be dragged before governors and kings because of me, as a testimony to them and the Gentiles. (19) When they hand you over, do not worry about how you are to speak or what you are to say; for what you are to say will be given to you at that time; (20) for it is not you who speak, but the Spirit of your Father speaking through you. (21) Brother will betray brother to death, and a father his child, and children will rise against parents and have them put to death; (22) and you will be hated by all because of my name. But the one who endures to the end will be saved. (23) When they persecute you in one town, flee to the next; for truly I tell you, you will not have gone through all the towns of Israel before the Son of Man comes. (24) A disciple is not above the teacher, nor a slave above the master; (25) it is enough for the disciple to be like the teacher, and the slave like the master. If they have called the master of the house Beelzebul, how much more will they malign those of his household!"

THIS PASSAGE IS SCARY. Jesus warn that you could be put "on the spot" at any moment with a demand (or question, or even a puzzled look from someone): What is it with you and Jesus?

There is good news and bad news. The bad news is that you'll be expected to say something. The good news is that you don't have to worry about what to say; Jesus assures you that "what you are to say will be given to you at that time." More good news is in the advice to just "be like the teacher." First and foremost that would mean don't resist or react to evil treatment.

In college there are many forces at work that aim at getting you not to commit to a position, a goal, a dream. Keep an open mind. Don't commit. Avoid big decisions. Be ready to argue all sides of every issue without ever picking the right one or the best one.

That may be okay for college, but it is not okay for life or for following Christ. He has already decided: he loves you. How can you not commit yourself to that offer?

Prayer: Strengthen me to depend on you and make the right choices. Amen.

36 – No Fear

Matthew 10:26–33 — (26) "So have no fear of them; for nothing is covered up that will not be uncovered, and nothing secret that will not become known. (27) What I say to you in the dark, tell in the light; and what you hear whispered, proclaim from the housetops. (28) Do not fear those who kill the body but cannot kill the soul; rather fear him who can destroy both soul and body in hell. (29) Are not two sparrows sold for a penny? Yet not one of them will fall to the ground apart from your Father. (30) And even the hairs of your head are all counted. (31) So do not be afraid; you are of more value than many sparrows. (32) Everyone therefore who acknowledges me before others, I also will acknowledge before my Father in heaven; (33) but whoever denies me before others, I also will deny before my Father in heaven."

"Do not fear" says Jesus three times in this passage. For Jesus, that is another way of telling disciples to "believe" or "trust." Fear can be easier than trust because sometimes it is hard to know how to trust, but it is usually pretty easy to fear: the next test, news from home, the bill for next semester. There is always plenty to worry about.

When I was about ten, I saw a really scary movie that was actually a comedy about some teenage boys in which a huge gorilla played a central role. At ten, however, instead of the humor, I found fear. For weeks I was pretty sure that gorilla was going to come to my house, enter the front door, pass the living room (where my folks somehow would not notice him), ascend the stairs, and . . . do something to me!

We grow out of a lot of our fears, but fear may still be useful—as long as we fear the right thing. Jesus urges that we fear the one "who can destroy both soul and body"—God. He urges that we fear that very God and fear nothing else.

Some of our college fears turn out to be inconsequential. In an English class I decided not to read a particular assignment (Don't ask me why. I have no idea and can't remember.). Every day I was terrified that I would be caught out in my ignorance of the story. I never was. What I feared was never materialized. Whom to trust and believe is much more substantive and consequential.

Prayer: Help me to know faith as a perfect substitute for fear. Amen.

37 – Discipleship's Collateral Damage

Matthew 10:34–39 — (34) "Do not think that I have come to bring peace to the earth; I have not come to bring peace, but a sword. (35) For I have come to set a man against his father, and a daughter against her mother, and a daughter-in-law against her mother-in-law; (36) and one's foes will be members of one's own household. (37) Whoever loves father or mother more than me is not worthy of me; and whoever loves son or daughter more than me is not worthy of me; (38) and whoever does not take up the cross and follow me is not worthy of me. (39) Those who find their life will lose it, and those who lose their life for my sake will find it."

SO MUCH FOR GENTLE Jesus, the pacifist who (according to some) advocated "family values." Perhaps the most powerful surprises about going to college are the profound changes—even disruptions—that it makes in your closest relationships. Parents—remember how dumb they were during your last year of high school? How out of it? Now, looking at them from a more mature perspective, they seem to be more reliable, a bit more "with it." Girlfriend/boyfriend—what was her (his) name, anyway? And high school friends? On a different planet.

Life in college can make for an entirely new set of relationships. One or two cool professors. A handful of new friends—some totally different from anyone that came before. Visits to their homes introduce you to new, surrogate parents. Perhaps even a new hero, a move from Mick Jagger to Karl Marx, or from Beyoncé to Bach.

In some ways a new "family" is coming into existence. Sociologists call this a "fictive" family, not biological, but real enough for you to recognize it. You may even begin to see it in Scripture: when Jesus answers this question, "Who is my mother?" with, "Whoever does the will of God" or when Paul calls Philemon his "son," or when Christians refer to one another as "brother" and "sister" and to God as "Father."

Against that background, it is not a total surprise to hear Jesus say "I have not come to bring peace." His coming—to the extent that you take him seriously—means a rearrangement of your relationships. But that's okay, because your new family is taking shape.

Prayer: Help me to understand the new family to which Jesus calls me. Amen.

38 – Not Just a Kiss and a Promise

Matthew 10:40—11:1 — (40) Whoever welcomes you welcomes me, and whoever welcomes me welcomes the one who sent me. (41) Whoever welcomes a prophet in the name of a prophet will received a prophet's reward; and whoever welcomes a righteous person in the name of a righteous person will receive the reward of the righteous; (42) and whoever gives even a cup of cold water to one of these little ones in the name of a disciple—truly I tell you, none of these will lose their reward." (11:1) Now when Jesus had finished instructing his twelve disciples, he went on from there to teach and proclaim his message in their cities.

ONE OF MY FONDEST memories of college was of something that occurred in the midst of what would have been one of the more dismal moments— my biology final exam freshman year. The fact that it was a final exam was dismal to begin; I always hated exams. The fact that it was in mid-January on the last Saturday of a two-week exam period was dismal. It was at night; dismal. It was snowing; dismal.

There we were, the "disciples" of the great biology teacher (John Bonner was world famous for his work on bees). We had learned some biology and it was our mission to demonstrate our meager achievements *via* the exam. I was in the pits. We were alone. Even the professor wasn't there. He had probably gone home and was warming himself in front of a cheerful fire.

But wait! Lo and behold, about an hour into the exam, Dr. Bonner returned—with refreshments! He had not left us alone. The teaching part of his work was done; but the caring part of his relationship with us wasn't.

This wasn't exactly the same as Jesus preparing the apostles for discipleship and then sending them out alone, but it was kind of like it. We had not been abandoned. We had been remembered.

Jesus remembers his own. And he calls on each of us to remember others who are alone. Do you ever think of how lonesome Jesus might have been and still did not forget the needs of others? What a rich blessing: to be comforted with the knowledge that Jesus does not forget us and to be challenged with the opportunity to remember others who feel their own abandonment. Can you think of anyone around you today who may need a visit?

Prayer: Lord, direct me in the best way to befriend the lonely. Amen.

39 – Playing "Yes" and "No"

Matthew 11:2-12 — (2) When John heard in prison what the Messiah was doing, he sent word by his disciples (3) and said to him, "Are you the one who is to come, or are we to wait for another?" (4) Jesus answered them, "Go and tell John what you hear and see: (5) the blind receive their sight, the lame walk, the lepers are cleansed, the deaf hear, the dead are raised, and the poor have good news brought to them. (6) And blessed is anyone who takes no offense at me." (7) As they went away, Jesus began to speak to the crowds about John: "What did you go out into the wilderness to look at? A reed shaken by the wind? (8) What then did you go out to see? Someone dressed in soft robes? Look, those who wear soft robes are in royal palaces. (9) What then did you go out to see? A prophet? Yes, I tell you, and more than a prophet. (10) This is the one about whom it is written, 'See, I am sending my messenger ahead of you, who will prepare your way before you.' (11) Truly I tell you, among those born of women no one has arisen greater than John the Baptist; yet the least in the kingdom of heaven is greater than he. (12) From the days of John the Baptist until now the kingdom of heaven has suffered violence, and the violent take it by force."

"Yes and no." Isn't that aggravating? You go to college, where you expect to pick up a ton of new information and get the straight story. Then your professor gives you this convincing picture of how things are. The next minute, she shows you what's wrong with the first picture, and offers a whole new story that's equally convincing. Part of any academic success you enjoy depends on adopting the "yes and no" approach. "A" papers and exams are those in which you present all sides in order to show off the breadth of your grasp of the material.

There is college (where you can get away with—and even benefit from—the game of "yes and no") and there is life (where sometimes you absolutely positively have to have the right answer): Is there enough in the checking account? Yes or no? Does she like me or not? Yes or no? Is it cancer or not? Yes or no?

Is Jesus the *One*? Yes or no? That was John the Baptist's question. A victim of "official" violence, things did not look good for him. If Jesus is the One, he can tough it out. If not . . . this can't be just "yes and no."

Prayer: Thank you, God, for the straight, clear answer you give us in Jesus Christ. Amen.

75

40 – Gripe, Gripe, Gripe

*Matthew 11:13–19 — (13) "For all the prophets and the law proph-
esied until John came; (14) and if you are willing to accept it, he is
Elijah who is to come. (15) Let anyone with ears listen! (16) But
to what will I compare this generation? It is like children sitting in
the marketplaces and calling to one another, (17) 'We played the
flute for you, and you did not dance; we wailed, and you did not
mourn.' (18) For John came neither eating nor drinking, and they
say, 'He has a demon'; (19) the Son of Man came eating and drinking, and they say, 'Look, a glutton and a drunkard, a friend of tax
collectors and sinners!' Yet wisdom is vindicated by her deeds."*

ALWAYS COMPLAINTS. THERE ARE folks who will complain about everything. If there is a problem and a solution is proposed, that person will find
something wrong with the solution.

Then there is God. In the stories of the Old Testament, God is constantly trying to fix the mess that people had gotten themselves into (but
couldn't get themselves out of). First he tries the exodus: a daring escape
from the despair that the Egyptians had put them through. Then he gave
them the Law (the Hebrews call it *torah*, which is more like "directions" or
"instructions" for how God would like his creatures to live). Later, those
folks told God that things would work out if they could have a king—like all
the other nations. God (reluctantly) went along.

It has gone without saying that none of God's efforts worked out very
well. (This was not God's fault, of course; the "chosen people" chose not to
"get it" or do it.) So he started inspiring individuals—prophets—to try more
personal relationships with leaders. A lot of them wound up in about the
same place as the last in that line, John the Baptist—in jail.

From the point of view of God's people, there was always something
wrong with God's efforts to help them to be the people they were created
to be. And Jesus concludes his praise of John the Baptist by pointing out
that the people complained that John was ignored because he was too different from Jesus, and that Jesus was being rejected because he was just the
opposite of John. Go figure. Shouldn't Christians be the least complaining
folks of all? Today can you think of some things for which you are grateful?
Shouldn't college be on that list?

*Prayer: In the midst of complaining, keep my mind and heart fo-
cused on Jesus. Amen.*

41 – "Eureka!" Moment

Matthew 11:20–27 — (20) Then he began to reproach the cities in which most of his deeds of power had been done, because they did not repent. (21) "Woe to you, Chorazin! Woe to you, Bethsaida! For if the deeds of power done in you had been done in Tyre and Sidon, they would have repented long ago in sackcloth and ashes. (22) But I tell you, on the day of judgment it will be more tolerable for Tyre and Sidon than for you. (23) And you, Capernaum, will you be exalted to heaven? No, you will be brought down to Hades. For if the deeds of power done in you had been done in Sodom, it would have remained until this day. (24) But I tell you that on the day of judgment it will be more tolerable for the land of Sodom than for you." (25) At that time Jesus said, "I thank you, Father, Lord of heaven and earth, because you have hidden these things from the wise and the intelligent and have revealed them to infants; (26) yes, Father, for such was your gracious will. (27) All things have been handed over to me by my father; and no one knows the Son except the Father, and no one knows the Father except the Son and anyone to whom the Son chooses to reveal him."

YOU KNOW HOW IT is when you try to figure something out and can't "get it." Then, after trying, and asking, and studying, and checking your notes, you finally do "get it," but not as a result of your conscious efforts. We even talk about it that way: "It suddenly came to me" as if it had been out there all along and had just decided on its own to make itself known to you. When you "get it" is it really coming to you as a gift?

In this text we encounter two things that might be surprising about Jesus. First, he gets mad at some cities. In these days of individualism, he reminds us that Christian faith is about us, not just me (or just you), and that he brought the whole "kingdom" of God, not just a slice of good feeling. Jesus reproaches whole cities who didn't "get it." The second surprise is to find out that only Jesus knows God and that others know God only if Jesus enables them to.

So here is the dilemma: Should you be able to recognize that Jesus is God's Son and repent as a consequence all on your own? But . . . how many get the same opportunity and reject Jesus? Whole cities. Perhaps we "get it" because he "gave it." Perhaps "it came to you" because Jesus delivered it.

Prayer: God, thank you for helping me to "get it" from Jesus. Amen.

42 – "Guts" and "Boats"

Matthew 11:28–30 — (28) "Come to me, all you that are weary and are carrying heavy burdens, and I will give you rest. (29) Take my yoke upon you, and learn from me; for I am gentle and humble in heart, and you will find rest for your souls. (30) For my yoke is easy, and my burden is light."

THE COMMON EXPRESSION FOR a really easy class in my college was "gut." (I have no idea why.) Later, at another school, a colleague referred to those easy classes as "boats." (When I asked why, he said, "Because they are classes that you can just float on through.") Even the best students take note of "guts" and "boats" because there are semesters when you know you will have a heavy load and an easy class would provide help.

Another thing students look out for is a great professor—that teacher who is charismatic, challenging, entertaining, famous, or distinguished above other instructors. In my undergraduate experience that prof was a chemistry teacher and his introduction to chemistry was that class. He combined pyrotechnics and theory with diabolically idiosyncratic behavior. It was unforgettable.

But you don't find the great professor teaching the "gut" or "boat." You really work hard for that great professor and consequently learn from them. Then there is Jesus, the Teacher, perhaps the greatest that ever lived. And here he is advertising his "class." Shockingly, he promises that the experience of learning from him will produce rest! And the reason we are to consider his invitation is that he seems merciful—not a quality usually on the top of the list of any teacher.

How can this be the case? First, remember that there is a difference between soul and mind. Disturbed minds and disturbed souls are two different things. The student with a disturbed mind—disturbed because you can't understand, can't remember, can't keep things straight—is one thing that can probably be overcome with more study. The student with a disturbed soul has a problem of quite a different character. A disturbed and unsettled soul is like a fear unto death. It is big trouble and needs settling of a permanent and transcendent nature. That is precisely what Jesus offers to do because he is not only the Teacher; he is also the Savior.

Prayer: Thank you, Lord, for being there with your rest when I need it. Amen.

43 – Changing Paradigm

Matthew 12:1–8 — (1) At that time Jesus went through the grain-
fields on the sabbath; his disciples were hungry, and they began
to pluck heads of grain and to eat. (2) When the Pharisees saw it,
they said to him, "Look, your disciples are doing what is not lawful
to do on the sabbath." (3) He said to them, "Have you not read
what David did when he and his companions were hungry? (4) He
entered the house of God and ate the bread of the Presence, which
it was not lawful for him or his companions to eat, but only for the
priests. (5) Or have you not read in the law that on the sabbath the
priests in the temple break the sabbath and yet are guiltless? (6) I
tell you, something greater than the temple is here. (7) But if you
had known what this means, 'I desire mercy and not sacrifice,' you
would not have condemned the guiltless. (8) For the Son of Man
is lord of the sabbath."

BY THIS TIME YOU'VE found out that one of the things that makes a college education last so long is that in so many classes you have to go through a lot of introductory material in order to know what the current status of the subject matter is. Physics offer a dramatic example: While religion provided the early "theories" on the nature of the material world, philosophers soon got into the act, proposing the basic substance as water (Thales), then air (Anaximander), then atoms (Democritus), later the four elements of fire, earth, air, and water (Greeks generally), and down through modern times with the ideas of quantum mechanics and the theories about quarks, strings, or simply (!) energy. Every new theory was an attack on entrenched notions that had held sway for years.

The Christian faith is both like and unlike this paradigm-changing story. With the coming of Jesus—particularly his death and resurrection—everything changed. That is the similarity. The dissimilarity is that the paradigm change has to be reaffirmed in every generation and in our individual lives almost daily.

We see the new paradigm in today's Scripture. The problem is not theft, it is work, which the law forbids on the sabbath. Jesus responds first as a teacher, out-maneuvering the Pharisees. Then he points out that while observance of the law is good, God prefers mercy. Finally, the change of paradigm kicks in: Jesus, a.k.a. the Son of Man, "is the lord of the Sabbath"; he is the one who says what may be done on the sabbath.

Prayer: Help me with my new mantra: Focus on Jesus, not on
rules, laws, habits, or customs. Amen.

44 – Turning Point

*Matthew 12:9–14 — (9) He left that place and entered their syna-
gogue; (10) a man was there with a withered hand, and they asked
him, "Is it lawful to cure on the sabbath?" so that they might accuse him. (11) He said to them, "Suppose one of you has only one
sheep and it falls into a pit on the sabbath; will you not lay hold of
it and lift it out? (12) How much more valuable is a human being
than a sheep! So it is lawful to do good on the sabbath." (13) Then
he said to the man, "Stretch out your hand." He stretched it out,
and it was restored, as sound as the other. (14) But the Pharisees
went out and conspired against him, how to destroy him.*

HAVE YOU BEEN FIRED from a job yet? Even though you are pursing a college education, that doesn't mean that you can't be considered the wrong
person for your job or that someone who had been a friend suddenly no
longer wants to be in contact—or even turns against you. I've been fired
from at least four jobs that I can remember. I turned out not to be the person, or not to do the job, my employer(s) wanted. This may or may not be
in store for you somewhere down the line. If it happens, you need to decide
what to do about it. Will you change into someone others want you to be?
Or—if you believe you were doing the right thing—will you continue along
your original path?

Today's story talks of a pivotal moment in Jesus' story. Enough is
enough, thought the Pharisees. We need to get rid of this Jesus. Not only
is he disturbing the peace (i.e., giving people who were oppressed by the
Romans the hope that a powerful rebel might overthrow the Romans and
free Israel from oppression) but he is breaking God's law.

Jesus surely is aware of their opposition and rejection. What should he
do? Short answer: keep on keeping on. As his story continues is your daily
readings, notice the integrity and commitment he displays as he continues
to proclaim and embody God's kingdom in the places where you find him.
Jesus' story can be a sustaining one in those moments when you get beat up
and feel rejected.

*Prayer: Dear Jesus, thank you for not giving up when you knew
they hated you. Amen.*

45 – Under the Radar

Matthew 12:15–21 — (15) When Jesus became aware of this, he departed. Many crowds followed him, and he cured all of them, (16) and he ordered them not to make him known. (17) This was to fulfill what had been spoken through the prophet Isaiah: (18) "Here is my servant, whom I have chosen, my beloved, with whom my soul is well pleased. I will put my Spirit upon him, and he will proclaim justice to the Gentiles. (19) He will not wrangle or cry aloud, nor will anyone hear his voice in the streets. (20) He will not break a bruised reed or quench a smoldering wick until he brings justice to victory. (21) And in his name the Gentiles will hope."

THERE WILL BE MANY discussions in college. Many in class; many in the dorm. Many will be agreeable; some will begin agreeably but later turn to disagreement. It is surprising how often friendly discussions can lead to moments when deep chasms between two previously agreeable people appear. But rather than avoid discussions with others, just be alert to the possibility that disagreements can erupt at unexpected moments.

Such an eruption occurred between Jesus and the religious people of his time. They may all have started out thinking they were (all) doing God's will, and then suddenly . . . .

In today's reading, Jesus has decided that this was not the time for him to add to his disagreement with the Pharisees by doing or saying anything more than he already had. Instead, Jesus asks that no one tell about their being healed by him. In addition, he leaves the area. He endeavors to maintain a quiet, nonviolent, low-key ministry despite the continual challenge from the religious establishment that wants to stop him.

Matthew concludes this section referring to what might be called Jesus' "job description"—the prophecies of the Old Testament. Some of the prophecies dealt with God's overthrowing of his enemies. Those were not the prophecies applied to Jesus. In this reference, Matthew points out that Jesus is not pushy, loud, or confrontive, but will continue in his quiet way until he has conquered injustice. This was really one side of the answer to the question, "How do you overcome injustice?" The popular answer seems to be, "With force." But Jesus' answer is different. Stay tuned on this matter because we haven't heard the last of it from Matthew.

Prayer: Teach me humility—what it is and how to have it. Amen.

46 – Tournament of Narratives

Matthew 12:22–31 — (22) Then they brought to him a demoniac who was blind and mute; and he cured him, so that the one who had been mute could speak and see. (23) All the crowds were amazed and said, "Can this be the Son of David?" (24) But when the Pharisees heard it, they said, "It is only by Beelzebul, the ruler of the demons, that this fellow casts out the demons." (25) He knew what they were thinking and said to them, "Every kingdom divided against itself is laid waste, and no city or house divided against itself will stand. (26) If Satan casts out Satan, he is divided against himself; how then will his kingdom stand? (27) If I cast out demons by Beelzebul, by whom do your own exorcists cast them out? Therefore they will be your judges. (28) But if it is by the Spirit of God that I cast out demons, then the kingdom of God has come to you. (29) Or how can one enter a strong man's house and plunder his property, without first tying up the strong man? Then indeed the house can be plundered. (30) Whoever is not with me is against me, and whoever does not gather with me scatters. (31) Therefore I tell you, people will be forgiven for every sin and blasphemy, but blasphemy against the Spirit will not be forgiven."

AT ONE TIME IT was theorized that bees could not fly. But of course they do fly. So much for theory?

One of the frustrations of the college experience could be too much theory. It can seem that in every class you have to sit through theory—not just one theory, but several. And they battle each other out for preeminence. Each theory wants to be the final explanation—for the cause of a disease or for a rise in the price of coffee.

When you get into your academic major, you will be expected to understand and explain the major theories that have played a central role in your area of study, whether it is art or zoology or anything in between. You may need to select and defend one theory over against others in the battles over what is really going on and how to understand it all.

As we see in today's narrative, those theoretical discussions (arguments) can get pretty serious. In Jesus' case, his explanation of his own behavior and mission was a matter of dispute. It would become a life-and-death matter. Don't be too eager to blow off theory. Theory can have serious, long-term consequences.

Prayer: When it comes to really serious matters, help me to be careful in drawing my conclusions. Amen.

47 – Loose Lips Sink Ships

Matthew 12:32-37 — (32) Whoever speaks a word against the Son of Man will be forgiven, but whoever speaks against the Holy Spirit will not be forgiven, either in this age or in the age to come. (33) Either make the tree good, and its fruit good; or make the tree bad, and its fruit bad; for the tree is known by its fruit. (34) You brood of vipers! How can you speak good things, when you are evil? For out of the abundance of the heart the mouth speaks. (35) The good person brings good things out of a good treasure, and the evil person brings evil things out of an evil treasure. (36) I tell you, on the day of judgment you will have to give an account for every careless word you utter; (37) for by your words you will be justified, and by your words you will be condemned."

Jesus said a lot of things. The first Christians remembered a lot of what he said. A lot of what he said is not always obvious in its meaning. As you read today's selection, you are free to stop and ponder one or another of the sayings strung together here; or, you can skip the ones that don't "grab" you at this moment. (Some other time, under some other circumstances, they will be just the thing you need.)

Right now—considering your immersion in college—perhaps the words that "grab" you are these: "you will have to give an account for every careless word you utter." Now that is scary. Then, "by your words you will be justified!" And you thought it would be "by your faith you will be justified." What's going on?

What if your words and your faith were identical? What if the words that came out of "the abundance of your heart" were words of faith? That could solve the problem. So instead of Jesus, or Matthew, being confused about exactly what justifies us, they both knew that words were a true representation of your faith.

That is a "quick and dirty" explanation of an apparent conflict in this text. If you are not satisfied with it, there might be a "longer and cleaner" interpretation in some theological tome . . . maybe another time. Right now, it's clear: your words are critically important.

Prayer: Jesus is your Word, O God; let him always be in my words. Amen.

48 – Sign Language

Matthew 12:38–45 — (38) Then some of the scribes and Pharisees said to him, "Teacher, we wish to see a sign from you." (39) But he answered them, "An evil and adulterous generation asks for a sign, but no sign will be given to it except the sign of the prophet Jonah. (40) For just as Jonah was three days and three nights in the belly of the sea monster, so for three days and three nights the Son of Man will be in the heart of the earth. (41) The people of Nineveh will rise up at the judgment with this generation and condemn it, because they repented at the proclamation of Jonah, and see, something greater than Jonah is here! (42) The queen of the South will rise up at the judgment with this generation and condemn it, because she came from the ends of the earth to listen to the wisdom of Solomon, and see, something greater than Solomon is here! (43) When the unclean spirit has gone out of a person, it wanders through waterless regions looking for a resting place, but it finds none. (44) Then it says, 'I will return to my house from which I came.' When it comes, it finds it empty, swept, and put in order. (45) Then it goes and brings along seven other spirits more evil than itself, and they enter and live there; and the last state of that person is worse than the first. So will it be also with this evil generation."

WE WERE PREPARING FOR a really big test. It covered more than one course or one year of study. It was a make-or-break point in our program. So a group of us students approached our professors and made a request: Give us a list of books to read so we will know we are exam ready. His answer stunned us: "No."

We were stuck! What to do? His answer to that question was more difficult than the first. He said, "You'll know when you're ready." We had asked for a sign. He gave us no sign other than our own state of preparation.

When we look to God for signs or proofs that we are on the right track with our faith we may feel directed in a certain way: look at the resurrection; look at Scripture. But we also know that these "signs" have often been rejected. The "sign" the Pharisees request is Jesus. Period.

You can't base Jesus' significance on something else, even if that something else is something that happened to him. Jesus' significance is Jesus himself. Whenever you look for a sign, you are really looking for proof, for certainty—and you are looking away from Jesus.

Prayer: Dearest Jesus, thank you for giving me yourself. That is everything. Amen.

49 –In Loco Parentis

Matthew 12:46–50 — (46) While he was still speaking to the crowds, his mother and his brothers were standing outside, wanting to speak to him. (47) Someone told him, "Look, your mother and your brothers are standing outside, wanting to speak to you." (48) But to the one who had told him this, Jesus replied, "Who is my mother, and who are my brothers?" (49) And pointing to his disciples, he said, "Here are my mother and my brothers! (50) For whoever does the will of my Father in heaven is my brother and sister and mother."

LATIN IS SO GREAT, isn't it? You can use it to show off that you've been to college. The phrase *in loco parentis* does not mean "in my crazy family." Instead, it means "in the place of parents" and is often used to refer to the college in its role "in the place of [your] parents." Can you think of the church as acting *in loco parentis* in the new family created by Christ, who calls you into a new family? (A really big family.)

As a Christian, you are placed—surprisingly and perhaps violently—in a new family. Paul writes letters to his "brothers" and "sisters" in Christ; he even claims Onesimus as a child that he (metaphorically) "fathered" while in prison (Phlm 10). Jesus speaks the hard words of how his presence divides families and in our passage for today he cavalierly dismisses his own mother and siblings in favor of "whoever does the will of my Father in heaven" as the new criterion for who is in the new "family." Jesus had already (i) answered a prospective disciple that he would need to leave his dead father to be buried by others (8:21), (ii) foreseen that brother would divide from brother because of himself (10:21), and (iii) predicted that all relatives would be at odds with each other because of the kingdom of heaven (10:35). For Paul and Jesus, water is thicker than blood. That would be the waters of Christian baptism—a rite of passage or sacrament that creates a new "fictive" (fictional) family in which you now are intimately connected to one another under a new parent, God.

Prayer: Help me to live so that all of my families can be one family, your family. Amen.

50 – It's Like . . .

Matthew 13:1–9 — (1) That same day Jesus went out of the house and sat beside the sea. (2) Such great crowds gathered around him that he got into a boat and sat there, while the whole crowd stood on the beach. (3) And he told them many things in parables, saying: "Listen! A sower went out to sow. (4) And as he sowed, some seeds fell on the path, and the birds came and ate them up. (5) Other seeds fell on rocky ground, where they did not have much soil, and they sprang up quickly, since they had no depth of soil. (6) But when the sun rose, they were scorched; and since they had no root, they withered away. (7) Other seeds fell among thorns, and the thorns grew up and choked them. (8) Other seeds fell on good soil and brought forth grain, some a hundredfold, some sixty, some thirty. (9) Let anyone with ears listen!"

IF "IT" IS A class, you could focus on a description of "it" by telling of the time it meets, the room in which it meets, the name of the professor who teaches it, and the textbook used. But that doesn't answer the real question: What's "it" like? Is it hard? Is it like beating your head against a brick wall? Is it like taking your medicine—really awful at the moment but with a great outcome? Is it like a "breath of fresh air" after all the other boring classes?

Efforts to describe something in a way that conveys important truth often has to resort to some sort of expression in which we "like"-en the thing needing description to something else that the listeners will understand. Everyone should understand banging one's head against a brick wall: it is painful. Everyone remembers taking some awful tasting medicine or a painful shot, but also knows that in the end it made them well again.

Parables are comparisons. The idea is to find something that the audience knows and understands and use that to describe what they are to understand. People do it all the time. Jesus did it all the time because he was trying to describe the rule of God (which no one had yet experienced). So he used comparisons—lots of them.

In this first of Jesus' parables recounted by Matthew, Jesus describes the nature of God to be (like a) sower, (like) what is sown, (like) the sowing action of the sower, (like) the soil—there are a lot of possibilities to explore here. They are not codes or secret messages but suggestions that move us from what we know to what do not know.

Prayer: Lord Jesus, may the riches of your parables find a place to grow and flourish in my imagination. Amen.

51 – In Plain English, Please

Matthew 13:10–17 — (10) Then the disciples came and asked him, "Why do you speak to them in parables?" (11) He answered, "To you it has been given to know the secrets of the kingdom of heaven, but to them it has not been given. (12) For to those who have, more will be given, and they will have an abundance; but from those who have nothing, even what they have will be taken away. (13) The reason I speak to them in parables is that 'seeing they do not perceive, and hearing they do not listen, nor do they understand.' (14) With them indeed is fulfilled the prophecy of Isaiah that says: 'You will indeed listen, but never understand, and you will indeed look, but never perceive. (15) For this people's heart has grown dull, and their ears are hard of hearing, and they have shut their eyes; so that they might not look with their eyes, and listen with their ears, and understand with their heart and turn—and I would heal them.' (16) But blessed are your eyes, for they see, and your ears, for they hear. (17) Truly I tell you, many prophets and righteous people longed to see what you see, but did not see it, and to hear what you hear, but did not hear it."

MOST OF THE SAYINGS of Jesus and the stories about Jesus are fairly easy to understand—or at least to get the general drift. Not so this one. Here's the deal. One of the main things Jesus does is to explain the "kingdom of heaven" (kingdom of God) to the public. The "kingdom of heaven" is when/where/how/what the world will be like with God in charge and with everyone living like God created them to live. Problem: that hasn't happened, so it is very difficult to explain in terms understandable to people who were not already experiencing it. How do you explain what no one has seen? In yesterday's reading, Jesus told his first parable. Immediately (today's reading), the disciples want to be spoon-fed an explanation.

Jesus' answer is unexpected. He tells them they have been given "the secrets of the kingdom." God invites everyone. Those who have accepted this invitation realize that they have been given a gift. Once they "get it," it is easier to understand Jesus, the kingdom, the gospel, and God's will. Those who haven't accepted the invitation keep on not getting it.

Prayer: Thank you for give me the gift of grasping glimpses of your truth. Please keep it coming. Amen.

87

52 – Simple Explanation

*Matthew 13:18–23 — (18) "Hear then the parable of the sower.
(19) When anyone hears the word of the kingdom and does not
understand it, the evil one comes and snatches away what is sown
in the heart; this is what was sown on the path. (20) As for what
was sown on rocky ground, this is the one who hears the word and
immediately receives it with joy; (21) yet such a person has no
root, but endures only for a while, and when trouble or persecution arises on account of the word, that person immediately falls
away. (22) As for what was sown among thorns, this is the one
who hears the word, but the cares of the world and the lure of
wealth choke the word, and it yields nothing. (23) But as for what
was sown on good soil, this is the one who hears the word and
understands it, who indeed bears fruit and yields, in one case a
hundredfold, in another sixty, and in another thirty."*

THE PARABLE OF THE sower is the first of Jesus' parables recorded in
Matthew's gospel; dozens of Jesus' parables are recorded in the Gospels; he
probably told many more that haven't been included. But it is only one of
two parables "explained" or "applied." Why? Is this an exemplary model of
interpretation that is to be used for every other parable?

More important: Is this the definitive interpretation of this parable? If
it is, then parables are really secret codes. You crack the code and have the
interpretation or application. If that is the case, why didn't Jesus say when he
gave the parable originally that the seed sown on rocky ground is a certain
kind of person? This exposes the problem. Jesus introduced the parables
with a key word: The kingdom is "like" . . . . He did not say, "In this story
about the kingdom, the seed is actually code for . . . and the rocky ground is
actually code for . . .".

But this is not code, this is more like poetry. Jesus invites you to use
your imagination to get a glimmer of God and God's possibilities among us.
Since there is no point of reference for us to use in trying to explain what
has never yet happened, imagination is critical to the success of his teaching.

So you can take this interpretation as a suggestion, only the beginning,
only an example, only the merest hint of a kind of trajectory that you are
challenged to take up and follow. The end is not even in sight. God has
given you imagination; Jesus challenges you to use it; college studies are
great things to exercise it on.

*Prayer: Fire my imagination to follow the hints that Scripture
gives me. Amen.*

53 – Discernment

Matthew 13:24-30 — (24) He put before them another parable: "The kingdom of heaven may be compared to someone who sowed good seed in his field; (25) but while everybody was asleep, an enemy came and sowed weeds among the wheat, and then went away. (26) So when the plants came up and bore grain, then the weeds appeared as well. (27) And the slaves of the householder came and said to him, 'Master, did you not sow good seed in your field? Where, then, did these weeds come from?' (28) He answered, 'An enemy has done this.' The slaves said to him, 'Then do you want us to go and gather them?' (29) But he replied, 'No; for in gathering the weeds you would uproot the wheat along with them. (30) Let both of them grow together until the harvest; and at harvest time I will tell the reapers, Collect the weeds first and bind them in bundles to be burned, but gather the wheat into my barn.'"

NOT EVERYONE AT COLLEGE is your friend. The fact that so many of the people you meet, and study, and eat with come from such different cultures—not necessarily from Timbuktu but just from different family environments—makes it harder to be sure you have correctly read their character, intentions, or reliability.

The same can be said about the ideas that you hear in lectures or read in your assignments. Some that sound good at the beginning can wind up not being so good.

The deal is that in college you find yourself in an environment that is full of a variety of new people, experiences, and ideas. And new facts and theories. When you add this to all the things you have brought with you—your moral, intellectual, and spiritual baggage—you wind up with a lot on your plate (pardon the mixing of metaphors, but when we hear Jesus' parables, metaphor is central). Your task in college is to sort things out.

In the parable, the farmer decides that trying to sort out the weeds from the good crop is not worth the effort; too much damage would be done if he tried to do that. So the alternative strategy is one of patience. Wait until it is time to bring in the harvest, then the sorting can be done.

It might be good to consider this advice for your situation in college: don't decide too quickly which people, ideas, or experiences are the ones that are good for you. You may need some time to sort things out.

Prayer: Lord, give me the patience to wait when waiting is the best thing to do. Amen.

54 – From Zero to Sixty in . . .

Matthew 13:31–35 — (31) He put before them another parable: "The kingdom of heaven is like a mustard seed that someone took and sowed in his field; (32) it is the smallest of all the seeds, but when it has grown it is the greatest of shrubs and becomes a tree, so that the birds of the air come and make nests in its branches." (33) He told them another parable: "The kingdom of heaven is like yeast that a woman took and mixed in with three measures of flour until all if it was leavened." (34) Jesus told the crowds all these things in parables; without a parable he told them nothing. (35) This was to fulfill what had been spoken through the prophet: "I will open my mouth to speak in parables; I will proclaim what has been hidden from the foundation of the world."

To SAY THAT A car—say a Porsche—can accelerate from a stopped position to sixty miles per hour in five seconds is to say that it is powerful. Our old VW bus took about ten to fifteen seconds to reach sixty, but we eventually got there. Despite the differences, there are similarities. Both cars can go sixty. And both start out at zero.

You started college pretty much at zero. Many of your instructors assume—and please don't take offense at this—that you know nothing (zero) about the subject, and will start class from the absolute beginning. By the end of the semester you will know something about the subject.

If you Google "zero to sixty" you will find that it can be used parabolically to refer to a big difference or the change from something insignificant and small to something big. One of the interesting thing about some of those changes is how you missed the beginning, because it was so small, almost a zero. When you reflect on the important teachers in your life, did they enter with a big splash? Or did they kind of grow on you slowly? Or what about some idea that has become significant? Did it explode full-grown instantly into your head?

Perhaps the idea of God being in charge of your life (e.g., "the kingdom of heaven" in this passage) is an idea that began in a really small way—small like a mustard seed (only 1/20 of an inch in diameter) or like yeast (of which your mother used a very small amount in baking those great rolls). Don't ignore the small stuff; it can grow on (in) you and even become like that mustard bush—a comfortable place to settle in and make your nest.

Prayer: Please give me the patience I need for the little things that don't seem important now. Amen.

55 – There Are No Dumb Questions

Matthew 13:36–43 — (36) Then he left the crowds and went into the house. And his disciples approached him, saying, "Explain to us the parable of the weeds of the field." (37) He answered, "The one who sows the good seed is the Son of Man; (38) the field is the world, and the good seed are the children of the kingdom; the weeds are the children of the evil one, (39) and the enemy who sowed them is the devil; the harvest is the end of the age, and the reapers are angels. (40) Just as the weeds are collected and burned up with fire, so will it be at the end of the age. (41) The Son of Man will send his angels, and they will collect out of his kingdom all causes of sin and all evildoers, (42) and they will throw them into the furnace of fire, where there will be weeping and gnashing of teeth. (43) Then the righteous will shine like the sun in the kingdom of their Father. Let anyone with ears listen!"

ONE OF THE HARDEST things in college is to understand what your professor means, or what the reading assignment means. There is so much to try to understand. What does it all mean?

One of the newest appointees to the US Supreme Court is Sonia Sotomayor. She came from a humble background and found herself in college feeling like a fish out of water. She says that for her whole first year she never said anything in class because she felt so inadequate. Perhaps you feel intimidated by college, or at least by some professors. It can be scary. You think, "Any question I ask would really be stupid. So I won't ask."

But if you want to understand things, you need answers. To get answers, you need questions to ask. And here is a fact: There are no stupid questions. Every question can be a door that opens to an answer or at least to another question that is a better, more appropriate, more direct, more-likely-to-help-you question.

Who to ask? Ask your roommate. Ask another person in your class. Google it. Ask your parents. Or . . . suck it up and ask your professor. Every time you ask, it gets easier to ask the next time. You're on your way to understanding. Justice Sotomayor finally began asking. She graduated first in her class!

In today's Scripture passage you see the disciples—who really had a hard time figuring things out—asking Jesus to explain one of his parables. Let's commend the disciples for (1) asking, and (2) asking Jesus, the real expert.

Prayer: I am still so frightened and ignorant; give me the humility and the courage to ask for help. Amen.

56 – Irrational Economics

Matthew 13:44–46 — (44) "The kingdom of heaven is like treasure hidden in a field, which someone found and hid; then in his joy he goes and sells all that he has and buys that field. (45) Again, the kingdom of heaven is like a merchant in search of fine pearls; (46) on finding one pearl of great value, he went and sold all that he had and bought it."

THESE ARE TWO WILD and crazy guys. From an economic point of view, their decisions seem extremely risky. The first one takes all of his resources and, without consulting others or evaluating the investment, buys a field that has (what he thinks is) a treasure. We don't know anything about how this fellow is doing later on. But we can imagine various versions of a major catastrophe: he goes broke.

The second fellow's situation seems both more reasonable and more risky. He is a professional dealer in pearls and finds one amazingly wonderful pearl. So he sells his entire business and buys just one pearl. Again, looking down the road, what is this man going to do? Just sit at home and look at his pearl?

Both of these fellows made economic decisions that do not seem very rational. When (not "if") you study economics, you will find that it is considered a science; in fact, it is often called the "dismal science." It is "science" because there is an understanding among economists that it has certain rules (the law of supply and demand; the law of diminishing returns). Perhaps it is "dismal" because it is about money. (Actually, Thomas Carlyle [1795-1881] was the first to use the adjective "dismal" because economics did not provide a justification for slavery, which he supported!) Anyway, it turns out—according to some economists—that a lot of our economic decisions are not as rational as they are emotional. (You pay $4 for a Starbucks coffee that costs $1 at McDonald's.)

Back to the two wild and crazy guys of the parables. It seems that instead of rational decisions, they are making decisions that are more like picking a girl-/boyfriend or picking a major. Instead of asking "How much will this cost?" you decide on the basis of what you hope might provide real, deep, permanent satisfaction.

That is probably why Jesus told these parables. He wanted you to get an idea of just how much "the kingdom of heaven"—living where God is at the center and makes sense of everything else for us—is worth.

Prayer: Direct my heart and help me to follow my guided heart. Amen.

57 – Line 'em Up, Move 'em Out

Matthew 13:47-50 — (47) "Again, the kingdom of heaven is like a net that was thrown into the sea and caught fish of every kind; (48) when it was full, they drew it ashore, sat down, and put the good into baskets but threw out the bad. (49) So it will be at the end of the age. The angels will come out and separate the evil from the righteous (50) and throw them into the furnace of fire, where there will be weeping and gnashing of teeth."

WHAT DO YOU CALL the student who graduates last in his class at medical school?

"Doctor!"

But think of all those who fell by the wayside. How many students were in your elementary school class? Did all of them graduate from high school? How many of your high school friends did not go on to college?

Education is a sorting process. "Many are called, but few are chosen [successful]." It seems cruel. On the other hand, think of how many drop-outs have made it big: Bill Gates, Clark Gable, Woodrow Wilson, Whoopi Goldberg, George Gershwin—and the list goes on. Of course, some of them dropped back in, but being sorted out is not always considered bad. If you get sorted out of school, there are lots of options open, including that of dropping back in.

But there are a few occasions where out is really out. Those occasions have to do with your deepest commitments, one of which is the question of your response and commitment to your creator, God. Some interpret this parable with the emphasis on a final judgment; others see it as emphasizing God's patience in not imposing a final sorting out until the last possible moment. Why not both? God's judgment and God's patience are both there for you to experience.

Prayer: God, whether it is soon or late, please sort me in. Amen.

58 – Can You Handle Growing Up?

Matthew 13:51–58 — (51) "Have you understood all this?" They answered, "Yes." (52) And he said to them, "Therefore every scribe who has been trained for the kingdom of heaven is like the master of a household who brings out of his treasure what is new and what is old." (53) When Jesus had finished these parables, he left that place. (54) He came to his hometown and began to teach the people in their synagogue, so that they were astounded and said, "Where did this man get this wisdom and these deeds of power? (55) Is not this the carpenter's son? Is not his mother called Mary? And are not his brothers James and Joseph and Simon and Judas? (56) And are not all his sisters with us? Where then did this man get all this?" (57) And they took offense at him. But Jesus said to them, "Prophets are not without honor except in their own country and in their own house." (58) And he did not do many deeds of power there, because of their unbelief.

Hasn't each of us been a smart aleck, or a goof-off, or a party animal at some time? Maybe through high school? Maybe through (some of) college? And then at some point you grow up. When that happens, it can be hard for people to adjust to. When I taught in college I had a student who was lovable, but totally goofy. Let's call him Ted. He was always the life of the party, but in class he was a flat-liner—nothing was happening. Somehow Ted did manage to graduate and I lost track of him. Fifteen years later I was the dean of the same college and was reviewing applications for a teaching position; there was one from Ted. His credentials included a bachelor's degree (the one we didn't think he'd ever get), a master's degree (how did he ever do that?) and a doctor's degree (say what?). This was the same person, but he had grown up. It was hard for me to see Ted as an adult, and a qualified one at that. The problem was not his; I was having the problem.

Warning: you may experience the same thing that Ted and Jesus experienced. When you go back home or to your old crowd, and you are no longer the kid from down the street. People may not accept the "new" you. It may be simple disbelief. It may be jealousy. Whatever the reason, the result may be that you simply cannot be effective or accepted on your old home turf. That is sad, but it might happen. At least you are in good company.

Prayer: Help me to accept those who cannot accept me. Amen.

59 – Who You Gonna Tell?

Matthew 14:1–12 — (1) At that time Herod the ruler heard reports about Jesus; (2) and he said to his servants, "This is John the Baptist; he has been raised from the dead, and for this reason these powers are at work in him."(3) For Herod had arrested John, bound him, and put him in prison on account of Herodias, his brother Philip's wife, (4) because John had been telling him, "It is not lawful for you to have her." (5) Though Herod wanted to put him to death, he feared the crowd, because they regarded him as a prophet. (6) But when Herod's birthday came, the daughter of Herodias danced before the company, and she pleased Herod (7) so much that he promised on oath to grant her whatever she might ask. (8) Prompted by her mother, she said, "Give me the head of John the Baptist here on a platter." (9) The king was grieved, yet out of regard for his oaths and for the guests, he commanded it to be given; (10) he sent and had John beheaded in the prison. (11) The head was brought on a platter and given to the girl, who brought it to her mother. (12) His disciples came and took the body and buried it; then they went and told Jesus.

IF THE EVENTS DESCRIBED in today's verses came across the news today, you might tell someone else about it under the rubric of "the weirdest thing I heard today." But what if it had been your friend who had been killed? (Crazier things have happened.) Among the survivors, stories are shared. It is so unsettling not to have that person around anymore that there is a necessity to speak about her in order to fill the gap and not forget.

Today's reading got into the Bible because the friends of John the Baptist told it. Who did they tell it to? According to Matthew, they told Jesus. When something terrible happens to you, whom do you tell? Your roommate, your girl-/boyfriend, your folks? Have you told Jesus? We don't know how well John's disciples got along with Jesus and his disciples, but at this horrific moment in their lives, John's disciples "went and told Jesus." Jesus is someone you can tell this kind of story to over and over and over again.

Prayer: Jesus, thank you for being there to listen to my complaints and stories. Amen.

60 – Not My Plan

Matthew 14:13–21 — (13) Now when Jesus heard this, he withdrew from there in a boat to a deserted place by himself. But when the crowds heard it, they followed him on foot from the towns. (14) When he went ashore, he saw a great crowd; and he had compassion for them and cured their sick. (15) When it was evening, the disciples came to him and said, "This is a deserted place, and the hour is now late; send the crowds away so that they may go into the villages and buy food for themselves." (16) Jesus said to them, "They need not go away; you give them something to eat." (17) They replied, "We have nothing here but five loaves and two fish." (18) And he said, "Bring them here to me." (19) Then he ordered the crowds to sit down on the grass. Taking the five loaves and the two fish, he looked up to heaven, and blessed and broke the loaves, and gave them to the disciples, and the disciples gave them to the crowds. (20) And all ate and were filled; and they took up what was left over of the broken pieces, twelve baskets full. (21) And those who ate were about five thousand men, besides women and children.

COLLEGE IS SUPPOSED TO develop mental quickness useful in all kinds of situations. But sometimes it develops the quickness to think of advantages for oneself rather than to come up with answers to problems that burden others. In today's Scripture, there is a problem. And the disciples understand it. They are far from town and the source of food that a town might provide. It's late and a lot of people are getting hungry. Things could get nasty if folks start fighting over the available food. People could get hurt; kids could get lost. This is definitely a crowd control problem. What to do?

The disciples come up with a neat—from their point of view—solution: send the people away to get their own food. Their suggestion is practical and has the advantage of shifting the responsibility from themselves to the people in the crowd. They not only came up with their own analysis and plan, they also told Jesus what he should do. Jesus shoots back to the disciples: "you give them something to eat."

What's the point? Better to keep your eye on Jesus rather than on yourself, your plan, your resources (or lack thereof). Focus on the main thing. That is a good thing in listening to a lecture, reading an article, writing a test or paper or having a class discussion. It is certainly the best thing to do in living the Christian life.

Prayer: Lord Jesus, let me make your answers my own, whatever the problem. Amen.

61 – Keep Your Eye on the Ball

Matthew 14:22–36 — (22) Immediately he made the disciples get into the boat and go on ahead to the other side, while he dismissed the crowds. (23) And after he had dismissed the crowds, he went up the mountain by himself to pray. When evening came, he was there alone, (24) but by this time the boat, battered by the waves, was far from the land, for the wind was against them. (25) And early in the morning he came walking toward them on the sea. (26) But when the disciples saw him walking on the sea, they were terrified, saying, "It is a ghost!" And they cried out in fear. (27) But immediately Jesus spoke to them and said, "Take heart, it is I; do not be afraid." (28) Peter answered him, "Lord, if it is you, command me to come to you on the water." (29) He said, "Come." So Peter got out of the boat, started walking on the water, and came toward Jesus. (30) But when he noticed the strong wind, he became frightened, and beginning to sink, he cried out, "Lord, save me!" (31) Jesus immediately reached out his hand and caught him, saying to him, "You of little faith, why did you doubt?" (32) When they got into the boat, the wind ceased. (33) And those in the boat worshipped him, saying, "Truly you are the Son of God." (34) When they had crossed over, they came to land at Gennesaret. (35) After the people of that place recognized him, they sent word throughout the region and brought all who were sick to him, (36) and begged him that they might touch even the fringe of his cloak; and all who touched it were healed.

TED WILLIAMS WAS ONE of the greatest batters in baseball history. His secret was that he kept his eye on the ball. There would be plenty of distractions: the pitcher's gyrations, the needling of opponents, the pressure of the moment, the boos of the fans. But he kept his eye on the ball.

Peter was terrified: was it a ghost or Jesus? Again, Peter tells Jesus what to do. This time Jesus "obeys," inviting Peter to "Come." Other than the fact that Peter knew that you can't walk on water, consider the other distractions he faced: waves, his own uncertainties; "he noticed the strong wind" (duh!) and it became his focus. When he "takes his eye off the ball" he sinks.

College can be a ginormous conglomeration of distractions. Peter and you both know it is hard to keep your eye on the ball. But that "ball"—Jesus—is the one fact out there that can redeem the situation.

Prayer: Help me to keep my eye on Jesus, in rough times and despite all the distractions. Amen.

62 – The Way We've Always Done It

Matthew 15:1–9 — (1) Then Pharisees and scribes came to Jesus from Jerusalem and said, (2) "Why do your disciples break the tradition of the elders? For they do not wash their hands before they eat." (3) He answered them, "And why do you break the commandment of God for the sake of your tradition? (4) For God said, 'Honor your father and your mother,' and, 'Whoever speaks evil of father or mother must surely die.' (5) But you say that whoever tells father or mother, 'Whatever support you might have had from me is given to God,' then that person need not honor the father. (6) So, for the sake of your tradition, you make void the word of God. (7) You hypocrites! Isaiah prophesied rightly about you when he said:

(8) This people honors me with their lips, but their hearts are far from me;

(9) in vain do they worship me, teaching human precepts as doctrines.'"

TRADITIONS—THE WAYS WE DO things—arise as we work the "how" of living out our lives as things change. They can be helpful in adapting a first-century religious faith or the challenges of a nation birthed in the eighteenth century to the needs and constraints of the twenty-first century.

The key issue about any tradition is whether it is "a way to do it" that is consistent with the original spirit of what you are trying to apply and keep relevant in a new situation. (For example, Christians agree that baptism expresses one's faith. But the "way to do it" varies. Some sprinkle water on the one being baptized; others submerge the whole person in water. Some want to get it baptism done as soon as possible—infant baptism. Others insist on waiting until the one being baptized is an adult, capable of his or her own decision.) Traditions can overshadow or change the original intention. Once that happens, we are in trouble and tradition becomes an impediment to our faithfulness.

How to sort it out? It's often difficult, but as happens in today's Scripture, let's look to Jesus the Teacher. In this particular conflict, Jesus is clear about the answer. In this case, he points his interrogators back to the law, the will of God as expressed in the basic texts of the Judeo-Christian tradition. Other times, his answer is different. If your hope is to find the will of God, then follow Jesus in his teaching and his examples to find the will of God in (or opposed to) the many traditions that we all hold so dearly.

Prayer: Lord Jesus, help me to let you be my teacher in every moment. Amen.

63 – G.I.G.O.

Matthew 15:10–20 — (10) Then he called the crowd to him and said to them, "Listen and understand: (11) it is not what goes into the mouth that defiles a person, but it is what comes out of the mouth that defiles." (12) Then the disciples approached and said to him, "Do you know that the Pharisees took offense when they heard what you said?" (13) He answered, "Every plant that my heavenly father has not planted will be uprooted. (14) Let them alone; they are blind guides of the blind. And if one blind person guides another, both will fall into a pit." (15) But Peter said to him, "Explain this parable to us." (16) Then he said "Are you also still without understanding? (17) Do you not see that whatever goes into the mouth enters the stomach, and goes out into the sewer? (18) But what comes out of the mouth proceeds from the heart, and this is what defiles. (19) For out of the heart come evil intentions, murder, adultery, fornication, theft, false witness, slander. (20) These are what defile a person, but to eat with unwashed hands does not defile."

"Garbage in, garbage out." A reasonable way to look at your computer's productivity. But is it reasonable for anyone to think of you in this way? For instance, is it reasonable for anyone to fear that your going to college will put you in an environment threatening to your faith and that all the "bad stuff" of the college experience will cause you to "lose your faith"?

Some people think we are like computers in that we are controlled by what we take in. Jesus never thought that anyone was defiled (made bad) by mere exposure to external influences. Instead, he knew it was what came from your heart that was definitive. (Think of heart as the same as mind; Jesus believed that the heart was the seat of personality and the core of one's understanding.)

Admittedly, college is a diverse and challenging environment and you are being exposed to so much that is new and different. But such diversity does not have to be a threat to your faith. Why not? Because you have been encouraged (by St. Paul) to "test everything; [but] hold fast to what is good; abstain from every form of evil" (1 Thess 5:21–22). That is Scripture's stamp of approval on the college experience. How do you "hold fast to what is good"? By keeping Christ at the center of your thinking, your studying, of who you are. If he is there, at your core (heart/mind), then what comes out will be good.

Prayer: Help me to really test everything and to hold fast to the good. Amen.

64 – Faith as Persistence

Matthew 15:21–31 — (21) Jesus left that place and went away to the district of Tyre and Sidon. (22) Just then a Canaanite woman from that region came out and started shouting, "Have mercy on me, Lord, Son of David; my daughter is tormented by a demon." (23) But he did not answer her at all. And his disciples came and urged him, saying, "Send her away, for she keeps shouting after us." (24) He answered, "I was sent only to the lost sheep of the house of Israel." (25) But she came and knelt before him, saying, "Lord, help me." (26) He answered, "It is not fair to take the children's food and throw it to the dogs." (27) She said, "Yes, Lord, yet even the dogs eat the crumbs that fall from their masters' table." (28) Then Jesus answered her, "Woman, great is your faith! Let it be done for you as you wish." And her daughter was healed instantly. (29) After Jesus had left that place, he passed along the Sea of Galilee, and he went up the mountain, where he sat down. (30) Great crowds came to him, bringing with them the lame, the maimed, the blind, the mute, and many others. They put them at his feet, and he cured them, (31) so that the crowd was amazed when they saw the mute speaking, the maimed whole, the lame walking, and the blind seeing. And they praised the God of Israel.

ONE REASON COLLEGE IS so great is that you can ask questions, and even follow-up questions. Usually you will learn in the process. So ask tough questions. Get your money's worth out of college.

As a teacher, I once had the opportunity to host the son of a candidate for US Congress in my class. While I actually admired the candidate, I couldn't let the opportunity pass to try some tough questions. I asked his campaigning son, "Did your father ever do anything wrong in his political career?" Reluctantly, but thoughtfully, the son admitted that his father had probably made errors in his political career.

My follow-up question: "What were some of those mistakes?"

His response? He couldn't actually think of any. End of questions.

At least the class got to hear a tough question. And to hear a response that . . . well, what did it reveal?

College does offer the opportunity for you to pursue the truth if you take the opportunity. The mother in today's gospel story is a good example of how you might go after what is really important. Like a dog after crumbs. Get your money's worth!

Prayer: Lord, I need answers. Thank you for promising to hear me out. Amen.

65 – Repeat the Lesson

Matthew 15:32–39 — (32) Then Jesus called his disciples to him and said, "I have compassion for the crowd, because they have been with me now for three days and have nothing to eat; and I do not want to send them away hungry, for they might faint on the way." (33) The disciples said to him, "Where are we to get enough bread in the desert to feed so great a crowd?" (34) Jesus asked them, "How many loaves have you?" They said, "Seven, and a few small fish." (35) Then ordering the crowd to sit down on the ground, (36) he took the seven loaves and the fish; and after giving thanks he broke them and gave them to the disciples, and the disciples gave them to the crowds. (37) And all of them ate and were filled; and they took up the broken pieces left over, seven baskets full. (38) Those who had eaten were four thousand men, besides women and children. (39) After sending away the crowds, he got into the boat and went to the region of Magadan.

ONE OF THE THINGS about being in college is that you are in college. A lot of folks aren't. Less than half of Americans have college experience. That puts you in a special category. Are you better than others?

On the "you're special" side of the ledger you have the following going for you: you have jumped through all the hoops necessary to get into college. You passed the tests and earned good grades. You have decided to devote a significant portion of your time and a lot of your resources—even though you may be in debt up to your neck!—to being in college. On the other hand, there are probably a lot of factors in your being in college that aren't due to how great you are: parental encouragement and support, a scholarship, the fact that the college was there, ready and waiting for you when you arrived.

In the narrative for today, Jesus' disciples again seem a bit too big for their sandals. They tell Jesus that he doesn't seem to understand that they do not have the resources to solve the problem of a lot of hungry people. Once again—remember the earlier occasion on which Jesus had to turn the disciples into waiters and busboys?—Jesus has to admonish the disciples. They are not in charge. They are disciples.

College folks need to be reminded occasionally that humility is called for—the recognition that what you are and what you have are gifts from God to be appreciated and to be used to serve others.

Prayer: Lord, help me to recognize that all I have is a gift from you. Amen.

66 – Prove It!

Matthew 16:1–4 — (1) The Pharisees and Sadducees came, and to test Jesus they asked him to show them a sign from heaven. (2) He answered them, "When it is evening, you say, 'It will be fair weather, for the sky is red.' (3) And in the morning, 'It will be stormy today, for the sky is red and threatening.' You know how to interpret the appearance of the sky, but you cannot interpret the signs of the times. (4) An evil and adulterous generation asks for a sign, but no sign will be given to it except the sign of Jonah." Then he left them and went away.

WEATHER FORECASTING CAN BE important. Will it rain on game day? Is that snow storm going to hit before, during, or after Thanksgiving? Then there are important questions about the future—the answers to which are less clear. How secure will Dad's job be if there is an economic downturn? How will Mom's next checkup with the doctor turn out? How will I do this semester in calculus (or French or physics)? What is going on in my relationship with John/Mary? Does God exist? For these latter questions, there is "evidence" but it's not always clear.

Take the question about God. Even Immanuel Kant, one of the most brilliant philosophers ever (1724–1804) concluded that there are equally persuasive arguments on each side of the "Does God exist?" debate. If Kant couldn't gain clarity on it, how can poor freshmen or sophomores (or even juniors or seniors) get it? Perhaps the best thing you can hope for in college (and in life) regarding some of these major questions is only a really cautious answer, or perhaps only a presentation of the evidence for each side of the argument.

When the religious leaders asked Jesus for a sign (proof) he was well into his public ministry, so they had already seen plenty of miraculous cures. He almost blew them off. What he did do was tell them what he thought of them: that they were "an evil and adulterous generation." Hadn't they already seen plenty of proof?

What was the "sign of Jonah"? Probably a prefiguring of Jesus' time in the tomb and then his resurrection. That certainly was a sign to the disciples and has been to many since then. Granted, the resurrection is pretty hard to believe sometimes. But that is the nature of our relationship with God and with Jesus: he spent his time doing amazingly good things for others and describing the indescribable. Jesus is his own "sign"; he is his own "proof."

Prayer: O God, thank you for showing me Jesus; help me to know him better. Amen.

67 – Don't Be So Literal

Matthew 16:5-12 — (5) When the disciples reached the other side, they had forgotten to bring any bread. (6) Jesus said to them, "Watch out, and beware of the yeast of the Pharisees and Saddu-cees." (7) They said to one another, "It is because we have brought no bread." (8) And becoming aware of it, Jesus said, "You of little faith, why are you talking about having no bread? (9) Do you still not perceive? Do you not remember the five loaves for the five thousand, and how many baskets you gathered? (10) Or the seven loaves for the four thousand, and how many baskets you gathered? (11) How could you fail to perceive that I was not speaking about bread? Beware of the yeast of the Pharisees and Sadducees!" (12) Then they understood that he had not told them to beware of the yeast of bread, but of the teaching of the Pharisees and Sadducees.

ONE OF COLLEGE'S BIG challenges is that you are expected to assume ever more responsibility for your own learning. Back in the earlier grades they would tell you exactly what you needed to know; you learned it; everyone was happy. In college there is more to learn, but not more time in which to teach it. So students are given big(ger) reading assignments, and things that weren't discussed in class begin to appear on tests.

The secret to success in this new environment is found in the ability to move from the known (what was explained and learned in class) to the unknown (and was never discussed in class). The trick is figuring out how what you learned but haven't tried yet can help deal with the as yet unknown.

You learn to "read" what is going on all around you in order to succeed socially. Some children lack the "wiring" to do this kind of work. They seem stuck in the known and are unable to make that jump to the new and unfa-miliar. They are stuck in the absolutely literal world they have known and do not have the ability to think that the new situation may be "like" the ones they already know and that they can apply the known to the new situation.

Jesus' disciples had a bit of this problem and it surfaces in the passage read today. When hanging onto the literal keeps you from moving ahead, it may be time to let go of it and make the leap of faith to the new. Disciples needed to let go of this story's "lunch" problem (the known) and leap out in faith to deal with the bigger, deeper problems.

Prayer: Thank you, God, for being there when I take that leap of faith. Amen.

68 – What's in a Name?

Matthew 16:13–20 — (13) Now when Jesus came into the district of Caesarea Philippi, he asked his disciples, "Who do people say that the Son of Man is?" (14) And they said, "Some say John the Baptist, but others Elijah, and still others Jeremiah or one of the prophets." (15) He said to them, "But who do you say that I am?" (16) Simon Peter answered, "You are the Messiah, the Son of the living God." (17) And Jesus answered him, "Blessed are you, Simon son of Jonah! For flesh and blood has not revealed this to you, but my Father in heaven. (18) And I tell you, you are Peter, and on this rock I will build my church, and the gates of Hades will not prevail against it. (19) I will give you the keys of the kingdom of heaven, and whatever you bind on earth will be bound in heaven, and whatever you loose on earth will be loosed in heaven." (20) Then he sternly ordered the disciples not to tell anyone that he was the Messiah.

DO YOUR TEACHERS ADDRESS you as Bill and Mary or as Ms. Jones and Mr. Smith? Would it make any difference? The argument seems to be that an informal address—first names only—shows more personal concern, more intimacy, a friendlier campus. The argument for more formality is that it shows that faculty are taking students more seriously—as adults, scholars, and even colleagues in the quest for knowledge. Regardless of which you prefer, do you agree that it is better if teachers know you by some name? Without a name, what are you?

Think for a moment about some of your other names—the pet names, the nicknames—and all the baggage they carry. How about that middle name that only your mother uses when she is really angry with you? Or that baby name that your family uses when telling you how cute you were? How about that special name that only your significant other uses to express intimate feelings? Those are all names that carry enormous meaning. In giving others the knowledge and permission to use your special names you are giving them special gifts and some power.

Using new names (titles) for Jesus gives Peter a new comprehension of who his companion is. Jesus, in turn, confers a new name onto Simon: "Peter" (a kind of nickname that could translate into English as "Rocky"). They have moved to a new level of mutual knowledge. This new relationship is more than the old names can handle.

Prayer: Thank you for naming me one of your own. Amen.

69 – Inevitability and Free Will

Matthew 16:21–28 — (21) From that time on, Jesus began to show his disciples that he must go to Jerusalem and undergo great suffering at the hands of the elders and chief priests and scribes, and be killed, and on the third day be raised. (22) And Peter took him aside and began to rebuke him, saying, "God forbid it, Lord! This must never happen to you." (23) But he turned and said to Peter, "Get behind me, Satan! You are a stumbling block to me; for you are setting your mind not on divine things but on human things." (24) Then Jesus told his disciples, "If any want to become my followers, let them deny themselves and take up their cross and follow me. (25) For those who want to save their life will lose it, and those who lose their life for my sake will find it. (26) For what will it profit them if they gain the whole world but forfeit their life? Or what will they give in return for their life? (27) For the Son of Man is to come with his angels in the glory of his Father, and then he will repay everyone for what has been done. (28) Truly I tell you, there are some standing here who will not taste death before they see the Son of Man coming in his kingdom."

OFTEN IN READING A story you can see that the scene you are reading now inevitably emerged from all that went before. It doesn't require a genius to figure these sorts of things out. The inevitability of much that happens around us can be depressing and boring but not hard to predict. Is that the way life is? Isn't there a commonly used expression about life: "Well, that's just the way things are"?

But what about free will? What about you? Will you be carried along in a set piece and crushed under the inevitability of the movement of the world? Some pretty heavyweight thinkers would have you believe just that. Thinkers as different as Hegel and Marx—one who believed in the spirit and the other only in matter. Both believed that the gigantic and inevitable movements of history ground forward and would destroy a lot of individuals in the process. They both believed that when you make an omelet (good) some eggs have to be broken (bad).

This is the kind of "discussion" Jesus and Peter had. Jesus could see what was coming. Peter's trust in free will was shortsighted. But Jesus saw that "human inevitability" could not triumph before God's ultimate will.

Prayer: Set my mind on things divine and not on human things. Amen.

70 – It Doesn't Get Any Better than This

Matthew 17:1–8 — (1) Six days later, Jesus took with him Peter and James and his brother John and let them up a high mountain, by themselves. (2) And he was transfigured before them, and his face shone like the sun, and his clothes became dazzling white. (3) Suddenly there appeared to them Moses and Elijah, talking with him. (4) Then Peter said to Jesus, "Lord, it is good for us to be here; if you wish, I will make three dwellings here, one for you, one for Moses, and one for Elijah." (5) While he was still speaking, suddenly a bright cloud overshadowed them, and from the cloud a voice said, "This is my Son, the Beloved; with him I am well pleased; listen to him!" (6) When the disciples heard this, they fell to the ground and were overcome by fear. (7) But Jesus came and touched them, saying, "Get up and do not be afraid." (8) And when they looked up, they saw no one except Jesus himself alone.

"WHAT IS THE MAIN point?" Haven't you wondered that often enough? You had to pick the right answer to questions like that on the ACT or the SAT. Then you had to "read for meaning" in those English classes. Then there were lectures, articles, and books that you had to get through and remember the main points of. "Getting the point" is really important in college. It can be the difference between pass and fail. Later on, potential employers will be wanting to hire you and your chances of landing the best job will depend a good deal on how quickly and how well you "get the point"—whatever the "point" is.

"Getting the point" usually requires developing the skills to distinguish—"discern" is the term that is totally applicable in this case—and is one of the main goals of a college education.

It is not unlike what happens in this story in which Jesus is "transfigured." Peter must be thinking: "Man, this is it! It doesn't get any better than this. Let's keep it this way forever!" He blurts out his second suggestion to Jesus in two days. (Remember yesterday when Peter suggested that Jesus avoid the crucifixion?) This time it has to do with building some structures so that Jesus, Moses, Elijah, John, James, and Peter can stay on the mountain forever. Forget the other disciples. Forget the trip to Jerusalem that Jesus just forecast. Forget the needy masses. Peter finally "gets the point"—he "saw no one except Jesus himself alone." That's the "point"—just Jesus.

Prayer: God, when I get distracted, keep pointing to Jesus so that I can get the point. Amen.

71 – Can You Keep a Secret?

Matthew 17:9-13 — (9) As they were coming down the mountain, Jesus ordered them, "Tell no one about the vision until after the Son of Man has been raised from the dead." (10) And the disciples asked him, "Why, then, do the scribes say that Elijah must come first?" (11) He replied, "Elijah is indeed coming and will restore all things; (12) but I tell you that Elijah has already come, and they did not recognize him, but they did to him whatever they pleased. So also the Son of Man is about to suffer at their hands." (13) Then the disciples understood that he was speaking to them about John the Baptist.

SECRETS. AREN'T THEY DELICIOUS? There is a curious cost/benefit aspect to secrets. If you promise not to tell, you might get to hear the secret. That's the upside. The downside is that you can't get the buzz you might get if you were to reveal that secret to someone else. So it might be better not to know the secret in the first place.

There is another upside to getting to hear secrets. If you have a reputation for really keeping secrets you may get to hear a lot of them. Then there are secrets that may not be hard to keep quiet. Like the ones that Jesus gave to his disciples—and to us. On any number of occasions, Jesus told others, "Don't tell (whatever just happened"—16:20, as well as Mark 7:36, 8:30, 9:9; Luke 5:14, 8:56, 9:21). Now that is the kind of command you can really get into: don't do something. Those are probably the commands that most of us have had the most success in keeping.

In today's report from Matthew you hear Jesus tell Peter, James, and John not to tell anyone about what had just happened. What was that? Only that Jesus sort of lit up like the sun, that Moses and Elijah dropped by for a chat, and that God spoke to the gathering! Just tell me that you're not going to mention that to somebody pretty soon.

In fact, there were people who broke Jesus' command and did tell what had happened. But he never got mad at them. If you have had a really powerful experience with Jesus should you tell? Or is it a secret?

> *Prayer: Give me the skill and the words to be able to tell what you have done to those who need to hear it. Amen.*

72 – Help My Unbelief

Matthew 17:14–20 — (14) When they came to the crowd, a man came to him, knelt before him, (15) and said, "Lord, have mercy on my son, for he is an epileptic and he suffers terribly; he often falls into the fire and often into the water. (16) And I brought him to your disciples, but they could not cure him." (17) Jesus answered, "You faithless and perverse generation, how much longer must I be with you? How much longer must I put up with you? Bring him here to me." (18) And Jesus rebuked the demon, and it came out of him, and the boy was cured instantly. (19) Then the disciples came to Jesus privately and said, "Why could we not cast it out?" (20) He said to them, "Because of your little faith. For truly I tell you, if you have faith the size of a mustard seed, you will say to this mountain, 'Move from here to there,' and it will move; and nothing will be impossible for you." (21) [Omitted by ancient authorities.]

WHEN SHE COLLAPSED OF what looked like an epileptic seizure, it was fortunate that she did it in the front yard as she was just leaving for school in the morning. She did not fall into fire or water, only onto the cement of the driveway. It was fortunate that I could call 911 and get help quickly. And it was fortunate that there were doctors and tests to evaluate her and prescribe medication to deal with it.

The father in today's reading was not so fortunate. His child "suffered terribly; he often falls." The man was desperate. He was so desperate that he came to the disciples! As far as we know the disciples had not done miracles. (Jesus had authorized them to heal [10:1] but Matthew gives no account of the success or failure of their mission.) This man was truly desperate to place his hope in the disciples who don't seem to have a great resume at this point in the gospel story!

Desperation drives us to do crazy stuff sometimes. Simply being a disciple didn't work for the disciples. Jesus was pretty critical of them. It is not clear whether the father "had faith"; it was clear that he felt desperate, that he knew he needed help that was beyond his own power to provide. Hmmm? Maybe that's what faith ultimately is.

Prayer: Lord, I believe; please help my unbelief (Mark 9:24). Amen.

73 – Good News, Bad News

Matthew17:22-23 — (22) As they were gathering in Galilee, Jesus said to them, "The Son of Man is going to be betrayed into human hands, (23) and they will kill him, and on the third day he will be raised." And they were greatly distressed.

DO YOU REMEMBER THE old joke: there is good news and bad news; which do you want first? Unfortunately, college students actually pay little attention to the news—good or bad. Perhaps paying attention to daily events and how they are reported would be educational. It could also help in other ways. It could put your deep grieving over the little things that happen to you into the larger context of major catastrophes that strike elsewhere.

What was it that distressed the disciples when Jesus told them—now for the second time—that he would be betrayed, killed, and raised? Is this one of those "good news/bad news" stories? If so, it sounds like this:

There is good news and bad news; which do you want first? The good news? Okay. The good news is that Jesus will be raised from the dead. The bad news is that the disciples will betray him and the government will kill him.

Or, what about this? There is good news and bad news; which do you want first? The good news? Okay. The good news is that Jesus says that he will be raised from the dead. The bad news is that everyone knows that is impossible.

Or how about this: There is good news and there is bad news; which do you want first? The bad news? Okay. The bad news is that Jesus will be betrayed and killed. The good news is that it is God's idea to do that. Does God really use Jesus' friends to betray him? Or what about his death and all the moments leading up to it that induce the false testimony and abuse of government power? Does God use governments to do his will in this way? Is that good news?

The story of Jesus is full of both good and bad news. Our hope is that the good news swallows up the bad.

Prayer: We hear so much bad news; remind me always of the good news in Christ Jesus. Amen.

74 – Discipleship Can Be Taxing

Matthew 17:24–27 — (24) When they reached Capernaum, the collectors of the temple tax came to Peter and said, "Does your teacher not pay the temple tax?" (25) He said, "Yes, he does." And when he came home, Jesus spoke of it first, asking, "What do you think, Simon? From whom do kings of the earth take toll or tribute? From their children or from others?" (26) When Peter said, "From others," Jesus said to him, "Then the children are free. (27) However, so that we do not give offense to them, go to the sea and cast a hook; take the first fish that comes up; and when you open its mouth, you will find a coin; take that and give it to them for you and me."

MY MOTHER'S ADVICE was always to refrain from being weird so that I might preserve enough normalcy to have something negotiable if I ever got in a position where everyone was thinking something I said or did was weird.

You may be tempted to argue with a prof or with a fellow student, protest conditions at work or a class assignment, refuse requirements from the college, violate the dress code, or just do something outrageous because it sounds like fun.

Remember—it's not all about you. It's about the other person. Sometimes the other person is wrong, and you know it. Even so, it is still a loving gesture to accede to their wishes.

It's about love. You will read (1 Cor 6:12 and 1 Cor 10:23–30) that Paul stated that in Christ he was free to do whatever he wanted, but if another Christian might be offended by something he did, he (Paul) would avoid doing it so as not to offend the more sensitive person. He preferred love to freedom; he preferred the other person to himself.

So in this passage Jesus pays a tax that he doesn't have to pay. In fact, he pays it for himself and for another person. Doing something you don't have to do can be "taxing"; but it can also be loving. And it can even be fun.

Prayer: Help me always to be considerate of the other person. Amen.

75 – Who Is the Greatest?

Matthew 18:1-14 — (1) At that time the disciples came to Jesus and asked, "Who is the greatest in the kingdom of heaven?" (2) He called a child, whom he put among them, (3) and said, "Truly I tell you, unless you change and become like children, you will never enter the kingdom of heaven. (4) Whoever becomes humble like this child is the greatest in the kingdom of heaven. (5) Whoever welcomes one such child in my name welcomes me. (6) If any of you put a stumbling block before one of these little ones who believe in me, it would be better for you if a great millstone were fastened around your neck and you were drowned in the depth of the sea. (7) Woe to the world because of stumbling blocks! Occasions for stumbling are bound to come, but woe to the one by whom the stumbling block comes! (8) If your hand or your foot causes you to stumble, cut it off and throw it away; it is better for you to enter life maimed or lame than to have two hands or two feet and to be thrown into the eternal fire. (9) And if your eye causes you to stumble, tear it out and throw it away; it is better for you to enter life with one eye than to have two eyes and to be thrown into the hell of fire. (10) Take care that you do not despise one of these little ones; for, I tell you, in heaven their angels continually see the face of my Father in heaven. (12) What do you think? If a shepherd has a hundred sheep, and one of them has gone astray, does he not leave the ninety-nine on the mountains and go in search of the one that went astray? (13) And if he finds it, truly I tell you, he rejoices over it more than over the ninety-nine that never went astray. (14) So it is not the will of your father in heaven that one of these little ones should be lost."

DON'T THE DISCIPLES HAVE anything better to do than but find out who "number one" is? Being first (or best) can be a mania. Okay, sometimes "best" can be helpful: Which therapy has the best record for curing a certain illness? But there are the really crazy ones: Who can eat the most hot dogs in ten minutes? Colleges are into this, too. The practice of ranking has become big stuff: "best" endowment, best "party" school, and all-around athletic program.

Looks like another case of disciples asking the wrong question. Jesus doesn't seem gripped by the question. What Jesus does seem to care about is children—or anyone hurt by others.

Prayer: Help me to excel in service. Amen.

76 – Iron Fists, Velvet Gloves

Matthew 18:15–20 — (15) If another member of the church sins against you, go and point out the fault when the two of you are alone. If the member listens to you, you have regained that one. (16) But if you are not listened to, take one or two others along with you, so that every word may be confirmed by the evidence of two or three witnesses. (17) If the member refuses to listen to them, tell it to the church; and if the offender refuses to listen even to the church, let such a one be to you as a Gentile and a tax collector. (18) Truly I tell you, whatever you bind on earth will be bound in heaven, and whatever you loose on earth will be loosed in heaven. (19) Again, truly I tell you, if two of you agree on earth about anything you ask, it will be done for you by my Father in heaven. (20) For where two or three are gathered in my name, I am there among them."

ARGUMENTS. SOME OF THESE have serious or even permanent consequences. Just because you have grown up enough to go off to college doesn't mean that everything will be smooth in your relationships. As you settle into college, you will have many potential flash points that could escalate into arguments.

There are a lot of techniques you can use to keep a cool head in such situations: count to ten; leave the room; try to see the situation from the other person's point of view. The wider and more diverse your circle of interactions and contacts, the more different kinds of people there are and the more possibilities there are for disagreements and misunderstandings.

At home, disagreements with your parents or siblings could be fierce but you always knew you could fall back on the fact that they loved you and you loved them. Here in college you have no such safety net. So disagreements have to be handled in a smart and constructive manner. Separation seems harsh, but sometimes it may be the only way to keep hard feelings from coming to the surface. Even if both of you are at the same college, there are plenty of ways to live completely separate lives. And there is always the possibility of the kind of second chance God has provided you in which arguments can become new conversations and ruptures can be healed.

Prayer: God, help me to live optimistically, even with the awareness of the relationships that have failed. Amen.

77– You've Got to Be Kidding

Matthew 18:21–35 — (21) Then Peter came and said to him, "Lord, if another member of the church sins against me, how often should I forgive? As many as seven times?" (22) Jesus said to him, "Not seven times, but, I tell you, seventy-seven times. (23) For this reason the kingdom of heaven may be compared to a king who wished to settle accounts with his slaves. (24) When he began the reckoning, one who owed him ten thousand talents was brought to him; (25) and, as he could not pay, his lord ordered him to be sold, together with his wife and children and all his possessions, and payment to be made. (26) So the slave fell on his knees before him, saying, 'Have patience with me, and I will pay you everything.' (27) And out of pity for him, the lord of that slave released him and forgave him the debt. (28) But that same slave, as he went out, came upon one of his fellow slaves who owed him a hundred denarii; and seizing him by the throat, he said, 'Pay what you owe.' (29) Then his fellow slave fell down and pleaded with him, 'Have patience with me, and I will pay you.' (30) But he refused; then he went and threw him into prison until he would pay the debt. (31) When his fellow slaves saw what had happened, they were greatly distressed, and they went and reported to their lord all that had taken place. (32) Then his lord summoned him and said to him, 'You wicked slave! I forgave you all that debt because you pleaded with me. (33) Should you not have had mercy on your fellow slave, as I had mercy on you?' (34) And in anger his lord handed him over to be tortured until he would pay his entire debt. (35) So my heavenly Father will also do to every one of you, if you do not forgive your brother or sister from your heart."

JESUS OFFERS PETER A different approach to conflict resolution: "forgive." Give up what you are owed. The "77 times" and "10,000 talents" are roughly equivalent to "every time" and "all the money in the world." The kingdom of God is like the situation where impossible disagreements (somebody not able to pay a ginormous debt) are forgiven. It doesn't make sense from a rational, business, or worldly point of view. But that is just the way God is and would like us to be. Maybe we don't feel like forgiving another. But this isn't about feelings. It's about forgiving. It's about God's kingdom.

Prayer: Thank God for that! Amen.

78 – Serious Sex

Matthew 19:1–12 — (1) When Jesus had finished saying these things, he left Galilee and went to the region of Judea beyond the Jordan. (2) Large crowds followed him, and he cured them there. (3) Some Pharisees came to him, and to test him they asked, "Is it lawful for a man to divorce his wife for any cause?" (4) He answered, "Have you not read that the one who made them at the beginning 'made them male and female,' (5) and said, 'For this reason a man shall leave his father and mother and be joined to his wife, and the two shall become one flesh'? (6) So they are no longer two, but one flesh. Therefore what God has joined together, let no one separate." (7) They said to him, "Why then did Moses command us to give a certificate of dismissal and to divorce her?" (8) He said to them, "It was because you were so hardhearted that Moses allowed you to divorce your wives, but from the beginning it was not so. (9) And I say to you, whoever divorces his wife, except for unchastity, and marries another commits adultery." (10) His disciples said to him, "If such is the case of a man with his wife, it is better not to marry." (21) But he said to them, "Not everyone can accept this teaching, but only those to whom it is given. (12) For there are eunuchs who have been so from birth, and there are eunuchs who have been made eunuchs by others, and there are eunuchs who have made themselves eunuchs for the sake of the kingdom of heaven. Let anyone accept this who can."

Is SEX WORTH IT? Would a cost/benefit analysis convincingly prove that the effort you put into a sexual relationship compensate for its possible side and after effects? College is definitely a time—for many students—of sexual experimentation.

In today's account Jesus doesn't directly address sexual issues but he does note that marriage (which, of course, involves sex) had been compromised by humans' hardness of heart in our seeming inability to maintain permanent relationships. When the disciples are reminded of this, they ponder another option: not marrying.

The great fifth-century theologian Augustine had had a long (about fifteen years!) illicit relationship that he had tried to end, but without serious effort. His famous prayer: "Lord, make me chaste, but not now." The point? Sex is serious stuff. Handle with care.

Prayer: Lord, let all I do be done in the context of the love that Jesus shows for all of us. Amen.

79 – Protecting Jesus?

Matthew 19:13–22 — (13) Then little children were being brought to him in order that he might lay his hands on them and pray. The disciples spoke sternly to those who brought them; (14) but Jesus said, "Let the little children come to me, and do not stop them; for it is to such as these that the kingdom of heaven belongs." (15) And he laid his hands on them and went on his way. (16) Then someone came to him and said, "Teacher, what good deed must I do to have eternal life?" (17) And he said to him, "Why do you ask me about what is good? There is only one who is good. If you wish to enter into life, keep the commandments." (18) He said to him, "Which ones?" And Jesus said, "You shall not murder; You shall not commit adultery; You shall not steal; You shall not bear false witness; (19) Honor your father and mother; also, You shall love your neighbor as yourself." (20) The young man said to him, "I have kept all these; what do I still lack?" (21) Jesus said to him, "If you wish to be perfect, go, sell your possessions, and give the money to the poor, and you will have treasure in heaven; then come, follow me." (22) When the young man heard this word, he went away grieving, for he had many possessions.

How do you get to heaven? The rich, young man always did the right thing, but couldn't get in because of his stuff. (Remember the "gate" is narrow [cf. 7:13-14]?) Jesus' ideas about entering the kingdom of heaven should offend just about everyone. But more pertinent for college people is the example (again) of the disciples. This time they feel they need to protect Jesus—from little kids! Are you kidding? From little kids? Surely Jesus can handle the situation.

Most well-intended "survival manuals" for Christians attending college don't say so explicitly. But implicitly, between the lines, is the fear that the college experience is so spiritually dangerous that Christians—and even Jesus himself—need to be protected from it. As in keeping them away from everything collegiate.

Like Jesus had never associated with people doing bad stuff or thinking naughty thoughts? Or like he wasn't aware of sex or had never had a drink of wine or been to a party where things got out of hand or had never had to deal with people who were peddling truly bad ideas?

Or was it that the disciples didn't want the kids' parents to hear about the "deal" Jesus offered to kids—"to such as these that the kingdom of heaven belongs"?

Prayer: Lord, I know you don't need my help but I sure need yours. Amen.

80 – Opportunity Costs

Matthew 19:23–30 — (23) Then Jesus said to his disciples, "Truly I tell you, it will be hard for a rich person to enter the kingdom of heaven. (24) Again I tell you, it is easier for a camel to go through the eye of a needle than for someone who is rich to enter the kingdom of God." (25) When the disciples heard this, they were greatly astounded and said, "Then who can be saved?" (26) But Jesus looked at them and said, "For mortals it is impossible, but for God all things are possible." (27) Then Peter said in reply, "Look, we have left everything and followed you. What then will we have?" (28) Jesus said to them, "Truly I tell you, at the renewal of all things, when the Son of Man is seated on the throne of his glory, you who have followed me will also sit on twelve thrones, judging the twelve tribes of Israel. (29) And everyone who has left houses or brothers or sisters or father or mother or children or fields, for my name's sake, will receive a hundred-fold, and will inherit eternal life. (30) But many who are first will be last, and the last will be first."

YOU PROBABLY ALREADY KNOW this, but it is worth repeating—and re-checking occasionally because it changes . . . upwards: on average, college graduates will made a lot more money than the folks who don't graduate from college. By the time you are ready to retire in about forty years you will be so far ahead of those who have no college experience that it will be mind-boggling. That's the good news.

Jesus warns his listeners of the possible downside: "It will be hard for a rich person to enter the kingdom of heaven." The problem to which Jesus alludes is probably not connected so much to the total income you may enjoy, but to the use(s) to which you put that income. If your income is small, you probably don't spend much. If your income is large, you probably spend more (duh!), have more, and get more stuff to which to be attached. This is not a mathematical certainty, but you get the idea. Jesus knew that people could use anything to separate themselves from God and from others. Just beware: you are going to have a lot more of everything just because you are in college. Don't let it be a barrier between yourself and God and between yourself and others.

Prayer: Lord, help me to commit myself and whatever I have in service to you and your creation. Amen.

81 – Hey! That's Not Fair!

Matthew 20:1–16 — (1) "For the kingdom of heaven is like a landowner who went out early in the morning to hire laborers for his vineyard. (2) After agreeing with the laborers for the usual daily wage, he sent them into his vineyard. (3) When he went out about nine o'clock, he saw others standing idle in the marketplace, (4) and he said to them, 'You also go into the vineyard, and I will pay you whatever is right.' So they went. (5) When he went out again about noon and about three o'clock, he did the same. (6) And about five o'clock he went out and found others standing around; and he said to them 'Why are you standing here idle all day?' (7) They said to him, 'Because no one has hired us.' He said to them, 'You also go into the vineyard.' (8) When evening came, the owner of the vineyard said to his manager, 'Call the laborers and give them their pay, beginning with the last and then going to the first.' (9) When those hired about five o'clock came, each of them received the usual daily wage. (10) Now when the first came, they thought they would receive more; but each of them also received the usual daily wage. (11) And when they received it, they grumbled against the landowner, (12) saying, 'These last worked only one hour, and you have made them equal to us who have borne the burden of the day and the scorching heat.' (13) But he replied to one of them, 'Friend, I am doing you no wrong; did you not agree with me for the usual daily wage? (14) Take what belongs to you and go; I choose to give to this last the same as I give to you. (15) Am I not allowed to do what I choose with what belongs to me? Or are you envious because I am generous?' (16) So the last will be first, and the first will be last."

THERE IS AN ANCIENT Jewish version of this parable that reads pretty much like what we learn from popular culture: work hard and you will succeed. In that version, the fellows who worked only one hour actually did as much work in that hour as the laborers who had worked since early in the morning. They worked hard and were successful.

The truth is that life is not fair. But more importantly, God is not fair! We don't deserve all the good we get; we don't earn forgiveness and salvation: It comes to us as a gift. If we learn anything from this parable, it is that God does not reward us for our work but he provides us what we need—like a "day's wage."

Prayer: God, thank you for giving me what I need, and not what I deserve. Amen.

82 – Your Mother Said What?

Matthew 20:17–28 — (17) While Jesus was going up to Jerusalem, he took the twelve disciples aside by themselves, and said to them on the way, (18) "See, we are going up to Jerusalem, and the Son of Man will be handed over to the chief priests and scribes, and they will condemn him to death; (19) then they will hand him over to the Gentiles to be mocked and flogged and crucified; and on the third day he will be raised." (20) Then the mother of the sons of Zebedee came to him with her sons, and kneeling before him, she asked a favor of him. (21) And he said to her, "What do you want?" She said to him, "Declare that these two sons of mine will sit, one at your right hand and one at your left, in your kingdom." (22) But Jesus answered, "You do not know what you are asking. Are you able to drink the cup that I am about to drink?" They said to him, "We are able." (23) He said to them, "You will indeed drink my cup, but to sit at my right hand and at my left, this is not mine to grant, but it is for those for whom it has been prepared by my Father." (24) When the ten heard it, they were angry with the two brothers. (25) But Jesus called them to him and said, "You know that the rulers of the Gentiles lord it over them, and their great ones are tyrants over them. (26) It will not be so among you; but whoever wishes to be great among you must be your servant, (27) and whoever wishes to be first among you must be your slave; (28) just as the Son of Man came not to be served but to serve, and to give his life a ransom for many."

STUDENT LIFE PERSONNEL REPORT that "helicopter parents" are more intrusive than ever. With universities no longer functioning *in loco parentis* ("in the place of parents") and the ubiquity of cell phones, parents feel free to intrude at will on behalf of their college children. College should be a time for you to be on your own, making your own decisions, carving out a new life for yourself—and suffering the consequences of your own decisions.

In today's reading, a "stage mom" and status-conscious disciples are doing their petty maneuvering in the context of more important concerns of Jesus. To begin this section, Jesus announces—for the third time—that he is to be betrayed, crucified, and resurrected. That might have elicited a more sensitive response than some disciples' mother asking, "Can my boys have special treatment?"

Prayer: God, teach me to be a servant—in thought and in deed. Amen.

83 – Possible Side Effects May Include . . .

Matthew 20:29–33 — (29) As they were leaving Jericho, a large crowd followed him. (30) There were two blind men sitting by the roadside. When they heard that Jesus was passing by, they shouted, "Lord, have mercy on us, Son of David!" (31) The crowd sternly ordered them to be quiet; but they shouted even more loudly, "Have mercy on us, Lord, Son of David!" (32) Jesus stood still and called them, saying, "What do you want me to do for you? (33) They said to him, "Lord, let our eyes be opened." (34) Moved with compassion, Jesus touched their eyes. Immediately they regained their sight and followed him.

WHEN YOU OPEN THE medicine that the doctor just prescribed for whatever ails you, do you ever read the insert? It's called the "indications" or something like that. It is supposed to give you all the clinical information on what could possibly happen when you take the medicine.

When you see one of those TV ads for some new medication that the manufacturer wants you to "ask your doctor" about, isn't it interesting how the afflicted persons are pictured "before" taking the medicine (sad face, physical limitations) and then how happy they are "after," when relief has come? What joy, what happiness, what laughter fills the screen, and their faces, and . . . wait, can you hear the voice-over by the announcer as the possible "indications" are catalogued? Cramps, depression, hair loss, rash, sleeplessness, difficulty breathing, blurred vision, weight gain, kidney failure, even death. A "fix"—quick and temporary, or long-term and permanent—will have consequences.

Today's tale is a miracle story. The blind men wanted sight. How much thought had they given to what their lives might be should that miracle occur? What would be the side-effects of a cure? Anything to worry about? Like having to go home and actually see the family? Or having to get a job?

If you are really up for it—for receiving the healing, whole-making, restorative makeover that trusting in Christ offers—have you thought through the "indications" of what being a "new person" might be for you? Are you truly ready to answer Jesus' call with "Lord, let our eyes be opened"?

Prayer: Lord, make me into the whole person God created me to be; and help to keep me there. Amen.

84 – Dashed Hopes

Matthew 21:1–11 — (1) When they had come near Jerusalem and had reached Bethphage, at the Mount of Olives, Jesus sent two disciples, (2) saying to them, "Go into the village ahead of you, and immediately you will find a donkey tied, and a colt with her; untie them and bring them to me. (3) If anyone says anything to you, just say this, 'The Lord needs them.' And he will send them immediately." (4) This took place to fulfill what had been spoken through the prophet, saying, (5) "Tell the daughter of Zion, Look, your king is coming to you, humble, and mounted on a donkey, and on a colt, the foal of a donkey." (6) The disciples went and did as Jesus had directed them; (7) they brought the donkey and the colt, and put their cloaks on them, and he sat on them. (8) A very large crowd spread their cloaks on the road, and others cut branches from the trees and spread them on the road. (9) The crowds that went ahead of him and that followed were shouting, "Hosanna to the Son of David! Blessed is the one who comes in the name of the Lord! Hosanna in the highest heaven!" (10) When he entered Jerusalem, the whole city was in turmoil, asking, "Who is this?" (11) The crowds were saying, "This is the prophet Jesus from Nazareth in Galilee."

YES? YES? WHAT HAPPENS then? Or is this another one of those big buildups that happens in politics, or sports, or romance? You get a big buildup, a lot of promises, excitement and anticipation, and then . . . it's a dud; nothing but disappointment.

You learn about it in your many relationships. Many of them that you have in college will not last beyond this semester. They will not flare up into a productive friendship. Only a few will survive and grow.

This can all be disappointing and might even lead to cynicism and to a reticence about any commitment for fear that whatever or whoever you choose will only disappoint you. Perhaps the lesson here is one of caution— waiting until you see more deeply into the person or possibility over which you got excited.

What are the religious expectations of those who surround and influence you? Are they realistic? What are Christians in your circle expecting from the Jesus who comes into their lives? What are you expecting? Looking for a king (a total revolution)? A magic wand wielder? A buddy? Ready for the kind of disappointment that challenges you to rethink Jesus—or that allows Jesus to reorient you in deeper and richer understanding?

Prayer: Lord, help me to distinguish the true from the popular in all things. Amen.

85 – Business as (Un-)usual?

Matthew 21:12 –17 — (12) Then Jesus entered the temple and drove out all who were selling and buying in the temple, and he overturned the tables of the money changers and the seats of those who sold doves. (13) He said to them, "It is written, 'My house shall be called a house of prayer'; but you are making it a den of robbers." (14) The blind and the lame came to him in the temple, and he cured them. (15) But when the chief priests and the scribes saw the amazing things that he did, and heard the children crying out in the temple, "Hosanna to the Son of David," they became angry (16) and said to him, "Do you hear what these are saying?" Jesus said to them, "Yes; have you never read, 'Out of the mouths of infants and nursing babies you have prepared praise for yourself'?" (17) He left them, went out of the city to Bethany, and spent the night there.

"THE CHURCH AS A Small Business." That was the theme of the meeting of area church leaders one year.

The church as a business? Is that good or bad? Is the local Christian bookstore kind of like the church with its music, books, wall plaques, greeting cards, seasonal ties, coffee mugs, and golf paraphernalia? Are those "Not of This World" products manufactured in a parallel universe by angels?

This Scripture account makes it sound like Jesus was antibusiness, and instead of using the temple space for selling and buying the legitimately "religious" goods that were clearly in demand by the customers—woops, sorry: the worshipers—he used it for healing and partying. While he (Jesus) healed people, kids were running around shouting praises to him. That really upset the *status quo* and those invested in protecting and benefiting from it.

Where do you come in? Since it is most likely that you are in college in order to prepare for a job (work, career, calling), and since business is the most popular major and career track in colleges today, the matter of business is always somewhere in the background. Where is the whole matter of job, career, money, business in your mental/spiritual landscape? Is it right at the (metaphorical) door of God's house? Is it something that needs to be attended to before you can enter what God has intended as his "house of prayer"? It's not too soon to begin to think through the relationship of your career to your faith.

Prayer: Help me to understand the "God vs. Mammon" dilemma. Amen.

86 – You Think You're Busy?

Matthew 21:18–27 — (18) In the morning, when he returned to the city, he was hungry. (19) And seeing a fig tree by the side of the road, he went to it and found nothing at all on it but leaves. Then he said to it, "May no fruit ever come from you again!" And the fig tree withered at once. (20) When the disciples saw it, they were amazed, saying, "How did the fig tree wither at once?" (21) Jesus answered them, "Truly I tell you, if you have faith and do not doubt, not only will you do what has been done to the fig tree, but even if you say to this mountain, 'Be lifted up and thrown into the sea,' it will be done. (22) Whatever you ask for in prayer with faith you will receive." (23) When he entered the temple, the chief priests and the elders of the people came to him as he was teaching, and said, "By what authority are you doing these things, and who gave you this authority?" (24) Jesus said to them, "I will also ask you one question; if you tell me the answer, then I will also tell you by what authority I do these things. (25) Did the baptism of John come from heaven, or was it of human origin?" And they argued with one another, "If we say, 'From heaven,' he will say to us, 'Why then did you not believe him?' (26) But if we say, 'Of human origin,' we are afraid of the crowd; for all regard John as a prophet." (27) So they answered Jesus, "We do not know." And he said to them, "Neither will I tell you by what authority I am doing these things."

Is THIS A BUSY week for you? How does it compare to that week in 374 CE when Aurelius Ambrosius (aka St. Ambrose [340–397])—an Italian civil servant—tried to resolve a dispute between two candidates for the job of Bishop in Milan. When he tried to calm things, someone shouted, "Ambrose for Bishop!" and everyone agreed! One problem: he was not yet even a member of the church. So he had a busy week: study, baptism, study, ordination to priest, study, installation as bishop.

Today's reading describes day two in Jesus' week. Day one was the "triumphal entry" and the "cleansing of the temple"; today would be for parables and disputes. Oh, yes, and for killing a fig tree. Later would come the Last Supper, his arrest, and crucifixion. And how about the resurrection? This is not only a busy week, it is a week of worthwhile doings.

It goes without saying that you will have a busy week, too. May what you do be worthwhile.

Prayer: Thank you for giving things to do that can be worthwhile. Amen.

87 – Clean Your Room

Matthew 21:28–32 — (28) "What do you think? A man had two sons; he went to the first and said, 'Son, go and work in the vineyard today.' (29) He answered, 'I will not'; but later he changed his mind and went. (30) The father went to the second and said the same; and he answered, 'I go, sir'; but he did not go. (31) Which of the two did the will of his father?" They said, "The first." Jesus said to them, "Truly I tell you, the tax collectors and the prostitutes are going into the kingdom of God ahead of you. (32) For John came to you in the way of righteousness and you did not believe him, but the tax collectors and the prostitutes believed him; and even after you saw it, you did not change your minds and believe him."

JESUS IS DOING WHAT he does most and best: tells a parable. It's a pretty simple parable. That is, it tells a common story about ordinary people doing what they frequently do. In this case, it is the story of two children responding to a parent's directions. How often have you heard this? "Clean your room."

The standard response when I was a kid was, "Okay." And then I would often not do it. Perhaps on a rare occasion I might have said, "No, I don't want to" and then done it anyway. This latter alternative was not usual but it is not totally out of the realm of possibility. Jesus tells stories that can fairly easily be imagined.

Jesus tells about the two sons and their different responses. Then he asks a question. He forces you (the listener) to say the obvious. The "obvious" is not what is normally considered the obvious. Normally we think prostitutes and tax-collectors (read: sleazebags, etc.) are not heading for the kingdom. Jesus has just upset your "obvious."

Are you ready to think of God's will and God's kingdom as contrary to conventional (and conventionally religious) wisdom? Self-proclaimed good people certainly did not like where the argument took them and they finally killed Jesus to express their disapproval. (That's one way to win an argument.)

If you occasionally despair about your fate, this illustration of God's kingdom leads to a wonderful conclusion: God's invitation is good for everyone. So wherever you find yourself on the spectrum of morally good through disobedient—there is good news for you.

Prayer: Thank you for being so hospitable to all of your creatures. Amen.

88 – Gotcha on CCTV

Matthew 21:33–41 — (33) Listen to another parable. There was a landowner who planted a vineyard, put a fence around it, dug a wine press in it, and built a watchtower. Then he leased it to tenants and went to another country. (34) When the harvest time had come, he sent his slaves to the tenants to collect his produce. (35) But the tenants seized his slaves and beat one, killed another, and stoned another. (36) Again he sent other slaves, more than the first; and they treated them in the same way. (37) Finally he sent his son to them, saying, 'They will respect my son.' (38) But when the tenants saw the son, they said to themselves, 'This is the heir; come, let us kill him and get his inheritance.' (39) So they seized him, threw him out of the vineyard, and killed him. (40) Now when the owner of the vineyard comes, what will he do to those tenants?" (41) They said to him, "He will put those wretches to a miserable death, and lease the vineyard to other tenants who will give him the produce at the harvest time."

I DON'T KNOW IF the town I live in is typical, but it seems that every day the news report includes a robbery: bank, convenience store, or individual victim. And every day the news report includes an arrest. These crooks are amazingly dumb. The cops always catch them.

Apparently, the "stick-up" guys think that their plan to get rich at the expense of others will work. That is mistake number one. It seems to be their only mistake, because their plan is obviously doomed to failure. Just like the plan the tenants in the story cooked up to relieve the landowner of his property.

How could anyone with a single brain cell make up such a fairy tale of a plan and expect it to work, no matter whether you lived in the first century or the twenty-first century, in Palestine or the US? And yet Jesus tells this story. It sounds outlandish, but according to my news sources, it is the kind of thing that people dream up and try on a daily basis.

Did Jesus tell this story to suggest that rejecting the son of the landowner (Jesus?) is an obviously catastrophic decision?

Rejection can be costly. Sometimes you don't know what you are rejecting. Aren't you glad that accepting Jesus' acceptance of you is something you don't need to second-guess?

Prayer: Dear Lord, life can be confusing, but help me avoid really stupid decisions. Amen.

89 – Stoned

Matthew 21:42–46 — (42) Jesus said to them, "Have you never read in the scriptures: 'The stone that the builders rejected has become the cornerstone; this was the Lord's doing, and it is amazing in our eyes'? (43) Therefore I tell you, the kingdom of God will be taken away from you and given to a people that produces the fruits of the kingdom. (44) The one who falls on this stone will be broken to pieces; and it will crush anyone on whom it falls." (45) When the chief priests and the Pharisees heard his parables, they realized that he was speaking about them. (46) They wanted to arrest him, but they feared the crowds, because they regarded him as prophet.

ONE OF THE COURSES I took in college was on Near Eastern literature—Persian poetry, Babylonian religious myths, history, etc. The instructor seemed too young, handsome, and smart; I couldn't get "into" the subject matter. I got a D in the class. So much for Near Eastern and Arabic literature. Why bring up this abject failure?

As it turns out, our nation now finds itself in desperate need to understand the history, cultures, religion, and languages of the Near East and we are in need of experts who can help our country make informed and wise choices in our relations with the peoples in that part of the world. What's the point?

The point is that you never know when you might need something that you don't think you need now or are sure you never will need. None of us knows how the world—and our own individual lives—might change and what will be demanded of us—in a decade, or in a year, or even tomorrow. This applies to big things like a whole college education. We all have a friend who decided that college was not worth it, dropped out, and then spent the rest of her life sad because of missed opportunities. It applies to smaller things too, like what you might learn in a class. You simply do not know at this moment what future moments will ask of you.

The odd parable about stones in today's reading is about the error of rejection. The parable depicts dramatic and tragic consequences. Not rejecting, but rather accepting, can offer immense opportunity, joy, peace—even job preparedness.

Prayer: Help me to hold to you, Lord, no matter what. Amen.

90 – Dressed to Kill

Matthew 22:1–14 — (1) Once more Jesus spoke to them in parables, saying: (2) "The kingdom of heaven may be compared to a king who gave a wedding banquet for his son. (3) He sent his slaves to call those who had been invited to the wedding banquet, but they would not come. (4) Again he sent other slaves, saying, 'Tell those who have been invited: Look, I have prepared my dinner, my oxen and my fat calves have been slaughtered, and everything is ready; come to the wedding banquet.' (5) But they made light of it and went away, one to his farm, another to his business, (6) while the rest seized his slaves, mistreated them, and killed them. (7) The king was enraged. He sent his troops, destroyed those murderers, and burned their city. (8) Then he said to his slaves, 'The wedding is ready, but those invited were not worthy. (9) Go therefore into the main streets, and invite everyone you find to the wedding banquet.' (10) Those slaves went out into the streets and gathered all whom they found, both good and bad; so the wedding hall was filled with guests. (11) But when the king came in to see the guests, he noticed a man there who was not wearing a wedding robe, (12) and he said to him, 'Friend, how did you get in here without a wedding robe?' And he was speechless. (13) Then the king said to the attendants, 'Bind him hand and foot, and throw him into the outer darkness, where there will be weeping and gnashing of teeth.' (14) For many are called, but few are chosen."

ERIC CORNELL CONFESSED THAT his main recollection of receiving the Nobel Prize for physics in 2001 was his *faux pas* at the moment the King of Sweden presented him with the award. Cornell had been coached in the proper etiquette for the moment: the king would hand him the award, then he would step back and bow to his highness. Cornell blew it. He took the prize, stood up, and shook hands with the king. Major no-no. His only hope was that his colleague in their noteworthy achievement would also forget etiquette and everyone would assume Cornell had acted appropriately. Unfortunately for him, his collaborator, Carl Weiman, had not forgotten and behaved according to expectations.

Fortunately, there were no negative consequences to Cornell's social blunder. But there is a message here: every situation calls for an appropriate response. For college students, serious study is your most appropriate response to the honor of being called to college.

Prayer: Teach me the etiquette for living in your kingdom. Amen.

91 – Something? Or Nothing?

Matthew 22:15–22 — (15) Then the Pharisees went and plotted to entrap him in what he said. (16) So they sent their disciples to him, along with the Herodians, saying, "Teacher, we know that you are sincere, and teach the way of God in accordance with truth, and show deference to no one; for you do not regard people with partiality. (17) Tell us, then, what you think. Is it lawful to pay taxes to the emperor, or not?" (18) But Jesus, aware of their malice, said, "Why are you putting me to the test, you hypocrites? (19) Show me the coin used for the tax." And they brought him a denarius. (20) Then he said to them, "Whose head is this, and whose title?" (21) They answered, "The emperor's." Then he said to them, "Give therefore to the emperor the things that are the emperor's, and to God the things that are God's." (22) When they heard this, they were amazed; and they left him and went away.

ONE OF MY FAVORITE sports clichés is the one that describes the commitment of a player: He gives 110 percent (or 150 percent; or even 200 percent). We understand that the hyperbole—and the bad math—is there because of the intention: to emphasize that this is a totally committed player. But we don't hear that kind of language applied in other arenas. Is your mother committed to cooking for the family 110 percent? Does your dad give 150 percent to home repairs? Nobody these days gives that much to anything. Instead, we are so spread out that serious commitment is found in "multitasking" in a desperate effort to get as much done toward each responsibility that you won't (i) flunk a class, (ii) get fired from your job, and (iii) appear to ignore your friends.

Commitment is not a numbers game but an integrity issue. That is made clear in the incident from Jesus' life described in today's reading. The Pharisees walked a fine line between maintaining their Jewish religion and accommodating Rome. When the Pharisees asked Jesus if it was okay to pay taxes to the emperor, it may not have been simply to entrap Jesus; they were asking one of the many questions to which they needed good answers for themselves. What may have "amazed" them about Jesus' answer was that they probably knew that for Jesus, giving the emperor what was the emperor's meant giving him nothing. Jesus gave at least 100 percent to God. That left nothing for the emperor—or to anything else. Jesus was totally committed—and did the math right.

Prayer: Lord, I know it's not good math, but help me to give you 110 percent. Amen.

92 – What Happens Then? (Trick Question?)

Matthew 22:23–33 — (23) The same day some Sadducees came to him, saying there is no resurrection; and they asked him a question, saying, (24) "Teacher, Moses said, 'If a man dies childless, his brother shall marry the widow, and raise up children for his brother.' (25) Now there were seven brothers among us; the first married, and died childless, leaving the widow to his brother. (26) The second did the same, so also the third, down to the seventh. (27) Last of all, the woman herself died. (28) In the resurrection, then, whose wife of the seven will she be? For all of them had married her." (29) Jesus answered them, "You are wrong, because you know neither the scriptures nor the power of God. (30) For in the resurrection they neither marry nor are given in marriage, but are like angels in heaven. (31) And as for the resurrection of the dead, have you not read what was said to you by God, (32) 'I am the God of Abraham, the God of Isaac, and the God of Jacob'? He is God not of the dead, but of the living." (33) And when the crowd heard it, they were astounded at his teaching.

I REALLY NEVER THOUGHT deeply about death until one of my daughters died. Previous deaths—even the deaths of students in colleges where I taught—had not moved me to ponder death.

As a result of reading "physics for idiots" (dumbed-down science), I think of heaven as a place incredibly far away and moving even farther away at increasing speed or—if it is right here—in some sort of anti-universe, accessible only through a wormhole or a quantum-esque transformation. In any case, it is something that is totally out of reach of my understanding and my imagination. When I go to a funeral and hear about the deceased busy with their favorite activities (fishing, knitting, caring for grandchildren) I have a really hard time taking any of it even remotely literally.

The point is: we are to trust God since he is the God of the living. He will provide life; leave the details on everything else up to him. You only need to be sure about God. You don't need to be sure about everything.

Prayer: Help me believe what I already confess: I believe in the resurrection of the body. Amen.

93– Ask a Simple Question

Matthew 22:34–40 — (34) When the Pharisees heard that he had silenced the Sadducees, they gathered together, (35) and one of them, a lawyer, asked him a question to test him. (36) "Teacher, which commandment in the law is the greatest?" (37) He said to him, "'You shall love the Lord your God with all your heart, and with all your soul, and with all your mind.' (38) This is the greatest and first commandment. (39) And a second is like it: 'You shall love your neighbor as yourself.' (40) On these two commandments hang all the law and the prophets."

WE LIKE TO GET simple answers to our questions. (Did I pass the course? Yes or no?) But in the classroom, simple questions often get complicated answers. I remember the first college test I took. It was in history and the question was: Explain the Reformation. It sounded like a simple question; I gave a simple answer: Martin Luther, the Protestant Reformer, protested against the Catholic Church. Okay as far as it went; the answer was worth a D- because there were a lot of other contributing factors that I had failed to take into account. That was a wake-up call. There is no such thing as a simple question in college. So any time a prof asks a "simple" question, be ready with an answer that has a least two parts.

In fact, you can really help your cause as a student by asking questions, even simple ones. Asking a good question—that is, a question that is pertinent, a question that will elicit information about the subject matter at hand—can accomplish a great deal.

First, a good question shows that you have some understanding of the subject and want to penetrate deeper into it. The professor will be impressed by this interest and commitment. Second, the question shows the professor that he is getting through to you and that his efforts have not fallen on deaf ears. Third, the question will give the professor a chance to explain some aspect of the subject that may not have been in the syllabus or in the lecture plan—a nice "stroke" for the professor.

What if you, the student, already know the answer to the question? Ask it anyway. The effort of speaking out in class and the reinforcement of hearing the professor tell you what you already know can only help to reinforce your confidence. And remember, Jesus is your special teacher; you can ask him anything.

Prayer: God, help my life be a simple answer to the command to love you and my neighbor. Amen.

94 – I'm My Own Grampa?

Matthew 22:41–46 — (41) Now while the Pharisees were gathered together, Jesus asked them this question: (42) "What do you think of the Messiah? Whose son is he?" They said to him, "The son of David." (43) He said to them, "How is it then that David by the Spirit calls him Lord, saying, (44) 'The Lord said to my Lord, "Sit at my right hand, until I put your enemies under your feet"'? (45) If David thus calls him Lord, how can he be his son?" (46) No one was able to give him an answer, nor from that day did anyone dare to ask him any more questions.

TO BE ACADEMICALLY SUCCESSFUL in college you need to be able to understand and answer questions on multiple levels.

For instance, if you are taking an interdisciplinary class in which two professors look at the same subject from two disciplinary perspectives, you might have two answers to the same question. A physicist and an artist will answer the question "What does the world look like?" differently. A psychologist and a political scientist will answer the question "Who am I?" differently.

In today's Scripture Jesus asked the Pharisees a question that could be boiled down to something like: We know that Jesus is descended from David (Jesus' great-, great-, great-, great-, etc. grandfather) so how could it be that David called him Lord (before Jesus was ever born)? While the Pharisees either didn't answer or their answer was not recorded, one way to answer the question is to see it in two ways. On the one hand, Jesus was a physical descendant of David. On the other, he was the Son of God who existed before David was even born. It is not only a puzzle but is also a profoundly important double truth for us—a double truth that combines two truths that are really (but only logically!) hard to hold together.

On the one hand it is important to note that Jesus is totally human. At the same time, it is of critical importance to understand that he is also God and that without his being divine and beyond time and space he would have lacked the power to do anything for us except perhaps be sympathetic.

Faith can be full of puzzles but it also is able to hold apparently contradictory realities simultaneously.

Prayer: Thank you, Lord, that you don't expect me to understand all the complexities of your love. Amen.

95 – Flat Earth Society

Matthew 23:1-12 — (1) Then Jesus said to the crowds and to his disciples, (2) "The scribes and the Pharisees sit on Moses' seat; (3) therefore, do whatever they teach you and follow it; but do not do as they do, for they do not practice what they teach. (4) They tie up heavy burdens, hard to bear, and lay them on the shoulders of others; but they themselves are unwilling to lift a finger to move them. (5) They do all their deeds to be seen by others; for they make their phylacteries broad and their fringes long. (6) They love to have the place of honor at banquets and the best seats in the synagogues, (7) and to be greeted with respect in the marketplaces, and to have people call them rabbi. (8) But you are not to be called rabbi, for you have one teacher, and you are all students. (9) And call no one your father on earth, for you have one Father—the one in heaven. (10) Nor are you to be called instructors, for you have one instructor, the Messiah. (11) The greatest among you will be your servant. (12) All who exalt themselves will be humbled, and all who humble themselves will be exalted."

THE FLAT EARTH SOCIETY was founded in 1547 and is devoted to the idea that the earth is geographically flat (see flatearthsociety.org). "Flat" is a term that also describes a type of organization—one with little hierarchy, where the one on top and the ones on the bottom are not separated (very much).

College prepares you for life in an un-flat world, with its hierarchy that looks like this: (1st) Board of Regents; (2nd) President; (3rd) Vice President(s); (4th) Deans; (5th) Professors; (6th) Associate Professors; (7th) Assistant Professors; (8th) Lecturers; (9th) Graduate Assistants; (10th) Graduate Students; (11th) Seniors; (12th) Juniors; (13th) Sophomores; (14th) Freshmen.

When Jesus discussed the "educational system," his first criticism of the "system" was that the teachers of the Jewish law didn't do what they taught. Primarily, they want the honor and respect that goes with their high office—particularly to be addressed as rabbi (read: Professor, Mr. President, Sir).

Jesus suggests a "flat" alternative: (1st) God; (2nd) Jesus; (3rd) you. Christians don't lord it over anyone nor are we subject to the tyranny of hierarchy; we have been invited into a heavenly version of the Flat Earth Society—not the one what got the science wrong, but the one that gets the message of Jesus right.

Prayer: Teacher God, thank you for being as close as you are to me. Amen.

96 – Blind Guides

Matthew 23:13–22 — (13) "But woe to you, scribes and Pharisees, hypocrites! For you lock people out of the kingdom of heaven. For you do not go in yourselves, and when others are going in, you stop them. (15) Woe to you, scribes and Pharisees, hypocrites! For you cross sea and land to make a single convert, and you make the new convert twice as much a child of hell as yourselves. (16) Woe to you, blind guides, who say, 'Whoever swears by the sanctuary is bound by nothing, but whoever swears by the gold of the sanctuary is bound by the oath.' (17) You blind fools! For which is greater, the gold or the sanctuary that has make the gold sacred? (18) And you say, 'Whoever swears by the altar is bound by nothing, but whoever swears by the gift that is on the altar is bound by the oath.' (19) How blind you are! For which is greater, the gift or the altar that makes the gift sacred? (20) So whoever swears by the altar, swears by it and by everything on it; (21) and whoever swears by the sanctuary, swears by it and by the one who dwells in it; (22) and whoever swears by heaven, swears by the throne of God and by the one who is seated upon it."

A MAN WAS PASSING a site where a large building was in the early stages of construction. (You have already read this anecdote—[Colossians #9]—but it's useful.) He approached two workers and asked what they were doing. One said, "I'm laying bricks." The second, clearly another bricklayer, responded, "I'm building a cathedral." On one level, both were doing the same thing—cementing one brick on another. While the first person could only see his piece of the work, the second saw the greater picture in which his small piece of work had its place.

Sometimes your education might seem like "laying bricks." You have no idea what the big picture is. Why do you have to study math if you intend to teach English? Or why do you need art if all you want to do is program computers? Teachers who leave you feeling like that are like the blind guides Jesus criticizes.

In this twenty-third chapter of Matthew, Jesus delivers a devastating critique of the teachers of his day—committed to their work but in such a way as to focus on the least important matters.

Jesus, on the other hand, consistently offers us the big picture: he wants to give you a rich overview of the kingdom of heaven. And he invites you into the frame of that new reality.

Prayer: Lord, thank you for lighting my way by sending Jesus, your Son and my Teacher. Amen.

97 – Temper, Temper

Matthew 23:23–36 — (23) "Woe to you, scribes and Pharisees, hypocrites! For you tithe mint, dill, and cumin, and have neglected the weightier matters of the law: justice and mercy and faith. It is these you ought to have practiced without neglecting the others. (24) You blind guides! You strain out a gnat but swallow a camel! (25) Woe to you, scribes and Pharisees, hypocrites! For you clean the outside of the cup and of the plate, but inside they are full of greed and self-indulgence. (26) You blind Pharisee! First clean the inside of the cup, so that the outside also may become clean. (27) Woe to you, scribes and Pharisees, hypocrites! For you are like white-washed tombs, which on the outside look beautiful, but inside they are full of the bones of the dead and of all kinds of filth. (28) So you also on the outside look righteous to others, but inside you are full of hypocrisy and lawlessness. (29) Woe to you, scribes and Pharisees, hypocrites! For you build the tombs of the prophets and decorate the graves of the righteous, (30) and you say, 'If we had lived in the days of our ancestors, we would not have taken part with them in shedding the blood of the prophets.' (31) Thus you testify against yourselves that you are descendants of those who murdered the prophets. (32) Fill up, then, the measure of your ancestors. (33) You snakes, you brood of vipers! How can you escape being sentenced to hell? (34) Therefore I send you prophets, sages, and scribes, some of whom you will kill and crucify, and some you will flog in your synagogues and pursue from town to town, (35) so that upon you may come all the righteous blood shed on earth, from the blood of righteous Abel to the blood of Zechariah son of Barachiah, whom you murdered between the sanctuary and the altar. (36) Truly I tell you, all this will come upon this generation."

ANGER. WHEN IS IT an appropriate response? It is remarkable that Jesus seems to have gotten angry so seldom. There was the time when he upset the tables of the money changers in the temple and virtually threw them out of the premises. And then there is the torrent of abuse that he hurled at the teachers of the Jewish religion. This is some big-time name-calling: hypocrites, blind guides, white-washed tombs, snakes and vipers.

Isn't it interesting that one of the only two things that Jesus really blew up over was bad teaching? Hmm.

Prayer: Lord, protect me—and all others—from the poison of my anger; and bad teaching. Amen.

98 – "Universe-City" Kills Prophets

Matthew 23:37-39 — (37) "Jerusalem, Jerusalem, the city that kills the prophets and stones those who are sent to it! How often have I [Jesus] desired to gather your children together as a hen gathers her brood under her wings, and you were not willing! (38) See, your house is left to you, desolate. (39) For I tell you, you will not see me again until you say, 'Blessed is the one who comes in the name of the Lord.'"

WE LIVE IN A weird but usually unnoticed paradox. On the one hand, we want to be unique, special, independent; and we think we are. We don't let anyone tell us what to do or think or how to dress or what music to favor. We are free operators. At the same time, if we really reflect on it, it turns out that we actually do, think, dress, and enjoy what most of our peers do, think, wear, and hear.

So, here you are in college, a free, independent, and groundbreakingly unique individual who—were the truth admitted—was not all that interested in trying something really new (i.e., that other people aren't doing).

When you go to class, you often hear about groundbreaking discoveries or ideas, most of which were scorned and rejected when they originally came on the scene. The people making these contributions are often called prophets—people who speak and act before their time. Prophets do not always suffer the fate Jesus describes—death or stoning. But they are not always recognized and applauded right away either.

When we hear about these people—scientists with a new theory, a politician with a new proposal, a composer with a new sound—we often think that if we had been there we would not have been among those who rejected them.

But the university is really a pretty unaccepting place when it comes to new things. Faculty members are pretty conservative. Alumni want things like they were. Administrators don't want the boat to rock. Students—as we suggested—are not terribly adventurous. (Being wild and crazy is not the same thing as being independent.)

Probably the last thing you may want as a student is to be gathered up by Jesus or anyone else as if you were a silly chicken. On the other hand, it is nice to have this promise of care from the Lord just in case you wind up in trouble.

Prayer: Lord, gather me to you when I lose myself in the crowd. Amen.

99 – When the World Ends

Matthew 24:1–14 — (1) As Jesus came out of the temple and was going away, his disciples came to point out to him the buildings of the temple. (2) Then he asked them, "You see all these, do you not? Truly I tell you, not one stone will be left here upon another; all will be thrown down."(3) When he was sitting on the Mount of Olives, the disciples came to him privately, saying, "Tell us, when will this be, and what will be the sign of your coming and of the end of the age?" (4) Jesus answered them, "Beware that no one leads you astray. (5) For many will come in my name, saying, 'I am the Messiah!' and they will lead many astray. (6) And you will hear of wars and rumors of wars; see that you are not alarmed; for this must take place, but the end is not near. (7) For nation will rise against nation, and kingdom against kingdom, and there will be famines and earthquakes in various places: (8) all this is but the beginning of the birth pangs. (9) Then they will hand you over to be tortured and will put you to death, and you will be hated by all nations because of my name. (10) Then many will fall away, and they will betray one another and hate one another. (11) And many false prophets will arise and lead many astray. (12) And because of the increase of lawlessness, the love of many will grow cold. (13) But the one who endures to the end will be saved. (14) And this good news of the kingdom will be proclaimed throughout the world, as a testimony to all the nations; and then the end will come."

WHILE FOR THOSE WHO keep up with the news, a day scarcely goes by without a report of some potentially catastrophic event that threatens "the end of life as we know it." But for most of us, things seem pretty normal on a day-to-day basis.

Jesus predicted "the end will come," but only after a whole series of signs. The list he gave was . . . well, like what we hear in the news on a daily basis: "wars and rumors of wars . . . famines and earthquakes," torture, murder, hate, betrayal, and "lawlessness." So how are you to know when "the end will come" unless you can fit specific current events into Jesus' list?

Forget it. Better to concentrate on where you are right now: the end of the beginning of your life and the beginning of the rest of your life. Jesus is accessible to you now, no matter what catastrophic events are happening elsewhere, or even if they should happen to you.

Prayer: In the midst of catastrophe, let me keep my eye and my faith on you, Lord Jesus. Amen.

100 – There Are Going to Be Changes

Matthew 24:15–31 — (15) So when you see the desolating sacrilege standing in the holy place, as was spoken of by the prophet Daniel (let the reader understand), (16) then those in Judea must flee to the mountains; (17) the one on the housetop must not go down to take what is in the house; (18) the one in the field must not turn back to get a coat. (19) Woe to those who are pregnant and to those who are nursing infants in those days! (20) Pray that your flight may not be in winter or on a sabbath. (21) For at that time there will be great suffering, such as has not been from the beginning of the world until now, no, and never will be. (22) And if those days had not been cut short, no one would be saved; but for the sake of the elect those days will be cut short. (23) Then if anyone says to you, 'Look! Here is the Messiah!' or 'There he is!'—do not believe it. (24) For false messiahs and false prophets will appear and produce great signs and omens, to lead astray, if possible, even the elect. (25) Take note, I have told you beforehand. (26) So, if they say to you, 'Look! He is in the wilderness,' do not go out. If they say, 'Look! He is in the inner rooms,' do not believe it. (27) For as the lightning comes from the east and flashes as far as the west, so will be the coming of the Son of Man. (28) Wherever the corpse is, there the vultures will gather. (29) Immediately after the suffering of those days the sun will be darkened, and the moon will not give its light; the stars will fall from heaven, and the powers of heaven will be shaken. (30) Then the sign of the Son of Man will appear in heaven, and then all the tribes of the earth will mourn, and they will see 'the son of Man coming on the clouds of heaven' with power and great glory. (31) And he will send out his angels with a loud trumpet call, and they will gather his elect from the four winds, from one end of heaven to the other."

THE BIGGEST, MOST TRAUMATIC, most anticipated change that ever can occur (in your college) is . . . finding a new football coach. This is a moment loaded with crisis and hope, with anxiety and promise. But if the new coach isn't a winner you hire another. Jesus knew that people will continue to seek a savior, one who will solve all the problems. People have tried a lot of saviors and they haven't worked. Jesus is the change that works.

Prayer: O God, if I am tempted by false promises, keep me faithful to Jesus. Amen.

101 – Signs of the Time

Matthew 24:32–35 — (32) "From the fig tree learn its lesson: as soon as its branch becomes tender and puts forth its leaves, you know that summer is near. (33) So also, when you see all these things, you know that he is near, at the very gates. (34) Truly I tell you, this generation will not pass away until all these things have taken place. (35) Heaven and earth will pass away, but my words will not pass away."

CHANGE IS NOT FUN; we do a lot to keep things from changing because of the discomfort that often comes with it. One of the most annoying changes is when the teacher changes the course syllabus halfway through the semester; it is especially annoying if you did some of the work that will no longer be required.

It can be really upsetting when friends change and are no longer friendly, or betray a confidence, or prove unreliable.

One of the earliest philosophical (and probably scientific) questions addressed by the first Greek philosophers was over whether change was the basic fact of life (so Heraclitus) or whether it was just the appearance that covered over a more fundamental permanence. Common sense seems to argue for change because that is what we see the most of and that is what bothers us more than the idea of permanence.

If you focus on the immediate, the events on a daily basis, you are almost certain to be disappointed. If you focus on the end or outcome, that is often elusive. What is it that you can really hang on to as permanent? Jesus' disciples had asked him about "the end." Many Christians today are looking for the "end" instead of living in the now. Or, while living in the now, they are looking to see how current events can be read to predict "the end." In either case, they are not looking at what is permanent but rather at what is changing.

Trying to read current events—wars, rumors of wars, disease, famine, earthquake (things that seem to be happening all of the time)—so as to be able to predict the end of the world or the second coming of Christ seems futile. Which set of wars, famines, and earthquakes is the exact set that will predict such final events?

Jesus said that his words will endure beyond the passing away of the earth and of the heavens. Would not attention to his words—words about loving and forgiving—be most rewarding?

Prayer: Lord, when I go in search of the signs of the end of the world, let me find you there. Amen.

102 – Jesus is Coming: Get Ready

Matthew 24:36–44 — (36) "But about that day and hour no one knows, neither the angels of heaven, nor the Son, but only the Father. (37) For as the days of Noah were, so will be the coming of the Son of Man. (38) For as in those days before the flood they were eating and drinking, marrying and giving in marriage, until the day Noah entered the ark, (39) and they knew nothing until the flood came and swept them all away, so too will be the coming of the Son of Man. (40) Then two will be in the field; one will be taken and one will be left. (41) Two women will be grinding meal together; one will be taken and one will be left. (42) Keep awake therefore, for you do not know on what day your Lord is coming. (43) But understand this: if the owner of the house had known in what part of the night the thief was coming, he would have stayed awake and would not have let his house be broken into. (44) Therefore you also must be ready, for the Son of Man is coming at an unexpected hour."

"BE READY." IT'S NOT always easy to know what that means. Did you feel "ready" for college? Do you feel "ready" for class? Do you feel "ready" for life?

A popular philosophical movement of recent years (existentialism) has been used by some biblical interpreters to read Scripture in such a way as to emphasize the immediate, "right now" nature and applicability of everything in Scripture—particularly of everything that Jesus said and did. This was not about what may have happened in the past (e.g., joining the church) or what might happen in the future (when . . . ?).

According to this way of reading Scripture and thinking about our relationship with Jesus, every encounter with Jesus should be seen as relevant to this very moment. When Jesus says "you also must be ready" he is inviting you to be "ready"—now! Are you "ready"? Okay—here we go . . . .

Prayer: Am I ready? I hope I'm ready; I believe I'm ready. Amen.

103 – Top Slave

Matthew 24:45–51 — (45) "Who then is the faithful and wise slave, whom his master has put in charge of his household, to give the other slaves their allowance of food at the proper time? (46) Blessed is that slave whom his master will find at work when he arrives. (47) Truly I tell you, he will put that one in charge of all his possessions. (48) But if that wicked slave says to himself, 'My master is delayed,' (49) and he begins to beat his fellow slaves, and eats and drinks with drunkards, (50) the master of that slave will come on a day when he does not expect him and at an hour that he does not know. (51) He will cut him in pieces and put him with the hypocrites, where there will be weeping and gnashing of teeth."

It's "GOOD NEWS/BAD NEWS" time again. You remember the drill. How about: The bad news is that you are a slave; but the good news is that you are Jesus' slave. Would that be terrible? At first blush it looks bad. Nobody in America today is—technically, legally—a slave. Nobody wants to be a slave. So why should we pay attention when Jesus wants to describe you, his follower, as a slave?

When Jesus wanted to illustrate what constituted good or bad relationships, the use of the institution of slavery offered one way of looking at relationships. He is trying to answer the question we considered yesterday: What does it mean to be ready? With that as background, let's play "good news/bad news."

The bad news is that you are a slave; the good news is that you are the "in charge" slave.

The good news is that you are in charge; the bad news is that you are responsible for all the other slaves.

The good news is that the master is not here at the moment; the bad news is that not only do you need to care for the other slaves, but you are to care for the master's possessions.

Here you are, wondering, "Why do I have to do all the work?"

The good news is that you are a slave; the even better news is that you are Jesus' slave.

Prayer: Lord, thank you for being the most loving and forgiving master anyone could have. Amen.

104 – Which of These Things Doesn't Belong?

Matthew 25:1–13 — (1) "Then the kingdom of heaven will be like this. Ten bridesmaids took their lamps and went to meet the bridegroom. (2) Five of them were foolish, and five were wise. (3) When the foolish took their lamps, they took no oil with them; (4) but the wise took flasks of oil with their lamps. (5) As the bridegroom was delayed, all of them became drowsy and slept. (6) But at midnight there was a shout, 'Look! Here is the bridegroom! Come out to meet him.' (7) Then all those bridesmaids got up and trimmed their lamps. (8) The foolish said to the wise, 'Give us some of your oil, for our lamps are going out.' (9) But the wise replied, 'No! there will not be enough for you and for us; you had better go to the dealers and buy some for yourselves.' (10) And while they went to buy it, the bridegroom came, and those who were ready went with him into the wedding banquet; and the door was shut.(11) Later the other bridesmaids came also, saying, 'Lord, Lord, open to us.' (12) But he replied, 'Truly I tell you, I do not know you.' (13) Keep awake therefore, for you know neither the day nor the hour."

REMEMBER ON *SESAME STREET* where you were asked, "Which of these things doesn't belong?" The goal was to learn to put "like" things together. This would develop critical skills of analysis and imagination that you would use in college.

Jesus—great teacher that he was—could not describe God in the kind of mathematical or scientific terminology that most of us might prefer. He resorted to comparisons, parables, metaphors—the language of "like." Whenever he told people about what God, or what being within God's care, was like, he would say "the kingdom of heaven will be like. . ." and then go on to describe something you could relate to. Sometimes he used imaginary "events" that may never have happened, like the time the pearl merchant sold all of his goods to buy one pearl. It may never happen, but you could imagine it.

Haven't you had this experience? You arrive somewhere, but . . . you're late, forgot the gift, wore the wrong outfit, just ate a Big Mac. What is Jesus' point? Being within God's care (kingdom) is a wonderful and happy thing. But if you are unprepared, you may miss it. A pretty simple point. Anybody with a *Sesame Street* education should be able to figure that out. It should be a piece of cake for a college person. Or at least "like" it.

Prayer: Give me the courage to use the imagination you gave me to see your truth. Amen.

105 – Know the Boss

Matthew 25:14-30 — (14) "For it is as if a man, going on a journey, summoned his slaves and entrusted his property to them; (15) to one he gave five talents, to another two, to another one, to each according to his ability. Then he went away. (16) The one who had received the five talents went off at once and traded with them, and made five more talents. (17) In the same way, the one who had the two talents made two more talents. (18) But the one who had received the one talent went off and dug a hole in the ground and hid his master's money. (19) After a long time the master of those slaves came and settled accounts with them. (20) Then the one who had received the five talents came forward, bringing five more talents, saying 'Master, you handed over to me five talents; see, I have made five more talents.' (21) His master said to him, 'Well done, good and trustworthy slave; you have been trustworthy in a few things, I will put you in charge of many things; enter into the joy of your master.' (22) And the one with the two talents also came forward, saying, 'Master, you handed over to me two talents; see, I have made two more talents.' (23) His master said to him, 'Well done, good and trustworthy slave; you have been trustworthy in a few things, I will put you in charge of many things; enter into the joy of your master.' (24) Then the one who had received the one talent also came forward, saying, 'Master, I knew that you were a harsh man, reaping where you did not sow, and gathering where you did not scatter seed; (25) so I was afraid, and I went and hid your talent in the ground. Here you have what is yours.' (26) But his master replied, 'You wicked and lazy slave! You knew, did you, that I reap where I did not sow, and gather where I did not scatter? (27) Then you ought to have invested my money with the bankers, and on my return I would have received what was my own with interest. (28) So take the talent from him, and give it to the one with the ten talents. (29) For to all those who have, more will be given, and they will have an abundance; but from those who have nothing, even what they have will be taken away. (30) As for this worthless slave, throw him into the outer darkness, where there will be weeping and gnashing of teeth.'"

THE FIRST TWO SERVANTS' "talent" was knowing and serving the master. When it came to "show time," the third servant served himself. Discipleship means knowing "the master," not serving yourself.

Prayer: Help me to know you, Master. Amen.

106 – On the One Hand . . .

Matthew 25:31–40 — (31) "When the Son of Man comes in his glory, and all the angels with him, then he will sit on the throne of his glory. (32) All the nations will be gathered before him, and he will separate people one from another as a shepherd separates the sheep from the goats, (33) and he will put sheep at his right hand and the goats at the left. (34)Then the king will say to those at his right hand, 'Come, you that are blessed by my father, inherit the kingdom prepared for you from the foundation of the world; (35) for I was hungry and you gave me food, I was thirsty and you gave me something to drink, I was a stranger and you welcomed me, (36) I was naked and you gave me clothing, I was sick and you took care of me, I was in prison and you visited me.' (37) Then the righteous will answer him, 'Lord, when was it that we saw you hungry and gave you food, or thirsty and gave you something to drink? (38) And when was it that we saw you a stranger and welcomed you, or naked and gave you clothing? (39)And when was it that we saw you sick or in prison and visited you?' (40) And the king will answer them, 'Truly I tell you, just as you did it to one of the least of these who are members of my family, you did it to me.'"

COLLEGE GIVES YOU THE opportunity to participate in amazing things, many of which can be really important.

Jesus lists at least six huge problems in this teaching. There are millions of people who suffer with these problems. You could (i) learn a lot and (ii) provide real help to the needy if you were to get involved in trying to solve these problems. From a purely academic point of view, working to feed the hungry (for example) would help to alleviate hunger and nutritional problems for people now suffering. At the same time that you work to get food to hungry people you would learn something about nutrition, about politics, about agriculture, about social systems, about . . . well, about a whole lot of things. (Some educators call this "service learning.")

You might learn how to solve some of the problems that humans have created for one another and in doing so it might turn out that you find yourself already in the kingdom of God.

Prayer: Give me insight and strength to give myself to the best experiences of all. Amen.

107 – . . . On the Other Hand

Matthew 25:41–46 — (41) "Then he will say to those at his left hand, 'You that are accursed, depart from me into the eternal fire prepared for the devil and his angels; (42) for I was hungry and you gave me no food, I was thirsty and you gave me nothing to drink, (43) I was a stranger and you did not welcome me, naked and you did not give me clothing, sick and in prison and you did not visit me.' (44) Then they also will answer, 'Lord, when was it that we saw you hungry or thirsty or a stranger or naked or sick or in prison, and did not take care of you?' (45) Then he will answer them, 'Truly I tell you, just as you did not do it to one of the least of these, you did not do it to me.' (46) And these will go away into eternal punishment, but the righteous into eternal life."

WHEN I WAS IN high school I was beginning to try to internalize what "being a Christian" meant—according to my home church. It was pretty simple: don't smoke; don't drink; don't swear. You could complain about having to miss out on some "fun," but on the other hand, the requirements were not hard to meet. "Being a Christian" meant keeping to my agenda; no need to notice anyone else. Unless it was to take pleasure in noting that I was better than they were.

Lesslie Newbigin insisted that the world sets the agenda for Jesus who saw human needs. The poor folks getting the bad news in this story saw the needs but it never connected with them. Instead of a "faith agenda" that we control, Jesus says something like: "You believe in and follow me? I am right here in the middle of famine, drought, refugees, sickness, prisons."

One more thing to consider. Confronting Jesus' agenda as a single individual (even with your tough individualism) is overwhelming in its demands. Confronting Jesus' agenda with others who are also called and energized by Jesus is just a little bit less intimidating. It may not even call you to be brilliant and imaginative. After all, do you remember the ones in yesterday's story who did—even without knowing it!—carry out Jesus agenda?

Sheep.

Prayer: Father, thy kingdom come, thy will be done. Please count me in. Amen.

108 – Cost/Benefit

Matthew 26:1–5 — (1) When Jesus had finished saying all these things, he said to his disciples, (2) "You know that after two days the Passover is coming, and the Son of Man will be handed over to be crucified." (3) Then the chief priests and the elders of the people gathered in the palace of the high priest, who was called Caiaphas, (4) and they conspired to arrest Jesus by stealth and kill him. (5) But they said, "Not during the festival, or there may be a riot among the people."

ONE OF THE FIRST things I had to deal with as the academic dean of a small school was the problem of scheduling. At a large school this is not such a problem because there is often more than one section of any class. In our small school, however, there was often only one section of many courses, so conflicts were inevitable despite our boast that we were small enough so that students could participate in any class and any activity they desired. I tried; and I worried; and I didn't always succeed. What to do when a student had a game and a test or a lab and a play rehearsal at the same hour? Students were being confronted with tough decisions even though professors tried to accommodate.

Then an older colleague took me aside and said, "Don't worry; this is really a positive problem for students. They need to make decisions. Sure, picking a test over a game, or a rehearsal over a lab may help in one area and penalize them in another, but more important is the fact that they have to make some tough decisions and accept the results—always a mixed bag. This is what 'cost/benefit' analysis is all about."

So there you are. The decision-making is hard, but it's always a "two-fer." You get the benefit of the choice you accept and the benefit of learning about choices.

There is only one caution: When you make a decision in this kind of situation, be sure you have thought through the impact of your decision. Who benefits? Who suffers? In the case of the game vs. the quiz, what are the broader and longer term implications?

When the politicians and religious leaders decided to eliminate Jesus, every aspect of their decision was governed by how it would affect them. The benefit was theirs; the cost was shrugged off onto others. You will always be facing tough decisions. Who will benefit and who will pay the cost?

Prayer: God, thank you for being with me when I have to make tough decisions. Amen.

109 – Speaking of Money

Matthew 26:6–16 - (6) Now while Jesus was at Bethany in the house of Simon the leper, (7) a woman came to him with an alabaster jar of very costly ointment, and she poured it on his head as he sat at the table. (8) But when the disciples saw it, they were angry and said, "Why this waste? (9) For this ointment could have been sold for a large sum, and the money given to the poor." (10) But Jesus, aware of this, said to them, "Why do you trouble the woman? She has performed a good service for me. (11) For you always have the poor with you, but you will not always have me. (12) By pouring this ointment on my body she has prepared me for burial. (13) Truly I tell you, wherever this good news is proclaimed in the whole world, what she has done will be told in remembrance of her." (14) Then one of the twelve, who was called Judas Iscariot, went to the chief priests (15) and said, "What will you give me if I betray him to you?" They paid him thirty pieces of silver. (16) And from that moment he began to look for an opportunity to betray him.

THE GOSPEL OF MATTHEW doesn't get to issues of money until now. That is a surprise because we know Matthew had been a tax collector. But that was before he became a disciple. For Jesus, there were a ton of things a lot more important. (Can you say the same? How important to you in the whole scheme of things is money?)

But the disciples were thinking about money. In the story of the woman who was anointing Jesus—symbolically preparing his body for the time after his death when it was customary to apply ointments to the corpse—the disciples decry the anointing on the grounds that the ointment could have been sold for money to help the poor. Jesus brushes that expression of social concern aside. Saying "you always have the poor with you" may have been a way of saying, "You can always help the poor." In the second part of the reported incident, we find money again. This time it is a reward for betraying Jesus to the authorities.

Even when money is involved in Jesus' story it does not seem to be important. What is important is whether Jesus is accepted (as he is by the woman with the ointment) or rejected (as he is by Judas and the religious politicians who want to destroy him). In these stories, the money follows the commitment.

Prayer: If the love of money is the root of evil, let my love of Jesus uproot the evil in me. Amen.

110 – When Friends Betray

Matthew 26:17–25 — (17) On the first day of Unleavened Bread the disciples came to Jesus, saying, "Where do you want us to make the preparations for you to eat the Passover?" (18) He said, "Go into the city to a certain man, and say to him, 'The Teacher says, My time is near; I will keep the Passover at your house with my disciples.'" (19) So the disciples did as Jesus had directed them, and they prepared the Passover meal. (20) When it was evening, he took his place with the twelve; (21) and while they were eating, he said, "Truly I tell you, one of you will betray me." (22) And they became greatly distressed and began to say to him one after another, "Surely not I, Lord?" (23) He answered, "The one who has dipped his hand into the bowl with me will betray me. (24) The Son of Man goes as it is written of him, but woe to that one by whom the Son of Man is betrayed! It would have been better for that one not to have been born." (25) Judas, who betrayed him, said, "Surely not I, Rabbi?" He replied, "You have said so."

YOU HAVE PROBABLY ALREADY experienced betrayal by someone you considered a dear friend. It really hurts. Sometimes the betrayer acts intentionally; sometimes the betrayal is an unintended consequence of some other act or word. In any case, the damage (to you) has permanent consequences. The acute pain and disappointment eventually pass; memories of it never do.

In the old days—really old, like before WWII, in the time of your grand- or great-grandparents—Americans were nowhere nearly as mobile as today. They were born, raised, schooled, parented, employed, retired, and buried pretty much in the same place. Personal betrayals had lifelong consequences, even family feuds.

Today, we are more mobile. As a college graduate, you will be even more mobile. Some 40 million Americans move each year; that's 1 out of every 7 or 8 people. And as a college grad you might even move more often. In a situation like that, personal betrayals can (sort of) be left behind.

And, of course, the cruelest kind of betrayal is dealt by those closest to you—"the one who has dipped his hand into the bowl" with you. Jesus seems less concerned with the official betrayal plot than the betrayal by Judas. He knows about betrayals. He knows about yours—that you were betrayed; and that you betrayed. But he never betrays.

Prayer: O Jesus, betrayed Lord and friend, forgive my betrayals and help me forgive those who betray me. Amen.

111 – Real Value Meal

Matthew 26:26–30 — (26) While they were eating, Jesus took a loaf of bread, and after blessing it he broke it, gave it to the disciples, and said, "Take, eat; this is my body." (27) Then he took a cup, and after giving thanks he gave it to them, saying, "Drink from it, all of you; (28) for this is my blood of the covenant, which is poured out for many for the forgiveness of sins. (29) I tell you, I will never again drink of this fruit of the vine until that day when I drink it new with you in my Father's kingdom." (30) When they had sung the hymn, they went out to the Mount of Olives.

IN COLLEGE YOU ARE finally free! Like—free to eat anything. Whenever. But however you decide, meals can easily slip into a routine—of time, place, and particular entrees. Special meals are reserved for dates or trips home. For the most part, however, it will be cafeteria, snacks, or fast food. Without mom there to urge a healthy diet, it is easy to slip into a regimen of tasty but too fattening and/or too salty and/or simply too much food. You know in your head that that is not good; but your taste buds tell you it's yummy.

Meal time can be lonesome or it can be a time of good fellowship with friends. It can be a celebration after a victory or comfort food after a defeat. Occasionally that "value meal" can have some value other than being cheap.

Most food, however, is eaten without a lot of thought, just to satisfy immediate need or because "it's time to eat."

But there is one meal that is truly special and that is the one that Jesus Christ offers us. His meal, taken at his table, with him at the center, is a meal that outdoes all other meals in terms of our true health and the significance it carries for us. Just look at what Jesus said when he first served that special meal—communion, the Lord's Supper, the Eucharist—on the night before his betrayal and death.

First, it is universal; it is open to everyone. Second, it is a meal that seals a deal; it is a "covenant" meal. In it, Jesus promises forgiveness, acceptance, and inclusion to those he feeds. Third, he promises that he will eat again with his guest when God's kingdom is a reality. Fourth . . . well, there are many dimensions to this meal that Christians throughout the ages have found nourishing. As you build your own diet around this meal, you will find layer after layer of healthy revelations for your own life. Now that's a "value meal"!

Prayer: O Lord, feed me 'til I hunger no more. Amen.

112 – On Your Own

Matthew 26:31–46 — (31) Then Jesus said to them, "You will all become deserters because of me this night; for it is written, 'I will strike the shepherd, and the sheep of the flock will be scattered.' (32) But after I am raised up, I will go ahead of you to Galilee." (33) Peter said to him, "Though all become deserters because of you, I will never desert you." (34) Jesus said to him, "Truly I tell you, this very night, before the cock crows, you will deny me three times." (35) Peter said to him, "Even though I must die with you, I will not deny you." And so said all the disciples. (36) Then Jesus went with them to a place called Gethsemane; and he said to his disciples, "Sit here while I go over there and pray." (37) He took with him Peter and the two sons of Zebedee, and began to be grieved and agitated. (38) Then he said to them, "I am deeply grieved, even to death; remain here, and stay awake with me." (39) And going a little farther, he threw himself on the ground and prayed, "My Father, if it is possible, let this cup pass from me; yet not what I want but what you want." (40) Then he came to the disciples and found them sleeping; and he said to Peter, "So, could you not stay awake with me one hour? (41) Stay awake and pray that you may not come into the time of trial; the spirit indeed is willing, but the flesh is weak." (42) Again he went away for the second time and prayed, "My Father, if this cannot pass unless I drink it, your will be done." (43) Again he came and found them sleeping, for their eyes were heavy. (44) So leaving them again, he went away and prayed for the third time, saying the same words. (45) Then he came to the disciples and said to them, "Are you still sleeping and taking your rest? See, the hour is at hand, and the Son of Man is betrayed into the hands of sinners. (46) Get up, let us be going. See, my betrayer is at hand."

BEING INDEPENDENT AND ON your own is great. Except when there is a crisis. That is when you need help. That is when it is helpful to know that even Jesus faced situations that he did not want to face and he wanted help. His friends aren't much help. Here is Jesus, our friend and Savior, scared, abandoned, alone, facing the painful end of his life. He knows what it means to face a crisis—alone. He knows. Thank God he knows.

Prayer: Jesus, thank you for always being with me. Amen.

113 – Dying by the Sword

Matthew 26:47–56 — (47) While he was still speaking, Judas, one of the twelve, arrived; with him was a large crowd with swords and clubs, from the chief priests and the elders of the people. (48) Now the betrayer had given them a sign, saying, "The one I will kiss is the man; arrest him." (49) At once he came up to Jesus and said, "Greetings, Rabbi!" and kissed him. (50) Jesus said to him, "Friend, do what you are here to do." Then they came and laid hands on Jesus and arrested him. (51) Suddenly, one of those with Jesus put his hand on his sword, drew it, and struck the slave of the high priest, cutting off his ear. (52) Then Jesus said to him, "Put your sword back into its place; for all who take the sword will perish by the sword. (53) Do you think that I cannot appeal to my Father, and he will at once send me more than twelve legions of angels? (54) But how then would the scriptures be fulfilled, which say it must happen in this way?" (55) At that hour Jesus said to the crowds, "Have you come out with swords and clubs to arrest me as though I were a bandit? Day after day I sat in the temple teaching, and you did not arrest me. (56) But all this has taken place, so that the scriptures of the prophets may be fulfilled." Then all the disciples deserted him and fled.

PROBABLY THE MOST POPULAR means of getting things done is through power: the power of money, of position, of knowledge, or of brute force. Religious faith is not really the main thing people rely on to get things done. Faith may be okay for the private world of religious thinking, but not for the public world of social position and professional advancement. This was asserted most powerfully a century ago by the German philosopher Friedrich Nietzsche, who labeled Christianity a faith of slaves who had given up being real people. Real people—Nietzsche called them the "supermen"—asserted themselves with expressions of power.

But you know the whole story, and it is a story in which God gets things done with justice and love in contrast to the story of the Romans and the religious authorities who used bribery, crowd appeasement, false witnesses, lies, a kangaroo court, and cold-blooded military to pursue their own agenda. God forbade it then; he forbids it now.

Prayer: Give me peace in my heart, Lord Jesus. Amen.

114 – Location, Location, Location

Matthew 26:57–68 — (57) Those who had arrested Jesus took him to Caiaphas the high priest, in whose house the scribes and the elders had gathered. (58) But Peter was following him at a distance, as far as the courtyard of the high priest; and going inside, he sat with the guards in order to see how this would end. (59) Now the chief priests and the whole council were looking for false testimony against Jesus so that they might put him to death, (60) but they found none, though many false witnesses came forward. At last two came forward (61) and said, "This fellow said, 'I am able to destroy the temple of God and to build it in three days.'" (62) The high priest stood up and said, "Have you no answer? What is it that they testify against you?" (63) But Jesus was silent. Then the high priest said to him, "I put you under oath before the living God, tell us if you are the Messiah, the Son of God." (64) Jesus said to him, "You have said so. But I tell you, From now on you will see the Son of Man seated at the right hand of Power and coming on the clouds of heaven." (65) Then the high priest tore his clothes and said, "He has blasphemed! Why do we still need witnesses? You have now heard his blasphemy. (66) What is your verdict?" They answered, "He deserves death." (67) Then they spat in his face and struck him; and some slapped him, (68) saying, "Prophesy to us, you Messiah! Who is it that struck you?"

WE SPEAK DIFFERENTLY TO different people. To grandparents it's one way, to store clerks another, to profs another, and to roommates still another. Topics differ, too. With grandparents it may be family; with clerks it could be the weather; with the prof an assignment; and with a roommate it might be anything.

Have you ever gotten in trouble because of what you said in one situation—say to a roommate—getting repeated in another—say to a girl- or boyfriend? A remark in the wrong place can mean big trouble.

In today's story, a statement quoted elsewhere (John 2:19) when Jesus was speaking of the "temple" of his body and foreseeing his own resurrection is torn from context, changed in meaning, and added to other fabricated and false testimony to condemn him. Jesus said nothing. What words might have worked in this situation when the audience was against him? Sometimes it is better just to say nothing.

Prayer: O God, thank you for sending your Word made flesh to us in Jesus Christ. Amen.

115 – A Real Pal

Matthew 26:69–75 — (69) Now Peter was sitting outside in the courtyard. A servant-girl came to him and said, "You also were with Jesus the Galilean." (70) But he denied it before all of them, saying, "I do not know what you are talking about." (71) When he went out to the porch, another servant-girl saw him, and she said to the bystanders, "This man was with Jesus of Nazareth." (72) Again he denied it with an oath, "I do not know the man." (73) After a little while the bystanders came up and said to Peter, "Certainly you are also one of them, for your accent betrays you." (74) Then he began to curse, and he swore an oath, "I do not know the man!" At that moment the cock crowed. (75) Then Peter remembered what Jesus had said: "Before the cock crows, you will deny me three times." And he went out and wept bitterly.

SOME CHRISTIANS WORRY ABOUT witnessing in college. In the days of the life of Jesus and the early church the only way any news about Jesus got around was by one person who had seen or heard Jesus telling others about it. This telling must have been powerful and persuasive because more and more people accepted the stories, trusted in their accuracy, and wound up believing them and believing and trusting in Jesus as the one who brought them into a positive relationship with God and with other people.

There have been at least three monumental revolutions in communication technology since Jesus' day: printing, electronics (phone, radio, TV), and the Internet. There was another big revolution, however. That was when the Christian faith changed from being illegal, unpatriotic, and despised to being legal and finally official. Before that revolution, witnessing was deadly serious; you could actually be killed for witnessing. Today, the worst is to be made fun of.

And remember poor St. Peter—at least before he was a saint. By the time we get to this sad time in Jesus' story, Peter has already failed to support Jesus several times. (He almost drowned through unbelief [14:31]; he rejected the cross as Jesus' fate [16:22]; he wanted to stay on the mount of transfiguration instead of following Jesus back into the world [17:4]; he fell asleep when Jesus wanted company while praying [26:40].) What a loser, we think. And in today's episode he fails an additional *three times!* It shouldn't be too hard to improve on Peter's performance.

Prayer: Thank you, Lord, for not depending on me to do your saving work. Amen.

116 – Suicide

Matthew 27:1–10 — (1) When morning came, all the chief priests and the elders of the people conferred together against Jesus in order to bring about his death. (2) They bound him, led him away, and handed him over to Pilate the governor. (3) When Judas, his betrayer, saw that Jesus was condemned, he repented and brought back the thirty pieces of silver to the chief priests and the elders. (4) He said, "I have sinned by betraying innocent blood." But they said, "What is that to us? See to it yourself." (5) Throwing down the pieces of silver in the temple, he departed; and he went and hanged himself. (6) But the chief priests, taking the pieces of silver, said, "It is not lawful to put them into the treasury, since they are blood money." (7) After conferring together, they used them to buy the potter's field as a place to bury foreigners. (8) For this reason that field has been called the Field of Blood to this day. (9) Then was fulfilled what had been spoken through the prophet Jeremiah, "And they took the thirty pieces of silver, the price of the one on whom a price had been set, on whom some of the people of Israel had set a price, (10) and they gave them for the potter's field, as the Lord commanded me."

EVERY YEAR ABOUT 1,100 college students commit suicide. Depending on which source you consult, suicide is the second or third most frequent cause of death for college-age Americans. There are plenty of reasons why one might feel depressed, distraught, helpless, hopeless, or any of the other feelings that could lead down the dark, lonesome, and cruel path toward self-destruction.

Admittedly there "seem" to be some positives to suicide: it ends the problem and it really puts all those folks who have created the difficulties in their places. But of course suicide doesn't end the problem for others. It is a cruel and permanent blow to the many people who know, care for, and love the self-destructive person. They would have done anything to have prevented the death.

Is there something on your mind? Something really heavy? There is somebody around who wants to hear about it. It could be your roommate. Or your advisor. Or a co-worker. You could call home—if not to a parent, maybe a sister or brother. Your minister at home; or the campus pastor. A school counselor. You have options even if, like Judas, you think you don't.

Prayer: Dear Lord, when I feel bad, please remind me that you care for me. Amen.

117 – Easy Way Out

Matthew 27:11–18 — (11) Now Jesus stood before the governor; and the governor asked him, "Are you the King of the Jews?" Jesus said, "You say so." (12) But when he was accused by the chief priests and elders, he did not answer. (13) Then Pilate said to him, "Do you not hear how many accusations they make against you?" (14) But he gave him no answer, not even to a single charge, so that the governor was greatly amazed." (15) Now at the festival the governor was accustomed to release a prisoner for the crowd, anyone whom they wanted. (16) At that time they had a notorious prisoner, called Jesus Barabbas. (17) So after they had gathered, Pilate said to them, "Whom do you want me to release for you, Jesus Barabbas or Jesus who is called the Messiah?" (18) For he realized that it was out of jealousy that they had handed him over.

DECISIONS, DECISIONS. IT SEEMS that you are always having to make decisions. Hamburger or taco? Channel 3 or channel 8? Study or go out for a Coke? Fortunately, most decisions are simple. Another way to say that is to say that most decisions are inconsequential—there are really no serious implications from deciding one way or the other. Then there are really important decisions that have important and far-reaching consequences. Complete a term paper or flunk the class? Break up with a steady or get engaged?

But let's consider the ways in which you handle decision-making. One way is the way that Pilate decided. He asked Jesus to help him, but Jesus remained silent. Pilate was going to have to do it on his own. Pilate was in a tough spot. He really couldn't see that Jesus had done anything wrong to justify condemning him.

So Pilate resorted to a tradition by which the populace could demand the release of a prisoner—a kind of popularity contest to reward the feisty crowds during the biggest Jewish religious celebration of the year (Passover).

Since the crowds had been encouraged to want Jesus killed, they called for the release of the other prisoner. When Pilate asked what to do with Jesus, the popular cry was for his death—which would provide the crowds with a continuation of the spectacle, this time of a crucifixion.

Often you decide in favor of immediate gratification. When Jesus doesn't help you decide with direct instructions it doesn't mean that you can't make the right choice by yourself. Don't be like Pilate.

Prayer: Lord, when I need to decide, help me to be part of the solution, not the problem. Amen.

118 – Everybody Has a Suggestion

Matthew 27:19-26 — (19) While he was sitting on the judgment seat, his wife sent word to him, "Have nothing to do with that innocent man, for today I have suffered a great deal because of a dream about him." (20) Now the chief priests and the elders persuaded the crowds to ask for Barabbas and to have Jesus killed. (21) The governor again said to them, "Which of the two do you want me to release for you?" And they said, "Barabbas." (22) Pilate said to them, "Then what should I do with Jesus who is called the Messiah?" All of them said, "Let him be crucified!" (23) Then he asked, "Why, what evil has he done?" But they shouted all the more, "Let him be crucified!" (24) So when Pilate saw that he could do nothing, but rather that a riot was beginning, he took some water and washed his hands before the crowd, saying, "I am innocent of this man's blood; see to it yourselves." (25) Then the people as a whole answered, "His blood be on us and on our children!" (26) So he released Barabbas for them; and after flogging Jesus, he handed him over to be crucified.

WHEN YOU READ SCRIPTURE through new and different lenses you will often be struck in new and helpful or maybe disturbing ways. Reading the original Greek text of this passage, I have had one of those disturbing thoughts.

Amidst the many voices telling Pilate what to do—his wife, chief priests (and elders), the crowd—it is the reference to "elders" that gets to me.

The Greek word for "elder" is *presbeuteros*. It might be a stretch for you, but can you see "Presbyterian" in there? I definitely can. Over and over again in this gospel, Matthew connects the *presbeuteroi* (plural) with the other bad guys: Pharisees and Elders, Chief Priests and Elders, etc. I keep getting the hint that instead of being on Jesus' side, people like me (Presbyterians) might be on the side of those who were keen on keeping the *status quo;* that would have meant getting rid of Jesus, who has been exciting people about new possibilities. My advice to Pilate in the midst of this problem—on the edge of a riot—might have been just to take the easy way out.

Sometimes these stories really point the finger right at somebody who is reading these meditations . . . or at the person who wrote them.

Prayer: Help me to really be independent when the crowd is making the wrong decision. Amen.

119 – Bullying

Matthew 27:27-44 — (27) Then the soldiers of the governor took Jesus into the governor's headquarters, and they gathered the whole cohort around him. (28) They stripped him and put a scarlet robe on him, (29) and after twisting some thorns into a crown, they put it on his head. They put a reed in his right hand and knelt before him and mocked him, saying, "Hail, King of the Jews!" (30) They spat on him, and took the reed and struck him on the head.

(31) After mocking him, they stripped him of the robe and put his own clothes on him. Then they led him away to crucify him. (32) As they went out, they came upon a man from Cyrene named Simon; they compelled this man to carry his cross. (33) And when they came to a place called Golgotha (which means Place of a Skull), (34) they offered him wine to drink, mixed with gall; but when he tasted it, he would not drink it. (35) And when they had crucified him, they divided his clothes among themselves by casting lots; (36) then they sat down there and kept watch over him. (37) Over his head they put the charge against him, which read, "This is Jesus, the King of the Jews." (38) Then two bandits were crucified with him, one on his right and one on his left. (39) Those who passed by derided him, shaking their heads (40) and saying, "You who would destroy the temple and build it in three days, save yourself! If you are the Son of God, come down from the cross." (41) In the same way the chief priests also, along with the scribes and elders, were mocking him, saying, (42) "He saved others; he cannot save himself. He is the King of Israel; let him come down from the cross now, and we will believe in him. (43) He trusts in God; let God deliver him now, if he wants to; for he said, 'I am God's Son.'" (44) The bandits who were crucified with him also taunted him in the same way.

HAZING IS ALIVE AND well in colleges. Students are still hazed and killed in the process of receiving some of the same abuse Jesus was submitted to: "mocking," spitting, hitting, taunting, humiliation. These are behaviors we might expect from immature and poorly raised kids. Christians have accepted a higher standard than the "heavies" in this biblical passage—priests, scribes, elders. We commit to treat others as we would be treated. Any way you look at it, this kind of behavior is unacceptable.

Prayer: Write the Golden Rule on my heart and in my mind, and in my actions. Amen.

Matthew 27:45–54 — (45) From noon on, darkness came over the whole land until three in the afternoon. (46) And about three o'clock Jesus cried with a loud voice, "Eli, Eli, lema sabachthani?" that is, "My God, my God, why have you forsaken me?" (47) When some of the bystanders heard it, they said, "This man is calling for Elijah." (48) At once one of them ran and got a sponge, filled it with sour wine, put it on a stick, and gave it to him to drink. (49) But the others said, "Wait, let us see whether Elijah will come to save him." (50) Then Jesus cried again with a loud voice and breathed his last. (51) At that moment the curtain of the temple was torn in two, from top to bottom. The earth shook, and the rocks were split. (52) The tombs also were opened, and many bodies of the saints who had fallen asleep were raised. (53) After his resurrection they came out of the tombs and entered the holy city and appeared to many. (54) Now when the centurion and those with him, who were keeping watch over Jesus, saw the earthquake and what took place, they were terrified and said, "Truly this man was God's Son!"

WHAT DO YOU DO for loneliness? Go out for a Coke? Turn on the tube? Look for someone to talk to? Call home? Usually, loneliness can be cured—at least temporarily—by getting in touch with others.

But there are deep and incurable times of alienation about which you seem to be able to do nothing—except maybe want to scream in anger against God. This bit of Scripture offers two assuring words.

First, in this account of the utterly bleak account of Jesus' feeling of abandonment is the assurance that Jesus knows what it means to be lonely and abandoned; his career as Savior was a "been-there-done-that" one, not one conducted from the safety of a heavenly throne.

Second, the fact that Jesus could rail against God himself and complain that he had been abandoned should be some comfort to you if/when you feel the need to complain to God about something that really, really pains you. God is not a delicate personality, subject to feeling bad if people get unhappy with him. And although we really don't know whether God had abandoned Jesus when Jesus said he had, it is clear at the end of the day that God raised Jesus from an undeserved death and drew him into a perfect and eternal relationship.

Prayer: Thank you for giving us a Savior who has been here and lived my kind if life already. Amen.

121 – I Don't Know What to Say (or Do)

Matthew 27:55-66 — (55) Many women were also there, look-ing on from a distance; they had followed Jesus from Galilee and had provided for him. (56) Among them were Mary Magdalene, and Mary the mother of James and Joseph, and the mother of the sons of Zebedee. (57) When it was evening, there came a rich man from Arimathea, named Joseph, who was also a disciple of Jesus. (58) He went to Pilate and asked for the body of Jesus; then Pilate ordered it to be given to him. (59) So Joseph took the body and wrapped it in a clean linen cloth (60) and laid it in his own new tomb, which he had hewn in the rock. He then rolled a great stone to the door of the tomb and went away. (61) Mary Magdalene and the other Mary were there, sitting opposite the tomb. (62) The next day, that is, after the day of Preparation, the chief priests and the Pharisees gathered before Pilate (63) and said, "Sir, we remember what that impostor said while he was still alive, 'After three days I will rise again.' (64) Therefore command the tomb to be made secure until the third day; otherwise his disciples may go and steal him away, and tell the people, 'He has been raised from the dead,' and the last deception would be worse than the first." (65) Pilate said to them, "You have a guard of soldiers; go, make it as secure as you can." (66) So they went with the guard and made the tomb secure by sealing the stone.

YOU ARE LEARNING THAT words are important. But knowing the right thing to say gets difficult when terrible things happen. Like when somebody dies. If you are the one bereft because of the death of someone really close, it really doesn't help to have somebody say something like, "They're in a better place now." Would it be better if that insensitive person just didn't bother to come to you at your time of such deep sorrow? I hope not. Better they should come if only to just be there with you.

Joseph of Arimathea couldn't do anything to bring Jesus back but he did something. Mary Magdalene, another Mary, and the mother of James and John are just there, sitting, saying nothing, but undoubtedly sharing their grief together; at least they did not leave each other alone.

Prayer: Lord, thank you for being with us in our sorrows and help-ing us to be with others in theirs. Amen.

122 – Facing the Future

Matthew 28:1–10 — (1) After the sabbath, as the first day of the week was dawning, Mary Magdalene and the other Mary went to see the tomb. (2) And suddenly there was a great earthquake; for an angel of the Lord, descending from heaven, came and rolled back the stone and sat on it. (3) His appearance was like lightning, and his clothing white as snow. (4) For fear of him the guards shook and became like dead men. (5) But the angel said to the women, "Do not be afraid; I know that you are looking for Jesus who was crucified. (6) He is not here; for he has been raised, as he said. Come, see the place where he lay. (7) Then go quickly and tell his disciples, 'He has been raised from the dead, and indeed he is going ahead of you to Galilee; there you will see him.' This is my message for you." (8) So they left the tomb quickly with fear and great joy, and ran to tell his disciples. (9) Suddenly Jesus met them and said, "Greetings!" And they came to him, took hold of his feet, and worshiped him. (10) Then Jesus said to them, "Do not be afraid; go and tell my brothers to go to Galilee; there they will see me."

THIS SEMESTER WILL END. What will be next? If it is graduation, what lies ahead? Really being on your own; more responsibility in a new job—sorry, career. (Less margin for error; less tolerance for messing up; on time and dressed up every day.) Exciting to think about, but it can still make you a little nervous. Perhaps it is vacation and the promise of travel to some place you've never been. You may be experiencing both excitement and a little bit of nervousness. Maybe just another semester. New classes, professors, new and perhaps more demanding subject matter. All of these turns in your life—necessary and expected though they may be—can be the occasion for great excitement along with understandable nervousness.

Jesus' disciples, on their way to meet the resurrected Jesus, were understandably excited to see the dear friend whom they had last seen dying or dead. But there was also a mixture of dread: What would this Jesus look like? A zombie? A see-through spirit? No one had ever engaged socially with a dead person before. Great joy? Yes. Fear? You bet.

Facing the new is an occasion for "fear and great joy." As Jesus said when they finally got together: "Do not be afraid" (28:10). Jesus was going to be with them. That promise holds good for you still today.

Prayer: Lord, you know my mixed feelings; thanks for helping me hold myself together. Amen.

123 – Just Take the Money and Run

Matthew 28:11-15 — (11) While they were going, some of the guard went into the city and told the chief priests everything that had happened. (12) After the priests had assembled with the elders, they devised a plan to give a large sum of money to the soldiers, (13) telling them, "You must say, 'His disciples came by night and stole him away while we were asleep.' (14) If this comes to the governor's ears, we will satisfy him and keep you out of trouble." (15) So they took the money and did as they were directed. And this story is still told among the Jews to this day.

It is said that everyone has their price. We know that people are still sold into various kinds of slavery—child soldiers, prostitutes, domestic workers. These deals don't involve much money. On the other end of the economic scale, we also know that there are big time, high-dollar deals in which people are bribed, bought off, or even legally hired to do things that are unethical.

We know that some of this high-end dealing even happens at colleges and universities. The lure of fame and riches can tempt coaches to bend or break the rules. The high salaries of some presidents fool them into thinking they can do as they want not only with their own money but with the college's money (i.e., your money).

Are you immune from this kind of sleaze? You will be getting a job. This means you will sell your time and skill and will be told what to do. Just what are you willing to do for your money? What if you were asked to do something that you regard as out of bounds? What if you were sure that you could not be detected?

That is the kind of deal that went down in the lesson for today. They—the leaders of the people—were still trying to silence Jesus and the Christians, this time by paying (read: bribing) the soldiers to lie about what had happened. The leaders desperately wanted to counter the possibility that the truth would get out and cause a political uprising.

They did not want this to happen, so they resorted to cheating—bribing someone to lie. What if your employer asks you to say something that is not quite true or that is a true but distorted version of the truth, wouldn't that be just like what was happening in the situation involving Jesus? Would you take the money and run?

Prayer: Don't let "the love of money is the root of all evil" be said about me. Amen.

124 – The Promise

Matthew 28:16–20 — (16) Now the eleven disciples went to Galilee, to the mountain to which Jesus had directed them. (17) When they saw him, they worshiped him; but some doubted. (18) And Jesus came and said to them, "All authority in heaven and on earth has been given to me. (19) Go therefore and make disciples of all nations, baptizing them in the name of the Father and of the Son and of the Holy Spirit, (20) and teaching them to obey everything that I have commanded you. And remember, I am with you always, to the end of the age."

WHEN YOU GET TO the end of college you will be off to something new. Whatever it is—a job, the military service, marriage, graduate school—it will be something where you will be on your own in a new way. Just leaving college will mean leaving certain comforts—the familiar places, the people, especially friends, the now-comfortable routines. As a college student you have been expected to take responsibility for your time, your work, your money. In the days and challenges ahead, you will be given more responsibility. You will be charged with getting projects done, and done on time—often with too little time. You will be expected to do big things with small resources.

This closing passage of Matthew's gospel is often called the "Great Commission" because the focus seems to be on Jesus telling the disciples that they need to go out into the whole world and teach everyone what he had taught. (How is that for a modest challenge!) This kind of commission—to do great things—can be daunting.

At your college graduation, you may hear this same kind of "commission." The commencement speaker may point out that your generation will provide tomorrow's leadership. She may cite the many problems left unsolved by her generation now bequeathed to your generation to solve. She may call upon you to commit yourself and your considerable talents to do what no previous generation has done.

Whatever part of that commission you accept as the piece for which you claim responsibility, you need not be overwhelmed. For just as Jesus promised his disciples that he would be with them as they went forth, so that promise will be just as good as it was when Jesus issued it—and it applies to you.

This is the enduring word from Jesus: "I am with you always." That is a great promise to hold to whether tomorrow is commencement, a new semester, or just another day in this semester.

Prayer: Lord God, I claim Jesus' promise to be with me always. Thank you. Amen.

First Corinthians
Over-Inflated & Self-Centered

CORINTH TODAY IS CITY of about 70,000 lying fifty miles west of Athens in Greece; in biblical times it was a city whose Christian inhabitants thought they were at the center of the world. And let it go to their heads. Today's college experience and the Christian community of ancient Corinth may be separated by centuries and great distances, but there are disturbing similarities.

Christians are individually called into the academic life—as students, teachers, college administrators. But collectively, we have let the colleges founded by Christians over the centuries go, ceding them to the service of other gods—job preparation, scholarship, social status, athletic supremacy.

Paul and other early Christians shared a biblical view as old as the Psalms (Ps 1). It can be summarized simply: There were two possible ways to live—according to God (planted solidly by a river that could provide nourishment) or according to another way (planted where there was no nourishment). These were two different possibilities resulting in different and opposing world views. As you read 1 Corinthians you will unpack many of the differences between the two ways. Paul uses a kind of shorthand to keep this difference before his readers. The "cross," from which the world flees, is the right way, the way of Christ, the way by which your gifts can be best nurtured and employed. The "world" is the other way—self-centered, oblivious to and regardless of others.

As a Christian, you can ask a bold question: How does the life, death, and resurrection of Jesus of Nazareth determine the way you are to live within the college setting to which you have been called? This question needs asking. First Corinthians puts Jesus Christ—and not just any Jesus but the one in conflict with the politics and intelligence of the world—into the center of your thinking about the college. That is what will help you to resist whatever the college experience offers that would compromise your faith.

First Corinthians offers an eerily familiar reflection of modern higher education. The Corinthians were exceedingly proud of their knowledge.

FIRST CORINTHIANS

Furthermore, they used their gifts to separate themselves from one another. To Paul, the most obvious and reprehensible results of this self-reliance—as opposed to reliance upon Christ—were disunity, fragmentation, disintegration of the community, and damage to others.

Frankly, the Corinthian community was coming apart at the seams, with individuals glorying in their own skills, touting their own group, speaking a language no one understood ("tongues"), alienating those inside and outside of the church—in short, using the values and methods of the dominant surrounding culture to hurt each other and benefit themselves. Which was why Paul wrote them this letter.

Education in America today is characterized by fragmentation, isolation, elitism, competition, and a vocational fervor with little moral direction. These features are both intellectual and social in nature, with negative consequences for you and the Christian church. Paul calls his readers to recognize the folly of their overblown self-importance, acknowledge the centrality of Christ, and come together at the central symbol of the Christian faith, the cross of Christ.

1 – You're Already Somebody

1 Corinthians 1:1-3 — (1) Paul, called to be an apostle of Christ Jesus by the will of God, and our brother Sosthenes, (2) To the church of God that is in Corinth, to those who are sanctified in Christ Jesus, called to be saints, together with all those who in every place call on the name of our Lord Jesus Christ, both their Lord and ours: (3) Grace to you and peace from God our Father and the Lord Jesus Christ.

POPULAR WISDOM TEACHES THAT you are an individual who must "make something of yourself." The college experience seems to offer the opportunity to do just that—"make something of yourself." College promises to be just that resource to aid students achieve their goals—whatever those goals might be.

But what a lonely and difficult task! In fact, it is hopelessly naive and naively hopeless. There is the real danger that you—privileged to be in college—might actually believe yourself to be "self-made" as a result of the efforts you invest to learn facts, earn grades, expand your "network," and acquire a degree. But as a Christian, you already are something prior to any performance on your part; you have been freed from the lonely responsibility the modern world would force on you to "make something of yourself."

Paul begins his letter in the style typical of his day: "Paul, [already] called . . . ." God had already made somebody out of him—"an apostle of Christ Jesus." Paul acknowledges his letter-writing partner: "Sosthenes, [already] our brother." He affirms that his readers—that includes you—are already "called to be saints." The result is that your vocation is to recognize that you are already put "together" (in the church) and that you need no longer exist as a lone and lonely individual. You are not given some big responsibility, but simply the gift and blessing of inclusion into God's people.

As you strive to be a member of a college, a team, or club, a class, a dorm, God promises you that you already have the gift of belonging to something larger—to God's people, "saints." The fact of God's call means that you are who and where you are because of God—not because you are the victim of blind forces or because of your own achievements. You are connected to everyone who is "called" and may "call on the name of the Lord Jesus Christ." You already are something and you are not alone; you don't need to bother about the impossibility of trying to make something of yourself.

Prayer: God, thank you for calling us all, everywhere, together. Amen.

2 – If Only I Had . . .

1 Corinthians 1:4–9 — (4) I give thanks to my God always for you because of the grace of God that has been given you in Christ Jesus, (5) for in every way you have been enriched in him, in speech and knowledge of every kind—(6) just as the testimony of Christ has been strengthened among you—(7) so that you are not lacking in any spiritual gift as you wait for the revealing of our Lord Jesus Christ. (8) He will also strengthen you to the end, so that you may be blameless on the day of our Lord Jesus Christ. (9) God is faithful; by him you were called into the fellowship of his Son, Jesus Christ our Lord.

PAUL BEGINS THE BODY of his letter in typical first-century–letter-writing style—with a prayer. In this case it is a prayer of thanksgiving for the wealth of abilities God has given the Corinthian Christians and an implicit reminder that they have both a purpose in life and the resources to achieve it. As you will discover, these folks—who must have aggrieved Paul mightily—are the same ones he thinks of as his "children" (4:14). And annoying children they were: they had everything and still couldn't get along. Though unworthy, they were "enriched in him, in speech and knowledge" individually and as a community,

You too are gifted—with mental powers, a family, scholarships, a library, fellow students, the teachers who daily bless your life. Do you ever feel that you are lacking something?

But perhaps you do lack—time, financial resources, recognition of your worth, cooperation from others. There always seems to be something more to need. Instead of promising to fulfill all these needs—which will never end—the promise is that God will strengthen you to the end. Forever! Your life may be too short for you to acquire and enjoy everything that you would like. Perhaps the main need you have is to be reminded of your ultimate purpose as you await the full revelation of Jesus Christ. You are already enriched; your main task is to wait, empowered and outfitted for a life that will finally be rewarded with a revelation. This is not something you achieve, but a gift that comes to you to enjoy in fellowship with others. With this in mind, a literal translation of Paul's literal Greek (v. 7) may be poor English, but the emphasis of the double negative is not contradictory but emphatic: "You are lacking in no gift!"

Prayer: Thank you for the abundance of your gifts; I shall not want (Ps 23). Amen.

3 – Can We All Get Along?

I Corinthians 1:10–11 — (10) Now I appeal to you, brothers and sisters, by the name of our Lord Jesus Christ, that all of you be in agreement and that there be no divisions among you, but that you be united in the same mind and the same purpose. (11) For it has been reported to me by Chloe's people that there are quarrels among you, my brothers and sisters.

THE INABILITY OF THE church members to agree or see things in the same way was a problem in Corinth. It is one that still plagues Christians and non-Christians alike. It is often particularly hard to agree with those closest to us. Agreement is certainly a challenge within the academy where skeletons of pitched battles litter the landscape: faculty vs. administration, department vs. department, students vs. administration. Gaps deepen every year; each of us has fell victim. The problem is real. Yet we are called upon by Paul to agree and to be "united in the same mind"—as in, have the same goal.

There is much in this exhortation to irritate the modern academic. We claim different ways of knowing and often come out with different conclusions—and we love to debate the alternatives. We resent those whom we perceive would tell us what to think or do. Our whole culture encourages disagreement; we agree to disagree.

The term "united" (v. 10) translates an original Greek term which means restored, whole, complete—as in the state of a broken bone or torn fishing net finally being reknit to its original condition. Our unity is to be in the same mind, the mind of Christ that provides our unity.

This is not uniformity, as you will see later when Paul explores the idea of the Christian community as the body of Christ. Each of us contributes to the whole with our ideas and support and helpful criticism. If you are "in Christ" and Christ is "in you" you do more than avoid conflict or topics of dissension. Christ provides the unity, the center. His gifts cannot lead us apart. Instead, your mental processes (gifts), submitted to God, move you toward participation in the same general understanding of life provided by Christ and to which we all are called. Christ provides a new and powerful understanding of life that draws us together and from which we draw new meaning. Let's have arguments (discussions) that lead to harmony.

Prayer: God, help me to know and to have the mind of Christ. Amen.

4 – Where Can We Meet?

1 Corinthians 1:12–17 — (12) What I mean is that each of you says, "I belong to Paul," or "I belong to Apollos," or "I belong to Cephas," or "I belong to Christ." (13) Has Christ been divided? Was Paul crucified for you? Or were you baptized in the name of Paul? (14) I thank God that I baptized none of you except Crispus and Gaius, (15) so that no one can say that you were baptized in my name. (16) (I did baptize also the household of Stephanas; beyond that, I do not know whether I baptized anyone else.) (17) For Christ did not send me to baptize but to proclaim the gospel, and not with eloquent wisdom, so that the cross of Christ might not be emptied of its power.

Is CHRIST DIVIDED? CHRISTIANS have done our best to split him up! We love dividing up in groups and derive much of our identity from the particular group that somebody established and that we joined. Not only do we divide up into groups, we compare and compete, and erect real and symbolic fences between ourselves and others. We prefer to spend our energies on defining criteria that divide (elevating us and putting others down in the process) than in seeking to find places to meet and unite (or at least "harmonize"). High school students occasionally do buck the divisiveness by holding "meet at the flagpole" events. Paul's implicit theme throughout this letter is to "meet at the cross."

You derive and reinforce identity by means of your allegiances. But in the light of the death and resurrection of Christ, those allegiances fade in significance. The cross is the one point of allegiance open to you that demands nothing from you or from anyone else. It interposes nothing between you and God or between you and others. At the cross, you find yourself without any basis for boasting or divisiveness. That is why it is at the cross that you can finally find unity with others. The "power" of the cross is not what the Roman inventors of that diabolical form of execution thought—to kill people. Its "power" is in providing a place where Christ can meet us and a way for us to come to God.

There is nothing about the cross that can provide any excuse for divisiveness. In your own life at the cross, you abandon every justification for divisiveness. In the words of the hymn: "In the Cross of Christ I Glory"!

Prayer: God, help me to see division as a rejection of the cross of Christ. Amen.

5 – Wisdom and Power

1 Corinthians 1:18–24 — (18) For the message about the cross is foolishness to those who are perishing, but to us who are being saved it is the power of God. (19) For it is written, "I will destroy the wisdom of the wise, and the discernment of the discerning I will thwart." (20) Where is the one who is wise? Where is the scribe? Where is the debater of this age? Has not God made foolish the wisdom of the world? (21) For since, in the wisdom of God, the world did not know God through wisdom, God decided, through the foolishness of our proclamation, to save those who believe. (22) For Jews demand signs and Greeks desire wisdom, (23) but we proclaim Christ crucified, a stumbling block to Jews and foolishness to Gentiles, (24) but to those who are the called, both Jews and Greeks, Christ the power of God and the wisdom of God.

AN OUTSTANDING STUDENT HAD died of alcohol poisoning and her funeral did what even a football game couldn't: it gathered hundreds of students together in one place for her funeral. In the shadow of death, students gathered voluntarily, were attentive for an hour, and were actually in a mood to listen. Unfortunately, the college was unable to take advantage of that "teachable moment" to offer hope in the face of loss or to work toward an improved campus in the face of a dismal failure.

The "message about the cross" is not only the good news that God is everywhere for everyone—including in death. The "message about the cross" is also a devastating critique of the message of the "world"—the message that the way the "world" does it (whatever "it" it does) is definitely not the wise and powerful (read: successful) way to do things. (Do they mean like drinking yourself to death at a fun party?) The "message about the cross" is that Christ is there—at the cross—so that when the wisdom of the "world" leaves a student dead, a family bereft, and a campus shaken, you can know that God is neither absent nor confused, but that he is there with love, and hope, and acceptance.

There is so much suffering because of human "wisdom" and the exercise of worldly power which so often overpowers and oversteps any legitimate limits of such humanly exercised force. But there is so much hope in God's wisdom in sending Christ and in the exercise of his power in raising Christ. Thanks be to God. It's all focused in the cross.

Prayer: God help me to let you to substitute your wisdom and power for my own. Amen.

6 – Define and Illustrate *Wisdom* and *Strength*

1 Corinthians 1:25 — (25) For God's foolishness is wiser than human wisdom, and God's weakness is stronger than human strength.

"TEST INSTRUCTIONS: YOU WILL be given several terms. Please write a brief definition of each and, if the terms are used differently in different contexts or by different users, point out the differences. Illustrate your answer(s)."

That would not be an unusual question for a quiz in a class. Let's say that the terms to be defined are "wisdom" and "power." After having read three portions of Scripture in which those terms appear, you should be able to do a passable job of it. How does this sound?

[Dear Prof.] Since I'm not sure what class this quiz is for, I will answer on the basis of my recent reading in the Christian Scriptures—1 Corinthians to be specific. Paul, the writer, wants to differentiate between how the members of the Corinth church are acting and how they should be acting as Christians. So that sets up two different ways to define the terms.

One way is "worldly." That seems to refer to how people think about the terms "wisdom" and "power" if they are not Christians and only operate with a worldly, or secular, point of view that doesn't include God. The other way is godly, only he doesn't use that term. I think that instead he substitutes the cross, or the cross of Christ, as a symbol for a context that makes for a completely opposite definition for the terms. So this is what wisdom looks like from those two points of view:

Worldly wisdom suggests that Jesus be gotten rid of because (if I remember from the Gospels) he was causing a lot of trouble for the political and religious authorities. That wasn't too smart since God just raised Jesus from the dead. The worldly wisdom plan was upset by God.

Worldly power suggests that the politicians (Roman ones) could use the soldiers to kill off people who threatened the *status quo*. Getting rid of people with subversive ideas could (here we are at worldly wisdom again) make everyone forget those ideas. God's power shown in the resurrection of Jesus pretty well undermined the success hoped for by the worldly guys. So there are two ways to use these terms. The worldly way seems popular and persistent, but when you look at the long-term success of that way it doesn't seem to work. The "wisdom/power" of the cross seems to be more helpful and doesn't seem to get destroyed by worldly power.

Prayer: Lord, help me pass this test. Amen.

7 – Your Résumé

1 Corinthians 1:26–31 — (26) Consider your own call, brothers and sisters: not many of you were wise by human standards, not many were powerful, not many were of noble birth. (27) But God chose what is foolish in the world to shame the wise; God chose what is weak in the world to shame the strong; (28) God chose what is low and despised in the world, things that are not, to reduce to nothing things that are, (29) so that no one might boast in the presence of God. (30) He is the source of your life in Christ Jesus, who became for us wisdom from God, and righteousness and sanctification and redemption, (31) in order that, as it is written, "Let the one who boasts, boast in the Lord."

AT SOME POINT YOU will need to write your résumé. This is a document that is all about you. You won't want to present yourself in the same categories Paul uses to characterize the Corinthians: "not . . . wise . . . powerful." Instead, you'll need to present the best picture possible. Frankly, you'll need to boast.

Paul would divide everyone into two groups—"the world" and "the cross." Focusing on "the cross" puts you in the "not wise according to worldly standards" category. You may be a called-to-college Christian but your résumé will be judged by "worldly standards" and you need to do your best to impress teachers with your learning. How do you live with one foot in "the world" and the other at "the foot of the cross"? How do you brag about your "call"?

Then you hear Paul's crashing judgment: God has "chosen what is foolish and weak in the world" to confound those things that the "world" affirms to be brilliant and strong—in fact, in the cross of Christ God has chosen to bring them to nothing, to show that worldly wisdom and power don't bring good results. This challenges your notions of what makes sense; it claims that the world's wisdom is a colossal and grinding failure, that the good is not sufficiently shared, that peace never lasts, that beauty is plundered, and that humans are discarded.

You are "called"; you have a vocation of which you can boast: to serve the Lord. Are you only to boast in the Lord and forget your résumé? No. In the Gospel according to John, you will see how Jesus calls his disciples to life "in" the world but not "of" the world. This is where God has put you and where he has called you. Do your best! And you can put that in your résumé.

Prayer: Give me the courage to abandon my wisdom and strength and let your wisdom rule my life. Amen.

8 – Don't Keep Your Cross in a Box—Even a See-Through One

1 Corinthians 2:1-5 — (1) When I came to you, brothers and sisters, I did not come proclaiming the mystery of God to you in lofty words or wisdom. (2) For I decided to know nothing among you except Jesus Christ, and him crucified. (3) And I came to you in weakness and in fear and in much trembling. (4) My speech and my proclamation were not with plausible words of wisdom, but with a demonstration of the Spirit and of power, (5) so that your faith might rest not on human wisdom but on the power of God.

THE HOUSE IS BURNING or the tornado is coming and you have to get out. You can take one item. What will it be? Paul "decided to know [take?] nothing . . . except Jesus Christ and him crucified . . . the power of God." For Paul, the crucified Jesus Christ is the one totally central reality. In this letter, he focuses on the cross as the answer to the wayward church's many failures. Hopefully, you will find that the cross and its multiple meanings and applications will serve you in reflecting on how to face many of the challenges college presents.

Speaking of "college" and the "cross," here is a "how not to do it" real-life anecdote about a college that had been established back in the seventeenth century and had displayed a cross in its chapel for more than 300 years. In the last century, the school became public and its constituency more varied, especially in matters of faith. Then, one day—well, not just "one day," but over the course of time—there were calls to put a broader, more diverse "face" on the religious profile of the institution. The cross that for years had graced the altar in the chapel was removed and boxed up and put into storage. It did make an occasional appearance during "Christian" services or in response to a special request. After some more controversy it was put on display in the chapel—but in a glass case and with a sign explaining its past history at the school.

Don't let your life be like that college where the cross is an artifact of some past time that can be on display (like jewelry). Instead, let your life be transformed by the cross and conformed to the cross. Let the powerless power of God shine forth in your cruciformity.

Prayer: If your cross is ever hidden, let it be hidden in me so all the world can see you. Amen.

9 – The Spirit

1 Corinthians 2:6–11 — (6) Yet among the mature we do speak wisdom, though it is not a wisdom of this age or of the rulers of this age, who are doomed to perish. (7) But we speak God's wisdom, secret and hidden, which God decreed before the ages for our glory. (8) None of the rulers of this age understood this; for if they had, they would not have crucified the Lord of glory. (9) But, as it is written, "What no eye has seen, nor ear heard, nor the human heart conceived, what God has prepared for those who love him"—(10) these things God has revealed to us through the Spirit; for the Spirit searches everything, even the depths of God. (11) For what human being knows what is truly human except the human spirit that is within? So also no one comprehends what is truly God's except the Spirit of God.

"EPISTEMOLOGY."

A word that covers the topic of how you know what you know. In college, you can't just say, "Well, I just know it." It will not go much better for you if you say, "My grandmother told me" or "I saw it on television." In college, you will need some authoritative source behind any assertion you make. When you do a research paper you will have to cite reliable sources. No more just making stuff up or copying it from someone else without telling.

But to get to the real, eternal, and redemptive truths of "God's wisdom," the gift of God's "Spirit" will help you to understand things that are from God (like the meaning of "the cross" or grace or salvation) that are virtually impossible to grasp if you are operating out of a "worldly" situation only.

Let's face it, this Corinthian letter so far has been pretty much focused on emphasizing the differences between "worldly" (bad!) and Godly (good!) and that you can't do both at the same time. Jesus said something like that in the gospel when he pointed out that you can't simultaneously serve two masters (Matt 6:24).

So you—the college student called to be a Christian (and theological) student in the "worldly" world of an American college—face a real challenge: maintain (and expand) your Christian faith and take advantage of (but not totally buy into) your mostly secular education. In other words: get the best of both worlds. The Holy Spirit is God's 24/7 way of helping you do that.

Prayer: Come, Holy Spirit; dwell in me and illuminate my thinking. Amen.

171

10 – Having the Mind of Christ

1 Corinthians 2:12–16 — (12) Now we have received not the spirit of the world, but the Spirit that is from God, so that we may understand the gifts bestowed on us by God. (13) And we speak of these things in words not taught by human wisdom but taught by the Spirit, interpreting spiritual things to those who are spiritual. (14) Those who are unspiritual do not receive the gifts of God's Spirit, for they are foolishness to them, and they are unable to understand them because they are spiritually discerned. (15) Those who are spiritual discern all things, and they are themselves subject to no one else's scrutiny. (16) "For who has known the mind of the Lord so as to instruct him?" But we have the mind of Christ.

PAUL SOUNDS PRETTY ARROGANT: "we have the mind of Christ"! But then, when you look at your own résumé it probably looks pretty arrogant, too. We are not afraid to pontificate on ourselves or our own special achievements; but we often fear to proclaim anything that might be claimed to be God's will, fearing that it might offend.

One of a teacher's fondest dreams is that of teaching a class of bright, mature, interested students; teachers seldom are so fortunate. Students occasionally take courses out of necessity; and ask the questions that are incredibly annoying to teachers: "Will it be on the test?" or "Sorry I missed class; did anything important happen?"

As a student, you want to learn what is truly important and not be encumbered by irrelevancies. But you learn according to the wisdom of the world—what can be proved, what will "work." The wisdom that satisfies you is often that popular wisdom of the world that serves the special interests of the rulers of the world.

Instead, God's wisdom is centered in the crucified Christ—and cannot have proofs or arguments from this world. Clearly the wisdom of this world, as Paul has already implied, is a wisdom of reason (Greek) and/or proofs (Jewish) that leads to what is popularly seen as success. If you would boast of having the "mind of Christ"—a mind oblivious to worldly machinations and scornful of worldly power—you truly would have God's wisdom. But God's wisdom has a long history and a high and universal purpose. Its etiology (origin) and its teleology (purpose) commend it. It ought to be that for which you most energetically seek and work.

Prayer: May the mind of Christ always be the model for my thinking. Amen.

11 – I'm a Tenor

1 Corinthians 3:1-4 — (1) And so, brothers and sisters, I could not speak to you as spiritual people, but rather as people of the flesh, as infants in Christ. (2) I fed you with milk, not solid food, for you were not ready for solid food. Even now you are still not ready, (3) for you are still of the flesh. For as long as there is jealousy and quarreling among you, are you not of the flesh, and behaving according to human inclination? (4) For when one says, "I belong to Paul," and another, "I belong to Apollos," are you not merely human?

MY FATHER HAD ENJOYED singing in the choirs of our local Baptist (his own), Lutheran (my mother's) and, Methodist (their compromise) churches. Late in life, and in the early stages of Alzheimer's disease, he was asked what his religious affiliation was. He answered, "I'm a tenor." How often do your strongly felt commitments sound equally obscure?

Our competitiveness shows up in a variety of ways. In general, our culture assumes that competitiveness is innate, part of our genetic inheritance, a normal and healthy dimension of our true being. But the Christian story offers no support for that idea and Paul makes it clear that the existence of competing factions in Corinth is proof of the Corinthians' immaturity and worldliness. This immaturity is both social and intellectual; it reveals a lack of practical and intellectual wisdom.

There are clear evidences of a lack of growth as a Christian: the extent to which you are jealous and in conflict is the extent to which you are an infantile Christian. You experience this in your passionate support of an athletic team, occasionally jingoist support of your college against others, or your commitment to your social groups. Every exclusionary barrier created by any of your affiliations is an infantile one.

You are called to be a Christian theological academic, to think and to live the life of unity in the cross, aware of your need to grow and to learn (cf. Heb 5:12—6:2). You know that the emptiness of the cross is filled with God's grace and you are reminded in the Lord's Supper that Christ regularly (re) fills you. True maturity means coming together at the cross.

I occasionally entertain the improbable fantasy that the confused commitment of my father to "tenor" rather than to a denominational tradition was a commitment to harmony over competition.

Prayer: Feed us, O God, the food to strengthen us to grow in your wisdom. Amen.

12 – Group Effort

1 Corinthians 3:5–9 — (5) What then is Apollos? What is Paul? Servants through whom you came to believe, as the Lord assigned to each. (6) I planted, Apollos watered, but God gave the growth. (7) So neither the one who plants nor the one who waters is anything, but only God who gives the growth. (8) The one who plants and the one who waters have a common purpose, and each will receive wages according to the labor of each. (9) For we are God's servants, working together; you are God's field, God's building.

HERE IS ANOTHER APPARENTLY arrogant claim by Paul: God and I work together! Most of us probably feel that we work on our own; we seem to prefer it that way. Another approach would be to operate within a group—particularly within a group that includes God. With this kind of attitude, the occasional disappointments that meet us in our work can be seen in the larger context of God's grace.

When we decided to build our own home, it was fascinating to watch the waves of experts who swept through the place, each building on the work of their predecessors; the work of one group might be covered up by that of the next and never seen again. So waves of workers exercised their skills and left behind work that lasted, even it would never be seen again.

Similarly, each of us is a worker adding one small contribution to the whole, and even our one contribution could be covered up in the larger picture. You see this clearly in your studies: you look back on the errors and triumphs of the past and see that present achievements rest on the foundation—or the rubble!—of the "certainties" of the past. The work of learning is enormously detailed and labor intensive. Hours trying to understand one page of a tough calculus problem, weeks on a term paper, five to six years on a degree. In the big picture, this labor is easily lost sight of. Work done with God is never lost. How wonderful that God has prepared a work for you to "walk in" (Eph 2:10).

Prayer: Show me the work prepared for me; thank you for your companionship as we work it together. Amen.

13 – Invisible, but Forever

1 Corinthians 3:10–15 — (10) According to the grace of God given to me, like a skilled master builder I laid a foundation and someone else is building on it. Each builder must choose with care how to build on it. (11) For no one can lay any foundation other than the one that has been laid; that foundation is Jesus Christ. (12) Now if anyone builds on the foundation with gold, silver, precious stones, wood, hay, straw—(13) the work of each builder will become visible, for the Day will disclose it, because it will be revealed with fire, and the fire will test what sort of work each has done. (14) If what has been built on the foundation survives, the builder will receive a reward. (15) If the work is burned up, the builder will suffer loss; the builder will be saved, but only as through fire.

GOING TO COLLEGE IS one way to "lay a foundation." Jesus Christ is a foundation. Your challenge is to pick the right foundation . . . and then use materials from every other source to build on it.

The choice of Jesus Christ as your foundation promises that work laid on that foundation will endure. But whether your work endures or not is not the ultimate question. In either case, you can be saved . . . even if only barely (v. 15). But for anyone investing herself daily in the academic venture of college, you would like to believe that your work will endure. To do so you must risk seeming to be a fool by ignoring the world's wisdom—that which is conventional, popular, and predictable. The only way you can risk ignoring worldly wisdom is by attaching yourself to Jesus Christ who does endure. Finally, the value of your commitment and the resilience of your foundation will be revealed in the crunch, when things are tough, when criticism is most severe, and when God weighs it in the judgment.

But throughout it all you are a fellow-worker with God and you know from the Genesis story that the work of God is to create good things. You are placed here to work with others in the creative activity of God. Jesus Christ is the one foundation on which the variety of all of our lives and skills can be united and can find a lasting place. Your work may be replaced or covered or removed, but the foundation that gave it significance and the building into which it found life will remain and will sustain you.

Prayer: Help me to focus on the foundation of Christ crucified, and guide me to build upon it. Amen.

14 – Body Beautiful

1 Corinthians 3:16–17 — (16) Do you not know that you are God's temple and that God's Spirit dwells in you? (17) If anyone destroys God's temple, God will destroy that person. For God's temple is holy, and you are that temple.

YOUR PARENTS THINK YOU'RE beautiful. Hopefully you think you're beautiful. God thinks you are; he made you (and he doesn't make junk). In addition to all the activities taking place in you—here you can refer to what you are learning in psychology (about the brain), chemistry (about cells), biology (all those internal organs), etc.—there is something else going on: God has long since taken up residence in you—in the *persona* of his Holy Spirit.

You already know that you don't want anybody or anything to mess with your precious body. Are you also aware that you can rely on God (via the Holy Spirit) to be a stalwart champion of your body—its health, integrity, maturation, learning?

College has a lot of ways to mess with your body. They range from the innocent food on offer in the cafeteria (if you eat too much or the wrong thing) to the downright stupid "opportunities" (binge drinking). Then there's the possibility of staying up all night to finish a paper or study for a test; not good for the paper, the test, or your health (physical or psychological). Then there are drugs to abuse (did I say "stupid"?) and sex to experiment with (always dangerous to experiment when you don't know what you're doing).

Remember: God made you and loves you just the way you are. And your parents were pretty active in making you also, and they love you pretty much the way you are. Isn't that enough to encourage you to love yourself just the way you are—with perhaps some improvements added through your attention to the benefits promised with a college education?

Prayer: I promise to honor my own and everyone else's bodies because they are God's. Amen.

15 – Fools for Christ

1 Corinthians 3:18–23 — (18) Do not deceive yourselves. If you think that you are wise in this age, you should become fools so that you may become wise. (19) For the wisdom of this world is foolishness with God. For it is written, "He catches the wise in their craftiness," (20) and again, "The Lord knows the thoughts of the wise, that they are futile." (21) So let no one boast about human leaders. For all things are yours, (22) whether Paul or Apollos or Cephas or the world or life or death or the present or the future—all belong to you, (23) and you belong to Christ, and Christ belongs to God.

"S/HE HAD IT ALL—MONEY, position, looks—and then . . . ." It is so hard to "arrive" and so easy to lose it all. We strive to arrive, struggle to stay, are often self-deceived into the belief that we have created who we are and that we can keep it that way. We academics are particularly susceptible, forgetting so many of the lessons that history can teach us about human achievement. We forget the multitude of examples of those who have achieved human favor through whatever means and who have deceived themselves into thinking that their achievement was something that could be grasped and held. This hope is utterly unlike the attitude of the Christ described in the letter to the Philippians—a Christ who didn't even feel that way about being God (Phil 2:6).

Being seen as foolish would be the last thing most of us would accept. And yet . . . .

The court fool or jester of the Middle Ages provides an interesting example—perhaps one worthy of admiration. He played the fool, dressed and spoke outrageously—even to the king—and got away with it. He could do so because he was considered to be a fool, and thought to be unencumbered by the "wisdom" of the court or kingdom. He seemed to know that the self-deception of the powerful and wise of his time would be seen as nonsense in the next age. And yet, in his outrageous commentaries were often found words of real wisdom, not a wisdom manufactured for the self-deception of the "self-made."

Paul quotes from the Old Testament to the effect that God knows and disregards the wise. Only those who have given that up and cling to the cross are freed from the burden of self-deception. While the world might see them as fools, they are truly God's because they wrap themselves in nothing but God's wisdom.

Prayer: Since I only see through a glass dimly, let me be seen and held by God. Amen.

16 – How Am I Doing? (No Navel Gazing)

1 Corinthians 4:1–5 — (1) Think of us in this way, as servants of Christ and stewards of God's mysteries. (2) Moreover, it is required of stewards that they be found trustworthy. (3) But with me it is a very small thing that I should be judged by you or by any human court. I do not even judge myself. (4) I am not aware of anything against myself, but I am not thereby acquitted. It is the Lord who judges me. (5) Therefore do not pronounce judgment before the time, before the Lord comes, who will bring to light the things now hidden in darkness and will disclose the purposes of the heart. Then each one will receive commendation from God.

BEING BUSY IS A hallmark of contemporary life. Everybody can claim that they are too busy. "No time" is the one excuse (along with "no money") that we all agree to accept as a legitimate excuse for not acting. The tragedy is that we might believe it and take pride in it and feel that it is our busyness that gives us worth.

But a servant always has time; having time—for the master—comes with the territory. Jesus' own ministry was one of interruptions, as he is constantly portrayed as doing something only to be interrupted by someone needing assistance. And, of course, he always turns away from his own agenda to the need pressed upon him. His first words to the blind Bartimaeus would be appropriate words for any Christian to say when asked to help: "What do you want me to do for you?" (Mark 10:51).

Do you present your personal agenda—political, athletic, academic, social—to God for approval and support? Do you see God as a supportive pal and ignore God as the creator-sustainer-judge who is to be faithfully served? Paul rightly dismisses his Corinthian brothers and sisters and indeed anyone who would evaluate him (v. 3). As a servant, his only concern is how the master will judge him, and he doesn't even waste energy on that.

You do not derive your significance from the judgment of others, nor even from your own good or negative judgments of yourself. Paul doesn't care what others think; nor is it even ultimately important what he thinks of himself. It is by focusing on God rather than self that gives the Christian her/his meaning and ultimate justification.

Prayer: Thank you for the gift to serve and find wholeness in loving others. Amen.

17 – Everything's a Gift

1 Corinthians 4:6–8 — (6) I have applied all this to Apollos and myself for your benefit, brothers and sisters, so that you may learn through us the meaning of the saying, "Nothing beyond what is written," so that none of you will be puffed up in favor of one against another. (7) For who sees anything different in you? What do you have that you did not receive? And if you received it, why do you boast as if it were not a gift? (8) Already you have all you want! Already you have become rich! Quite apart from us you have become kings! Indeed, I wish that you had become kings, so that we might be kings with you!

"NOTHING BEYOND WHAT IS written." What a peculiar phrase; and Paul wants his readers to "learn through us the meaning of the saying." I'm not sure I understand what he means, and a number of commentaries I've looked at are puzzled about it also. It seems to mean: stick with what is written and don't add anything to that.

But here you are in college with everything new—people, ideas, choices, possibilities. Can you just pull out your old list that says "do this" and "don't to that" and find instructions for each new thing? I don't think so.

Don't let this kind of sticking-to-the-past literalism keep you from employing and cultivating your imagination. Don't remain in your early childhood view of your faith and be "childish." Don't let it keep you from growing all of those intellectual gifts you have been given.

Indeed, few places are as replete with "gifts" and gifted people as is a college. Think of the gifts you encounter daily: the science building given by the Smiths; the library by the Carnegie Foundation; the solarium furnished by an anonymous donor; scholarships for so many students.

In *1493: Uncovering the New World Columbus Created,* Charles C. Mann mentions the European priests who condemned the use of the newly imported potato from the New World on the grounds that the potato was never mentioned in Scripture. Think of some of the other things we use with no guilt today that are absent from Scripture: oranges, radios, coffee, penicillin. Need I continue?

Just because Scripture, or Jesus, or Paul didn't mention something doesn't mean you can't use it or do it. What you should use is the gift of your imagination—especially in your studies.

Prayer: Thank you, Lord, for all of you gifts—the ones I know and the ones I will come to know. Amen.

18 – Turning the Other Cheek

1 Corinthians 4:9-13 — (9) For I think that God has exhibited us apostles as last of all, as though sentenced to death, because we have become a spectacle to the world, to angels and to mortals. (10) We are fools for the sake of Christ, but you are wise in Christ. We are weak, but you are strong. You are held in honor, but we in disrepute. (11) To the present hour we are hungry and thirsty, we are poorly clothed and beaten and homeless, (12) and we grow weary from the work of our own hands. When reviled, we bless; when persecuted, we endure; (13) when slandered, we speak kindly. We have become like the rubbish of the world, the dregs of all things, to this very day.

REJECTION.

No doubt you have had some experience with that. Granted, rejection and its various consequences may not have been on the scale that early Christian missionaries experienced it—"sentenced to death . . . spectacle to the world . . . fools . . . weak . . . in disrepute . . . hungry and thirsty . . . poorly clothed and beaten and homeless . . . reviled . . . persecuted . . . slandered . . . the rubbish of the world . . . the dregs." Even so, it would not be a useless exercise to evaluate the rejections you have experienced, why they happened, and—most importantly—how you responded to them.

Our natural and automatic response to rejection is often anger. Or is it "I don't get angry, I get even"? But looking at things with a calm view you can realize that neither response is a productive one. Paul's response to those who revile, persecute, or slander him is to "bless . . . endure . . . speak kindly."

Admittedly that is hard work. Especially since it is often the case—as Paul concludes—that he and his colleagues are still treated like garbage.

Prayer: God, remind me when I am rejected for whatever reason to turn the other cheek. Amen.

19 – Teacher's Pet

1 Corinthians 4:14–21 — (14) I am not writing this to make you ashamed, but to admonish you as my beloved children. (15) For though you might have ten thousand guardians in Christ, you do not have many fathers. Indeed, in Christ Jesus I became your father through the gospel. (16) I appeal to you, then, be imitators of me. (17) For this reason I send you Timothy, who is my beloved and faithful child in the Lord, to remind you of my ways in Christ Jesus, as I teach them everywhere in every church. (18) But some of you, thinking that I am not coming to you, have become arrogant. (19) But I will come to you soon, if the Lord wills, and I will find out not the talk of these arrogant people but their power. (20) For the kingdom of God depends not on talk but on power. (21) What would you prefer? Am I to come to you with a stick, or with love in a spirit of gentleness?

ONE OF MY MAIN teachers in school was a man named Norman Perrin. He came from a humble coal mining background in England. After serving in the British army in World War II in Africa, he went to Germany where he studied for his doctorate in New Testament studies with the famous Joachim Jeremias, whom Perrin always referred to as his *doktor vater* (loosely, German for "father of [the] doctor's degree"). Of course, Perrin had had many instructors, but he always saw Jeremias as his *vater*.

This is not how we view our teachers today. Nor are our relationships with teachers as close as we trundle from one large lecture hall to another, then to a website for an online class with an instructor many miles away. (It is likely that some of your teachers are actually also real human beings. Hard as it might be to think that way given how college education works today, please stay open to that possibility. It could become a joyous possibility for you when you least expect it.)

Paul claims a teaching style that is fatherly and loving rather than one based on ridicule and threats of punishment. Paul likes to speak of creating his listeners or of becoming their "father" (see his letter to Philemon).

That did not dilute his instruction. It was universally the same for all the churches. Can you, as a student, see yourself as one of the "beloved children" listening attentively to Paul who has just catalogued the difficulties the Corinthian Christian face? The relationship the apostle seeks with you is both one of father-child and fellow worker.

Prayer: Thank you for teachers who care for me. Amen.

20 – Time to Decide, Maybe

1 Corinthians 5:1-5 — (1) It is actually reported that there is sexual immorality among you, and of a kind that is not found even among pagans; for a man is living with his father's wife. (2) And you are arrogant! Should you not rather have mourned, so that he who has done this would have been removed from among you? (3) For though absent in body, I am present in spirit; and as if present I have already pronounced judgment (4) in the name of the Lord Jesus on the man who has done such a thing. When you are assembled, and my spirit is present with the power of our Lord Jesus, (5) you are to hand this man over to Satan for the destruction of the flesh, so that his spirit may be saved in the day of the Lord.

I ONCE HAD A colleague who could almost never decide anything. This instructor hesitated to commit midterm grades to paper, then failed to decide on the preliminary grades needed to validate graduating seniors. Finally, after the end of the school year, his grades would finally appear—belatedly—in the registrar's office.

Academic life has many enjoyments, a secret one of which may be that of not having to make decisions. Teachers will assemble all of the information available, and pass an hour lecturing with, "On the one hand . . . but then on the other hand" or "Yes . . . but . . . ." If not enough information is available, judgment is withheld. And, of course, there is never enough information available. Perhaps that is why the academy is occasionally referred to as the "ivory tower"—a place where we are protected from decision-making.

But outside of the classroom there are problems that demand action. Sexual immorality is a problem Paul faced. He acted fast and decisively: "Kick him out!" His insistence that this man be thrown out of the church was the only time in any of his letters that Paul made such a demand. Paul may have been too harsh and in error, but he decisively faced the problem.

Sexual immorality is still a problem—especially in college. Be like Paul: be clear and decisive, and totally intolerant . . . especially with yourself!

Prayer: God, give me the courage and the clarity to make and keep the decisions I have to make. Amen.

21 – Only Know Christ

1 Corinthians 5:6–13 — (6) Your boasting is not a good thing. Do you not know that a little yeast leavens the whole batch of dough? (7) Clean out the old yeast so that you may be a new batch, as you really are unleavened. For our paschal lamb, Christ, has been sacrificed. (8) Therefore, let us celebrate the festival, not with the old yeast, the yeast of malice and evil, but with unleavened bread of sincerity and truth. (9) I wrote to you in my letter not to associate with sexually immoral persons— (10) not at all meaning the immoral of this world, or the greedy and robbers, or idolaters, since you would then need to go out of the world. (11) But now I am writing to you not to associate with anyone who bears the name of brother or sister who is sexually immoral or greedy, or is an idolater, reviler, drunkard, or robber. Do not even eat with such a one. (12) For what have I to do with judging those outside? Is it not those who are inside that you are to judge? (13) God will judge those outside. "Drive out the wicked person from among you."

IN THE MIDDLE OF campus there was a wire model of the earth—basically a wire ball with continents outlined. A mischievous student placed a large lump of dough inside of it. After several hours, the dough ball that had been easy enough to insert had "risen" to the size where removal from the sculpture was a major maintenance challenge.

Such it was with the Corinthians. They were bloated with the worldly "yeast" of self-satisfaction and they were seriously "into" themselves. There was need for something new to fill their lives. Jesus had worried about the "yeast of the Pharisees and Sadducees" and didn't want his disciples poisoned by their hypocritical teaching (Matt 16:6, 11).

It was time, Paul said, to clean out the bad stuff from the Christian fellowship. They could leave the ultimate judgment of the world to God. Their task was to clean up their own act. If they wanted to boast they had plenty to boast about in Jesus Christ (1:31—"Let the one who boasts boast in the Lord"). If it appears repetitive, it is. In Corinth, as in college, boasting—even if it is only to yourself—is a sin that keeps on giving . . . God pains.

Prayer: God, clean me out, fill me with you, and keep me uncontaminated by my own pride. Amen.

22 – Being Deciders

1 Corinthians 6:1-6 — (1) When any of you has a grievance against another, do you dare to take it to court before the unrighteous, instead of taking it before the saints? (2) Do you not know that the saints will judge the world? And if the world is to be judged by you, are you incompetent to try trivial cases? (3) Do you not know that we are to judge angels—to say nothing of ordinary matters? (4) If you have ordinary cases, then, do you appoint as judges those who have no standing in the church? (5) I say this to your shame. Can it be that there is no one among you wise enough to decide between one believer and another, (6) but a believer goes to court against a believer—and before unbelievers at that?

PRINCETON COLLEGE PROFESSOR AND (college) president Woodrow Wilson, commenting wryly on the politics of campus life, observed that college arguments are so nasty because the stakes were so petty. A lot of times, the arguments among Christians are equally petty. Even so, they can get so big that Christians go to court—worldly court. Example: When one congregation gets in a spitting contest with its denomination, wants to quit the "offending" denomination, and has to sue in court to take the church building with them as they go out the door.

We are prone to set our own agendas and then call God in to approve our plans and assist us in carrying them out. We chuckle at the brother who asked Jesus to intervene on his behalf in a family dispute over money (Luke 12:13) or even the mother who asked Jesus, who was on the verge of being crucified (!), if he would arrange for her sons to sit next to him in the kingdom of God (Matt 20:21). Hello? Our focus is so often on the trivial. When it is on something big—like the issue of getting along with others that the Corinthians seemed not to be able to adjudicate according to today's passage—we are not always wise (read: unselfish) enough to address it.

The issue as Paul saw it was the embarrassment of submitting an intra-Christian dispute to non-Christian adjudication. The Corinthians—enamored as you have seen with the non-Christian visions of life rampant in Corinth (not irreligious but religious in other ways)—were willing to allow non-Christian criteria and people who wielded them to have the say.

Paul expects us to make decisions and we should be able to as long as we keep Jesus in the picture.

Prayer: O God of peace, let me find the blessedness Jesus promised in peacemaking. Amen.

23 – A New Paradigm

1 Corinthians 6:7–11 — (7) In fact, to have lawsuits at all with one another is already a defeat for you. Why not rather be wronged? Why not rather be defrauded? (8) But you yourselves wrong and defraud—and believers at that. (9) Do you not know that wrong-doers will not inherit the kingdom of God? Do not be deceived! Fornicators, idolaters, adulterers, male prostitutes, sodomites, (10) thieves, the greedy, drunkards, revilers, robbers—none of these will inherit the kingdom of God. (11) And this is what some of you used to be. But you were washed, you were sanctified, you were justified in the name of the Lord Jesus Christ and in the Spirit of our God.

As LONG AS WE'RE on the topic of being sued and people taking advantage and running over you . . . Paul has a new idea of how to deal with situations in which you are being jerked around or even totally shipwrecked.

Here the hypothetical situation is that you might be defeated in a lawsuit; serious business with serious consequences. Later (in chapter 8) you will read a about those Christians with weak (uninformed, frightened) consciences who might freak out if they saw you eating meat offered to (nonexistent) idols or going to the movies or . . . whatever freaked them out anyway.

What will be Paul's solution to the idol-offered–meat problem? That the Christian with the strong (informed, knowledgeable) conscience—although free to eat such meat since idols don't exist—was not only free to eat, but was also free not to eat because of the conscience of another soul for whom Christ had died. Freedom is to be used to support, not wreck, another person—not primarily to do your own thing.

Here, Paul says if you are being "wronged . . . defrauded," so what? So what difference does the decision of the world's institutions, or world-informed people, or even misguided fellow Christians make to you, a Christian? It may very well hurt, but it hurt Jesus to be executed as a criminal by an unjust conspiracy of two institutions—the Jewish religion and the Roman government—and a lot of uninformed, worldly, and unwise people. One of the greatest gifts accompanying the great gift of freedom is the freedom to forget the past, the freedom to forgive. And then you have the freedom to move on!

Prayer: Let me be able to suffer being sinned against rather than to sin against others. Amen.

24 – Free For All

1 Corinthians 6:12 — (12) "All things are lawful for me," but not all things are beneficial. "All things are lawful for me," but I will not be dominated by anything.

BEGINNING WITH A SLOGAN that biblical critics think might be the theme of his freewheeling and irresponsible opponents, Paul says (agreeing with them), "All things are lawful for me." This freedom thing has a modern ring to it—"that's my kind of religion," you might say.

But the slogan of the Corinthian "Christians" is qualified: what is chosen in freedom must be helpful, otherwise it will result in further and unpleasant enslavement. And freedom is not total, nor is there any such thing as perfect freedom. Freedom is not only *from* but also *for*. Paul also says: "I will not be dominated by anything"; like enslaved by anything? Indeed, being enslaved, trapped, or bound by anything or anyone is the last thing you want; it is no kind of freedom at all.

In our modern American fixation on individualism it is easy to imagine that your actions will not affect others. In fact, denying responsibility for others is almost a hallmark of popular ethical thought today. There is something exhilaratingly freeing about going to college. But how often do you see that freedom squandered in choices that everyone knows can have bad consequences? Freedom is not limitless; its use always has consequences. Freedom is always *for* something, not just *from* something. In the case of Christians, it is *for* being of help to others. How is that not a new slavery? The contrast of freedom with the possibility of enslavement appears superficially curious, but within the limitless spectrum of freedoms facing the Christian, some choices would not only be bad choices, but actually enslaving. For example, using freedom to choose for self is a self-limiting freedom since it is enslavement to yourself. Freedom *for* others is true freedom since it encounters the mysterious freedom of unlimited and unexpected possibilities inherent in the other person; you are not enslaved *by* them but enslaved *for* them.

Your freedom in Christ becomes the field upon which the answers to the other's needs takes shape. The development of those answers calls for the creativity and commitment only available in your new freedom (from self/ for others) and your new enslavement (to God). In Christ you are firmly bound and forever free.

Prayer: O God who gives us freedom, help my choices be made in my freedom for others. Amen.

25 – The Student Body

1 Corinthians 6:13–20 — (13) "Food is meant for the stomach and the stomach for food," and God will destroy both one and the other. The body is meant not for fornication but for the Lord, and the Lord for the body. (14) And God raised the Lord and will also raise us by his power. (15) Do you not know that your bodies are members of Christ? Should I therefore take the members of Christ and make them members of a prostitute? Never! (16) Do you not know that whoever is united to a prostitute becomes one body with her? For it is said, "The two shall be one flesh." (17) But anyone united to the Lord becomes one spirit with him. (18) Shun fornication! Every sin that a person commits is outside the body; but the fornicator sins against the body itself. (19) Or do you not know that your body is a temple of the Holy Spirit within you, which you have from God, and that you are not your own? (20) For you were bought with a price; therefore glorify God in your body.

THE BODY IS NOT meant for fornication. For sex, yes, but not fornication. Not only is it true that "your body is a temple of the Holy Spirit"; it is also a member of the body of Christ (12:27).

Do you get a bit embarrassed if you have to say that you are a Christian; or that you are a "member of Christ"? What if you had to say, "I'm a member of a prostitute"? That would impress (negatively!) a lot of folks.

When Jesus said you can't serve two masters (Matt 6:24), he might just as well have said that you can't be a member of two bodies—Jesus' and a prostitute's. That is a kind-of-gross way of pointing out that your basic and ultimate commitment can only be in one direction. If your body (i.e., you) gets involved in an inappropriate sexual relationship you are selling out Christ and his body—the whole church—into a relationship with your new "best friend" or partner. You can't do that and maintain a faithful relationship with Christ at the same time. People that walk the fence wind up falling off. People committed to many things cannot be committed very seriously to any one thing. And it's not just that Paul is suggesting you pick Jesus over prostitutes but that he is reminding you that in Jesus, God paid a whole lot for you already.

Prayer: Lord, I worship and honor you with my body. Amen.

26 – You Can't Always Find an Expert

1 Corinthians 7:1-6 — (1) Now concerning the matters about which you wrote: "It is well for a man not to touch a woman." (2) But because of cases of sexual immorality, each man should have his own wife and each woman her own husband. (3) The husband should give to his wife her conjugal rights, and likewise the wife to her husband. (4) For the wife does not have authority over her own body, but the husband does; likewise the husband does not have authority over his own body, but the wife does. (5) Do not deprive one another except perhaps by agreement for a set time, to devote yourselves to prayer, and then come together again, so that Satan may not tempt you because of your lack of self-control. (6) This I say by way of concession, not of command.

IN THIS CHAPTER, PAUL reveals that he is not an expert; he has taken criticism down through history for his allegedly negative views on marriage. But, remembering that this letter is written in the heat of a response to a virtual meltdown within the Corinthian church, we cannot expect it to be perfect in all its recommendations for all Christians in all subsequent situations. How often have you been confronted with questions far beyond your abilities to answer?

The personal questions that students raise have not always been well received by teachers and counselors. Sometimes they have been handed off to "experts." Setting aside the content of Paul's answers on the relative merits of marriage (how "expert" could a single fellow be on the question of marriage?), his approach itself is instructive.

He is not hesitant to answer. He certainly has opinions, some firmly rooted in his own experience. But he balances and qualifies his own opinions so that his hearers get the whole story. He knows that the Lord Jesus had spoken on many topics, but in those areas where the Lord had not spoken, Paul hazards his own opinion. He lets his readers know which is the Lord's and which are merely his own views.

We know that Jesus has not given us a word to cover every eventuality. You will have to be responsible for coming up with solutions to problems previously unaddressed. Remember how Paul tried to do it—with "the mind of Christ." In such situations, you are to shut out the opinions of this world and then through prayer and imagination seek "the mind of Christ."

Prayer: Help me to be helpful but keep me from insisting that my opinion is yours, too. Amen.

27 – Why Can't a Woman Behave like a Man?

1 Corinthians 7:7–13 — (7) I wish that all were as I myself am. But each has a particular gift from God, one having one kind and another a different kind. (8) To the unmarried and the widows I say that it is well for them to remain unmarried as I am. (9) But if they are not practicing self-control, they should marry. For it is better to marry than to be aflame with passion. (10) To the married I give this command—not I but the Lord—that the wife should not separate from her husband (11) (but if she does separate, let her remain unmarried or else be reconciled to her husband), and that the husband should not divorce his wife. (12) To the rest I say—I and not the Lord—that if any believer has a wife who is an unbeliever, and she consents to live with him, he should not divorce her. (13) And if any woman has a husband who is an unbeliever, and he consents to live with her, she should not divorce him.

THE PROFESSOR OF ELOCUTION in the movie *My Fair Lady*—Henry Higgins—is bothered by some quite understandable outbursts of crying by his student Liza Doolittle; he has been quite hard on her in his efforts to teach her proper English speech. In utter frustration, he sings, "Why can't a woman be more like a man?" Higgins fancies himself a perfectly rational being and he would prefer Eliza to behave like him.

Many of your professors would also like you to be like them, adopt their ideas at least, or perhaps even follow in their professional shoes.

Paul was a great founder and nurturer of churches and solver of problems; he had great insight into the Christian faith; he was super-courageous as a missionary facing great challenges. But, as my college professor of New Testament, W. D. Davies, said once off-handedly, "Paul would have made a terrible house guest." Just think of him visiting in your home and expounding his views on how to solve the problems he saw there.

Just as you should not be wanting everyone to be like you, you need not worry too much about copying Paul in every detail. He might not have known all there was to know about marriage. A good piece of advice in studying Scripture is to "keep your eye on the prize"—Jesus. All the rest of us are, in the words of Paul, fellow laborers.

Prayer: Help me to encourage others to be like Jesus. Amen.

28 – Yoked to Unbelievers – What Rubs Off?

1 Corinthians 7:14–16 — (14) For the unbelieving husband is made holy through his wife, and the unbelieving wife is made holy through her husband. Otherwise, your children would be unclean, but as it is, they are holy. (15) But if the unbelieving partner separates, let it be so; in such a case the brother or sister is not bound. It is to peace that God has called you. (16) Wife, for all you know, you might save your husband. Husband, for all you know, you might save your wife.

"Unbelieving partner."

Again, forget about the marriage angle in this passage and think about the "unbelieving partners" you have acquired in college: roommates, suite mates, lab partners, buddies at work, teammates, dates; the list will go on. The question is: What rubs off from whom to whom? Does bad stuff rub off of the unbeliever onto the believer, thrusting a Christian into a pagan, secular, worldly contaminated zone? Or, does good stuff (i.e., Christian faith, virtuous behavior, good deeds) rub off onto others?

Paul hopes that the holiness of a Christian spouse might just rub off on a mate; he is already certain that the holiness of a Christian parent "holy-ifies" (sorry if that isn't a word yet) the children. In the Gospel accounts of Jesus, it is clear that Jesus had no fear of contamination from contact with any of the people deemed "unclean" or sinful by the popular religion or cultural opinion: instead, the power of good (healing, forgiveness) went zooming from Jesus to the needy and did its thing in direct contradiction to the way most people thought about such a question.

"Unbelieving partner"? Welcome the opportunity; don't worry about being infected with whatever it is you might be afraid of because if you don't let it seem real it won't be real . . . because it isn't real. Remember your larger vocation—even larger than that of student: "it is to peace that God has called you."

Prayer: As Jesus loved the "other," let me love and not be afraid. Amen.

29 – Happy with Yourself

1 Corinthians: 7:17–20 — (17) However that may be, let each of you lead the life that the Lord has assigned, to which God called you. This is my rule in all the churches. (18) Was anyone at the time of his call already circumcised? Let him not seek to remove the marks of circumcision. Was anyone at the time of his call uncircumcised? Let him not seek circumcision. (19) Circumcision is nothing, and uncircumcision is nothing; but obeying the commandments of God is everything. (20) Let each of you remain in the condition in which you were called.

IN *ACRES OF DIAMONDS,* an astonishingly popular lecture and book from the late nineteenth century, Russell Conwell proclaimed that each person had all the opportunities for success in life right in their own backyard. His lecture was incredibly popular and struck the competitive, capitalistic chord in the American soul at that moment in our history. It is reported that he gave this message in lectures some 6,000 times around the country!

Paul had somewhat the same idea and saw no need, when he addressed those in his Corinthian audience who were slaves, for them to seek freedom—something with which we today seem almost obsessed. He knew that each individual was involved in a web of social, political, and economic relationships that simultaneously confined them and gave them the structures necessary for framing their lives. Flight from one servitude (say, slavery) meant involvement in another (say, the freedom to choose to become a slave in any other number of ways).

Paul saw that your present circumstances—whatever they might be—offered opportunities to serve others and thereby to fulfill God's call in your life. His advice was to take advantage of the situation in which each person found herself.

Prayer: Thank you, Lord, for finding me where I am; stay with me wherever I am. Amen.

30 – Houston, We May Have a Problem . . . in Translation

1 Corinthians 7:21-24 — (21) Were you a slave when called? Do not be concerned about it. Even if you can gain your freedom, make use of your present condition now more than ever. (22) For whoever was called in the Lord as a slave is a freed person belonging to the Lord, just as whoever was free when called is a slave of Christ. (23) You were bought with a price; do not become slaves of human masters. (24) In whatever condition you were called, brothers and sisters, there remain with God.

THE ORIGINAL GREEK TEXT of the twenty-seven "books" in the New Testament has enjoyed amazing integrity in the nearly 2,000 years of copying, translating, editing, and printing. Just think of the 1,400 years before printing during which all that copying was done by hand, under conditions you wouldn't tolerate, using materials inferior to those available now. The consistency and faithfulness with which the text of Scripture has been preserved with so few human mistakes is astonishing. But every once in a while you will run into . . . .

There is a textual challenge here where there could be one of two different meanings: does the text of v. 21—translated here: "if you can gain your freedom, make use of your present condition"—mean (i) take the opportunity to become free, or (ii) use the situation in which you find yourself a slave to serve your master (instead of trying to free yourself)? The whole thrust of the letter would suggest that Paul would prefer the latter. The probability is that you would prefer the former.

Whether slave or free, circumcised or uncircumcised, married or single—these are big alternatives, and Paul is not immune to preferring one to another—you are to be content within the condition or status you already occupy, and your effort should not go into chasing change but into "taking the opportunity" to live faithfully and in the service of others. The efforts to change or dwell on the greener pastures that lie elsewhere are both selfish and wasteful. The truth is that you can find God present and available to you in whatever state you find yourself. So look for the ways to "make use of your present condition"—classes, tests, papers, roommates, job—to live out your calling.

Prayer: Thank you, Lord, for being accessible no matter what my condition. Amen.

31 – Too Much Sex?

1 Corinthians 7:25–31 — (25) Now concerning virgins, I have no command of the Lord, but I give my opinion as one who by the Lord's mercy is trustworthy. (26) I think that, in view of the impending crisis, it is well for you to remain as you are. (27) Are you bound to a wife? Do not seek to be free. Are you free from a wife? Do not seek a wife. (28) But if you marry, you do not sin, and if a virgin marries, she does not sin. Yet those who marry will experience distress in this life, and I would spare you that. (29) I mean, brothers and sisters, the appointed time has grown short; from now on, let even those who have wives be as though they had none, (30) and those who mourn as though they were not mourning, and those who rejoice as though they were not rejoicing, and those who buy as though they had no possessions, (31) and those who deal with the world as though they had no dealings with it. For the present form of this world is passing away.

YOU HAVE PROBABLY NOTICED that all the Scripture writers were men. And maybe you are beginning to think that Paul is spending too much time on marriage and sex. And that maybe women aren't as focused on that stuff as men are. And maybe you have noticed that most of the students in college these days are female. So . . .

Christians need to recognize that there are different ways to think about faith now than the way in which people in our part of the world have thought about it for literally centuries. That way has been mostly white (Caucasian), male, Western. Patriarchal.

Over the last several decades it has become clear that other perspectives were being asserted (women, people of color, people of the Third World). And there are so many other problems other than sex that those people face. College can help you to notice, consider, study, and even commit yourself to do something about alleviating "the impending crisis" faced by so many others for whom "the present form of this world is passing away" leaving them to face persecution, poverty, climate change damage, displacement, disease.

Even if you are not facing an impending cataclysmic disaster that will totally change your life right now, aren't there enough pressing issues that merit your focused attention and energy in ways that haven't occurred to classmates obsessed with fun, partying, drinking, sex, etc.?

Prayer: God, you are so big; help me to see the bigger you. Amen.

32 – Big Decisions

*1 Corinthians 7:32–35 — (21) I want you to be free from anxieties.
The unmarried man is anxious about the affairs of the Lord, how
to please the Lord; (33) but the married man is anxious about the
affairs of the world, how to please his wife, (34) and his interests
are divided. And the unmarried woman and the virgin are anxious about the affairs of the Lord, so that they may be holy in body
and spirit; but the married woman is anxious about the affairs of
the world, how to please her husband. (35) I say this for your own
benefit, not to put any restraint upon you, but to promote good
order and unhindered devotion to the Lord.*

SOME OF THE TOUGHEST decisions are tough precisely because the options
are not all that different. The classic ethical dilemma of the runaway street-
car conductor about to hit five workmen on the tracks and confronted with
the possibility of avoiding them only by turning onto a siding where a playing child will be killed presents the student with two bad options: kill the
workmen or the child? Or consider the good options available at a church
carry-in dinner where ham, chicken, and meatloaf in abundance challenge
one's decision-making powers, but there are no "wrong" choices.

For Paul, marriage was one of those situations; either way was okay.
Paul did consider remaining single to be preferable but he based his choice
on the expectation that Christ would soon return and that by remaining
single he could better serve the Lord in the short time remaining before
Jesus' return.

Too often in our lives we conceal the motives on which we base our
choices. Too seldom do we involve others by frankly exposing our reasons
to see if they are reasons that will allow God into our lives and direct our
lives toward active and loving concern for others. Too seldom are our decisions as students informed in any way by reasoning that could be construed
as Christian. How often instead do you tend to make decisions on the basis
of the thinking of the day?

We do not know the totality of Paul's several exchanges of letters with the
Corinthians, nor do we know much of the Corinthians' side of the conversation. But we do know there was a dialogue, and an extended one at that. How
often do you have those kinds of conversations over the important matters of
life? How often do you—being trained in critical thinking—work at making
your decisions in the way God in Christ would have you think and decide?

*Prayer: God, help me make good choices by considering your will
in my life. Amen.*

33 – Getting a Second Opinion

1 Corinthians 7:36–40 — (36) If anyone thinks that he is not behaving properly toward his fiancée, if his passions are strong, and so it has to be, let him marry as he wishes; it is no sin. Let them marry. (37) But if someone stands firm in his resolve, being under no necessity but having his own desire under control, and has determined in his own mind to keep her as his fiancée, he will do well. (38) So then, he who marries his fiancée does well; and he who refrains from marriage will do better. (39) A wife is bound as long as her husband lives. But if the husband dies, she is free to marry anyone she wishes, only in the Lord. (40) But in my judgment she is more blessed if she remains as she is. And I think that I too have the Spirit of God.

PAUL ISN'T AS ASSERTIVE on this—hopefully last!—consideration of marriage (sex). Note the "but in my judgment" (v. 40) and the following, almost hesitant, "And I think that I too have the Spirit of God." Does Paul think others can't have different opinions and still be inspired by "the Spirit of God"?

Let's just try something. If you're a guy, get a female (a Christian, but she could be your mother, a girl down the hall, the janitor) and ask her the two questions Paul answers here: (first) should engaged people marry "if . . . passions are strong"? And (second), if a spouse dies, is remarriage advisable (and is remarriage to a non-Christian okay)?

If you're a girl, find a Christian of the male variety and do the same questioning.

These can be fairly important questions. In your discussion, are you able to agree? Completely? A little? If you disagree, are you able to see the viewpoint of the other? Can they see yours?

One of the tensions in Corinth and in your life now is achieving that being "united in the same mind and the same purpose" business (1:10) at the same time that each of you is being true to the "body of Christ" model of Christian fellowship in which occasionally an "ear" will have to notify a "hand" that there is a problem needing resolution.

Prayer: Help me to practice hospitality to others instead of just tolerance. Amen.

34 – Being Known

1 Corinthians 8:1–3 — (1) Now concerning food sacrificed to idols: we know that "all of us possess knowledge." Knowledge puffs up, but loves build up. (2) Anyone who claims to know something does not yet have the necessary knowledge; (3) but anyone who loves God is known by him.

FINALLY! AFTER ALL THE chapters on the cross, internal church disputes, freedom and slavery, and marriage, we get to a topic that is probably a lot more pressing for you: knowledge. Are you ready for today's test? Have you mastered today's assignments? How can you find more information for your term paper, and will you be able to evaluate it so that the information becomes useful knowledge?

During the oral examination for my doctor's degree, I kept trying to decide how many times I could say "I don't know" and still pass the exam. Knowing seemed to be better than not knowing.

But being "known" is a different matter. Imagine the fact, statistic, or datum you want to know. And all of a sudden, you *are* that fact, statistic, or datum. You are now the object of someone else's knowing. It could be scary. There are probably some things about yourself that you would rather not have anyone uncover.

In the Bible, knowledge is often about being "known" instead of knowing. If you concentrate on it, knowing can get you out of shape—puffed up because you are the subject. Love, on the other hand, results in being "known," being who you are and being accepted for who and what you are.

In dealing with another problem—the one in Galatia where the church had added the observation of the Jewish law to their list of requirements to be a Christian—Paul writes that in Christ the Galatian Christians have all they need. In Christ, he assures them, they "have come to know God . . ." (Gal 4:9a). Immediately he qualifies his statement: ". . . or rather to be known by God (Gal 4:9b)." We are assured that the omniscient (all knowing) God who can know us still loves and cares for us regardless of what there is to know. That good news needs processing. You know that what God knows about you may not be all that great, and that the fact that God knows it is not all that important, because even though he knows some bad stuff it doesn't keep him from loving and accepting you. What a comfort to know that God knows and loves you and that your knowing sometimes isn't that important.

Prayer: Know me, O God. Amen.

35 – Using Your Smarts

1 Corinthians 8:4–8 — (4) Hence, as to the eating of food offered to idols, we know that "no idol in the world really exists," and that "there is no God but one." (5) Indeed, even though there may be so-called gods in heaven or on earth—as in fact there are many gods and many lords—(6) yet for us there is one God, the Father, from whom are all things and for whom we exist, and one Lord, Jesus Christ, through whom are all things and through whom we exist. (7) It is not everyone, however, who has this knowledge. Since some have become so accustomed to idols until now, they still think of the food they eat as food offered to an idol; and their conscience, being weak, is defiled. (8) "Food will not bring us close to God." We are no worse off if we do not eat, and no better off if we do.

SOME CHRISTIAN TRADITIONS DOWNPLAY knowledge, suggesting that it interferes with or is even opposed to faith. This passage doesn't take that approach, and it offers an example in which a lack of understanding—not knowing that idols actually don't exist—can put a Christian in a vulnerable position. When a Christian who is informed about the nonexistence of idols comes along and does something that appears to play into the hands of a (nonexistent) idol, it can devastate a Christian who hasn't yet matured to the point of dismissing idols.

Paul solves the problem for both: let the one who is more mature back off from what she knows is permissible and use her freedom to "let it go" and not risk offending the weaker sister.

In this part of his letter, Paul reveals a good deal of knowledge that he wished that Christians shared: (i) idols do not exist; (ii) there is only one God; (iii) our behaviors don't decide our relationship with God; and, finally, (iv) there are people who do not know these things who nonetheless are beloved of God and who can be ruined by the actions of Christians who misuse this important knowledge for their own satisfaction. That is a lot of useful and helpful information for today's living. Use it for the edification of others.

Prayer: Help me to never let another fall because of my knowledge. Amen.

36 – Stumbling on Freedom

1 Corinthians 8:9-13 — (9) But take care that this liberty of yours does not somehow become a stumbling block to the weak. (10) For if others see you, who possess knowledge, eating in the temple of an idol, might they not, since their conscience is weak, be encouraged to the point of eating food sacrificed to idols? (11) So by your knowledge those weak believers for whom Christ died are destroyed. (12) But when you thus sin against members of your family, and wound their conscience when it is weak, you sin against Christ. (13) Therefore, if food is a cause of their falling, I will never eat meat, so that I may not cause one of them to fall.

THE HIGH SCHOOL YOUTH group was meeting to plan for Youth Sunday, when they would be in charge of the morning worship service. Lyn, the brightest of the group, offered the initial suggestion: "Let's do something really gross that will blow everyone away!"

That set the bar pretty high. Or low. The youth had been entrusted with a serious responsibility: lead the congregation (of parents, friends, and others) in a religious service that would be helpful, uplifting, challenging, soothing—pick the criterion that would mark a good worship experience. But to use the freedom afforded by this opportunity to focus on "blowing them away" (offending, embarrassing, confusing) seems to exemplify exactly what Paul was trying to prevent.

It is hard to find any scriptural support for the idea that Christians are supposed to go around grossing other people out—whether sisters and brothers in the faith, or those outside the faith. In fact, Paul will soon make it clear that when he was engaged with others he took pains not to offend them; in fact he made every effort to appear as a Jew to Jews or as a Gentile to Gentiles by avoiding behaving in ways that could distance himself from others whose culture and/or religious ideas and behaviors were different from his.

Are there things in your daily life and behavior that might be creating a distance between you and those with whom you want to be closer? Why not abandon those behaviors that might put them off?

Prayer: God free me from idolizing my own freedom so much that I risk tripping others. Amen.

37 – Rhetorical Questions

1 Corinthians 9:1–12a — (1) Am I not free? Am I not an apostle? Have I not seen Jesus our Lord? Are you not my work in the Lord? (2) If I am not an apostle to others, at least I am to you; for you are the seal of my apostleship in the Lord. (3) This is my defense to those who would examine me. (4) Do we not have the right to our food and drink? (5) Do we not have the right to be accompanied by a believing wife, as do the other apostles and the brothers of the Lord and Cephas? (6) Or is it only Barnabas and I who have no right to refrain from working for a living? (7) Who at any time pays the expenses for doing military service? Who plants a vineyard and does not eat any of its fruit? Or who tends a flock and does not get any of its milk? (8) Do I say this on human authority? Does not the law also say the same? (9) For it is written in the law of Moses, "You shall not muzzle an ox while it is treading out the grain." Is it for oxen that God is concerned? (10) Or does he not speak entirely for our sake? It was indeed written for our sake, for whoever plows should plow in hope and whoever threshes should thresh in hope of a share in the crop. (11) If we have sown spiritual good among you, is it too much if we reap your material benefits? (12) If others share this rightful claim on you, do not we still more?

THIS PASSAGE IS FULL of questions. But don't worry, they are not the kind of questions that are on a quiz. They are rhetorical questions—questions that were never intended to elicit an answer but were asked to make a point. Paul's "right" to be treated like other apostle-missionaries and receive support so that he could carry out his vocation had apparently been questioned. And he was mad! So he lets fly a barrage of rhetorical questions—sixteen to be exact!—to express his astonishment and anger. He throws in his credentials and supportive examples. He quotes Scripture and brings up the example of others in his position.

Until the time of the English philosopher John Locke (1632–1704), "inalienable rights" were thought to be possessed only by royalty. Centuries earlier, Paul had claimed his "right" to support. This could get interesting.

Pray: I'm confused; what are my rights as a follower of Jesus? Amen.

38 – Calm Down

1 Corinthians 9:12b–18 — (12b) Nevertheless, we have not made use of this right, but we endure anything rather than put an obstacle in the way of the gospel of Christ. (13) Do you not know that those who are employed in the temple service get their food from the temple, and those who serve at the altar share in what is sacrificed on the altar? (14) In the same way, the Lord commanded that those who proclaim the gospel should get their living by the gospel. (15) But I have made no use of any of these rights, nor am I writing this so that they may be applied in my case. Indeed, I would rather die than that—no one will deprive me of my ground for boasting! (16) If I proclaim the gospel, this gives me no ground for boasting, for an obligation is laid on me, and woe to me if I do not proclaim the gospel! (17) For if I do this of my own will, I have a reward; but if not of my own will, I am entrusted with a commission. (18) What then is my reward? Just this: that in my proclamation I may make the gospel free of charge, so as not to make full use of my rights in the gospel.

PAUL FINALLY COOLS DOWN. He concludes that if he is denied exercise of his "right" to (financial) support, he is not going to let that ruin his day. He is clear about his vocation; he is clear about his "right" to get support. If he can't get the due support, he is certainly not going to let that mess up his vocation, which is to bring the good news about Jesus Christ to those who need it.

So what have you learned?

First, that it's okay for Christians to be angry. Remember Job? He was so angry about what had happened to him that he swore he wished he had never been born (one example: Job 3:11). The Psalmist gets angry with God (Ps 44:24, etc.). Jesus seems angry as he throws the money-changers out of the temple (Matt 21:12). And on the cross he cries out the question why God has abandoned him there (Matt 27:46).

Second—and this is really big—it's okay not to use all the freedom or all the "rights" you (think you) have. Especially if not using them will help others or help the situation.

Prayer: Lord, thank you from reminding me that I don't have to be a slave to my own rights. Amen.

39 – Freedom, Again

I Corinthians 9:19–23 — (19) For though I am free with respect to all, I have made myself a slave to all, so that I might win more of them. (20) To the Jews I became as a Jew, in order to win Jews. To those under the law I became as one under the law (though I myself am not under the law) so that I might win those under the law. (21) To those outside the law I became as one outside the law (though I am not free from God's law but am under Christ's law) so that I might win those outside the law. (22) To the weak I became weak, so that I might win the weak. I have become all things to all people, that I might by all means save some. (23) I do it all for the sake of the gospel, so that I may share in its blessings.

Do you remember your first "overnighter"? Your mom took you to a friend's home and left you there. (She was really nervous about the whole thing.) You were anxious, unsure about things. Everything was different. Maybe you met your friend's dad for the first time. He was very different from your dad. Your friend's room was different from yours. Your friend's stuff was different from your stuff. These people were acting different than your family did in an evening. You were having fun, but . . . .

Then bedtime approached. You got more anxious. Would you make it, or would you have to have your friend's mom call your mom to come and take you home? (Of course, your mom was sitting at home wondering the same thing.) Everything was different. Your friend didn't have a bathing and tooth-brushing routine like you did at home. And when the parents said "Lights out" they meant it! The lights went out—like totally!

Then morning came and more different things happened. Instead of pancakes, like your mom always fixed, there were two boxes of cereal that you had never seen before—even in TV ads. You had to pick one, or go hungry. When you finally got home, you had some real stories to tell your family. You had had to behave like your friend, and to an extent you were able to do that. You did it because you were a friend. You didn't like some of things you had to do, but because of your friendship, you did them. Even though you didn't feel comfortable doing some of those things, you were still friends.

You and Paul experienced the kind of freedom we have in Christ.

Prayer: Thank you for the freedom to be like others without having to be others. Amen.

40 – Self-Control

1 Corinthians 9:24–27 — (24) Do you not know that in a race the runners all compete, but only one receives the prize? Run in such a way that you may win it. (25) Athletes exercise self-control in all things; they do it to receive a perishable wreath, but we an imperishable one. (26) So I do not run aimlessly, nor do I box as though beating the air; (27) but I punish my body and enslave it, so that after proclaiming to others I myself should not be disqualified.

PAUL CALLS FOR A discipline within our freedom that enables freedom in Christ to be true freedom. As the great athlete or dancer appears nonchalant in the execution of a move, so Christian life is to be lived with an air of freedom. But that freedom comes only at the cost of total surrender. For the athlete or dancer it is physical giftedness combined with countless hours of practice; for the Christian it is the world-changing work of Christ on the cross that redefines life.

Our freedom in Christ comes as a result of his self-discipline. In the ancient hymn quoted in Philippians 2, Christ starts out as equal to God, but gives that up to "descend" or come down to where we are as humans—even all the way down to the most debased of human conditions, as the victim of capital punishment. In this self-abasement, Jesus is able to become the one who, by that same discipline, lifts us all up.

Incidentally, Paul did not do his "become as a Jew" evangelism to remove individuals from their Jewish or gentile or Native American or Hispanic culture. That would be ludicrous even if you were successful. To what culture would you move someone? To American culture? But you know American culture brings us no closer to God than do Jewish or French or Congolese cultures. The more you can learn about all people through your college experience the more effective (disciplined) you can be in making the gospel clear to others and to yourself.

Prayer: Let me not seek shelter from the race but involve me to connect with others. Amen.

41 – The Past—Don't Knock It

1 Corinthians 10:1-6 — (1) I do not want you to be unaware, brothers and sisters, that our ancestors were all under the cloud, and all passed through the sea, (2) and all were baptized into Moses in the cloud and in the sea, (3) and all ate the same spiritual food, (4) and all drank the same spiritual drink. For they drank from the spiritual rock that followed them, and the rock was Christ. (5) Nevertheless, God was not pleased with most of them, and they were struck down in the wilderness. (6) Now these things occurred as examples for us, so that we might not desire evil as they did.

IF YOU LOOK AT the publication dates on the texts you use in your classes, it is likely that you will find that the date is fairly recent; it is seldom that you are asked to look far into the past for authoritative instruction. The old is suspect and out; the new is in and trusted. In our culture there is almost an idolatrous attitude towards the new.

Yes, this section of 1 Corinthians is about idolatry. You have probably seen a lot of bad movies in which supposedly primitive or deranged people worship some weird god who is represented by a statue or wild animal. Those statues are idols. Avoiding them—the ones in the movies—is a no-brainer. But there are many more subtle kinds of idolatry and you ought not forget that the second commandment is: Make no idols (Exod 20:4-6).

Paul directs his first-century readers to resources from the past that he offers as particularly useful in protecting them from idolatry, that sin of considering something more important than God. Paul interprets texts/stories from the distant past in a way that they become instructive to his readers. The way in which he is able to do this is to read those texts with Christ as the explanatory key.

What this all means is that the past, seen through the "mind of Christ," can provide instruction for the present. Christians believe that you can more fully comprehend the Old Testament because you can read it through the lens that is Jesus Christ. Christ has become for you the key or tool for understanding Scripture, the past, the present, the future—everything.

Prayer: God of the past, present, and future, help me to understand you through Jesus Christ. Amen.

42 – Am I Pushing It?

1 Corinthians 10:7–14 — (7) Do not become idolaters as some of them did; as it is written, "The people sat down to eat and drink, and they rose up to play." (8) We must not indulge in sexual immorality as some of them did, and twenty-three thousand fell in a single day. (9) We must not put Christ to the test, as some of them did, and were destroyed by serpents. (10) And do not complain as some of them did, and were destroyed by the destroyer. (11) These things happened to them to serve as an example, and they were written down to instruct us, on whom the ends of the ages have come. (12) So if you think you are standing, watch out that you do not fall. (13) No testing has overtaken you that is not common to everyone. God is faithful, and he will not let you be tested beyond your strength, but with the testing he will also provide the way out so that you may be able to endure it. (14) Therefore, my dear friends, flee from the worship of idols.

DURING THE FINAL ORAL exam for my doctoral degree, I had to answer "I don't know," (spoken, of course, as thoughtfully as possible so as to give the impression that I was still awake) way too many times. I was "pushing the envelope" about as far as anyone in that position could.

How many times do we test Christ, our mediator with God? In the examples from history—that ancient history of God's people—it is clear that God isn't always Mr. Cuddly, going along with all the bad stuff we do like an overly solicitous uncle. And those examples . . . aren't they totally appropriate ones to bring up in a college setting?

Sexual immorality. As I write these words, female US senators are crafting legislation to force colleges to get serious about ridding campuses of sexual harassment; too many students have been destroyed by sexual misconduct.

Testing Christ: Or does Christ quietly test us? How are we doing?

Complaining: That's what we do. About everything. And most of us have very little to complain about compared to, say, the 50,000,000-plus refugees around the world now having things a bit harder than most US college students.

As you learn day by day, are you learning for your vocation as a Christian?

Prayer: Thank you for good warnings and help me to learn from them. Amen.

43 – Time for Supper

1 Corinthians 10:15–22 — (15) I speak as to sensible people; judge for yourselves what I say. (16) The cup of blessing that we bless, is it not a sharing in the blood of Christ? The bread that we break, is it not a sharing in the body of Christ? (17) Because there is one bread, we who are many are one body, for we all partake of the one bread. (18) Consider the people of Israel; are not those who eat the sacrifices partners in the altar? (19) What do I imply then? That food sacrificed to idols is anything, or that an idol is anything? (20) No, I imply that what pagans sacrifice, they sacrifice to demons and not to God. I do not want you to be partners with demons. (21) You cannot drink the cup of the Lord and the cup of demons. You cannot partake of the table of the Lord and the table of demons. (22) Or are we provoking the Lord to jealousy? Are we stronger than he?

MURPHY'S LAW GOES SOMETHING like this: If something can possibly be messed up, it will be messed up. So it is no surprise to find out that the Corinthians had messed up the communal meal that Jesus had instituted in his last night on earth. Consequently, Paul has to give them a brief and absolutely clear little talk about just what that meal is about. First, the drink and the bread. They are "a sharing in the blood of Christ"—probably thinking of his death—and of the body of Christ—perhaps the very person and being of Christ or/and the church; he refers to the Christian community as the body of Christ. So the meal is a sharing, a getting/being together, with each other and with Jesus Christ.

Then, when the meal or "table of the Lord" is shared, Christians are totally and exclusively committed to him and can't possibly join up with or commit to any other leader who would in turn demand their commitment.

As the church grew, the meal's importance only grew. For example, it can now be called "communion" (com = with; union = united with); Lord's Supper (established by Jesus); Eucharist (thanksgiving). When we celebrate—together—we join in remembering Jesus, appreciating his sacrifice on the cross, and in expecting his return. So there is a lot of stuff that goes on when we eat that meal. Together.

Prayer: Lord Jesus, thank you for giving us the best meal of all. Amen.

44 – Just Eat It!

1 Corinthians 10:23-27 — (23) "All things are lawful," but not all things are beneficial. "All things are lawful," but not all things build up. (24) Do not seek your own advantage, but that of the other. (25) Eat whatever is sold in the meat market without raising any question on the ground of conscience, (26) for, "the earth and its fullness are the Lord's." (27) If an unbeliever invites you to a meal and you are disposed to go, eat whatever is set before you without raising any question on the ground of conscience.

WE'RE BACK ON FREEDOM again because it is one of the biggest things you have to handle right or to mess up on in college. Your mom isn't here to wake you up, feed you, check your clothes before you leave for class. You are on your own. You can use that freedom to sleep in late, or sleep with someone. You can use it to eat the right stuff or drink the wrong stuff. You can use it to stumble or to study.

Laws don't decide what should be allowed and what shouldn't be allowed. History proves that. Just think of our own US Supreme Court decisions declaring the legitimacy of laws that we know should never have been passed, defended, and approved by that body—laws that were later declared unconstitutional. Our highest court approved slavery (1857, *Dred Scott v. Sanford*), school segregation ("separate but equal schooling for different races" in 1896, *Plessy v. Ferguson*), and miscegenation (1883, *Pace v. Alabama*.) You can look that up.

Paul's "opponents" at Corinth took the total, exact opposite approach—also wrong—when they basically said that "all things are lawful." They were assuming that somehow Christ freed them to do whatever they wanted or felt like doing.

Paul's view was not "somewhere in the middle" but was based on the fact that (i) God created everything, (ii) so you can do everything (like eat anything), except that (iii) what you do do should be to "build up" other people. (Note: He doesn't say "Just don't offend others." That is not enough; that is an ethic that is designed only to protect you. Seeking the advantage of others is a proactive posture that challenges you to use your freedom creatively for others.)

So if nobody else's conscience is going to be bothered by your behavior, eat up!

Prayer: Lord, keep my antennae alert to the needs of others and make me fearless in advantaging them. Amen.

45 – Just Don't Eat It!

1 Corinthians 10:28-30 — (28) But if someone says to you, "This has been offered in sacrifice," then do not eat it, out of consideration for the one who informed you, and for the sake of conscience— (29) I mean the other's conscience, not your own. For why should my liberty be subject to the judgment of someone else's conscience? (30) If I partake with thankfulness, why should I be denounced because of that for which I give thanks?

WE'RE BACK TO THE topic of "rights" again. My "rights," your "rights," the "rights" of the person whose conscience is so sensitive she would be offended by something you have the "right" to do. This is not an arcane argument about who should and who shouldn't eat "idol burgers"—those ancient fast food specials with two all-beef patties, a couple of slices of cheese, some mayo, maybe an additional slab or two of bacon . . . .

This is a contemporary issue: your "rights" vs. the "rights" of others. And questions about where those rights come from (the Constitution, natural law, the Bible, their feelings, or "the way we've always done it"—there are many ways to try to justify "rights"). Our world is a litigious one; we are not slow to establish our "rights," get a lawyer to defend or assert our "rights," or try to make sure no one takes them from us.

Earlier (6:1–5) Paul expressed his astonishment that members of the Corinthian church would sue one another in a worldly court. His sad conclusion: "to have lawsuits at all with one another is already a defeat for you (6:7). Why not rather be wronged?" he asks—a whole new idea for most of us. But when it comes to "rights," the right thing is to exercise your "right" not to insist on your "rights."

> *Prayer: Lord, strengthen me so that I can easily and graciously concede my rights and love others. Amen.*

46 – The *Imitator*

1 Corinthians 10:31—11:1 — (31) So, whether you eat or drink, or whatever you do, do everything for the glory of God. (32) Give no offense to Jews or to Greeks or to the church of God, (33) just as I try to please everyone in everything I do, not seeking my own advantage, but that of many, so that they may be saved. (11:1) Be imitators of me, as I am of Christ.

IT SOUNDS LIKE A Hollywood movie: *The Imitator.* Relax, it's just my bad joke on the title of the very famous book of devotional readings by Thomas à Kempis, a priest who lived and wrote in the early 1400s. In his book, *The Imitation of Christ,* Thomas calls the reader to focus on Christ, focus on his suffering on the cross. It is this call to the cross that makes Thomas's book so appealing and powerful and so often foreign to modern readers.

On the cross, Christ is empty, naked, and dead, with no hope other than that God will help him. On the cross, Christ does not stand on his performance or his platform, his promise or his principles. On the cross, there is nowhere to stand; one hangs suspended, at the mercy of others, completely vulnerable and accessible—a fierce embodied paradigm of the mission of Jesus.

Paul found his salvation and his model for life in the crucified Jesus; "the cross" was his shorthand for this overwhelming constellation of factors, events, and significance (for example: Gal 5:11; Eph 2:16; Col 2:14).

We have not discussed Christian music—hymns, choruses, etc. But we should. Can you imagine Paul singing "In the Cross of Christ I Glory"? The powerful second line—"towering o'er the wrecks of time"—offers a devastating critique of all that humans have tried to accomplish under their own power and outside of God's will. Whenever we act without God, we wreck. Or could you follow Paul singing "Beneath the Cross of Jesus," "When I Survey the Wondrous Cross," or "Jesus, Keep Me near the Cross"? This kind of sacred music can help you unpack Paul's call to "be imitators of me" when you are singing in the shower or walking across campus.

Prayer: Help my life to be a brave, sweet, and harmonious imitation of Christ. Amen.

47 – Who's in Charge?

I Corinthians 11:2–12 — (2) I commend you because you remember me in everything and maintain the traditions just as I handed them on to you. (3) But I want you to understand that Christ is the head of every man, and the husband is the head of his wife, and God is the head of Christ. (4) Any man who prays or prophesies with something on his head disgraces his head, (5) but any woman who prays or prophesies with her head unveiled disgraces her head—it is one and the same thing as having her head shaved. (6) For if a woman will not veil herself, then she should cut off her hair; but if it is disgraceful for a woman to have her hair cut off or to be shaved, she should wear a veil. (7) For a man ought not to have his head veiled, since he is the image and reflection of God; but woman is the reflection of man. (8) Indeed, man was not made from woman, but woman from man. (9) Neither was man created for the sake of woman, but woman for the sake of man. (10) For this reason a woman ought to have a symbol of authority on her head, because of the angels. (11) Nevertheless, in the Lord woman is not independent of man or man independent of woman. (12) For just as woman came from man, so man comes through woman; but all things come from God.

MISSION CONTROL IN HOUSTON heard the message: "Houston . . . we have a problem."

Apparently another problem in Corinth is "good order." Among the things that are out of whack is the issue of people not knowing "their place" and behaving with selfish and disorderly use of freedom. Then we get to the place where women are instructed to be veiled or have their heads shaved. That will show the kind of order that Paul wants to see. It is hard for you to get worked up about good order when it depends on hairdos. The temptation is to move on.

But wait a moment. Here is a problem: What if in class today (it could be psych, art appreciation, sociology, political science) the prof claims that there is a long history of controlling and subjugating women by forcibly shaving their heads? And that such practices have been justified by using religious texts—especially the Bible? The quick take-away from this "conflict" should be your firm commitment never to use Scripture or faith to demean any of God's creatures—not even to enforce "good order." Love and kindness trump hurting people.

Prayer: When I have confusion about how things ought to be, direct my focus to Jesus and his love. Amen.

48 – Order in the . . . Place

1 Corinthians 11:13–16 — (13) Judge for yourselves: is it proper for a woman to pray to God with her head unveiled? (14) Does not nature itself teach you that if a man wears long hair, it is degrading to him, (15) but if a woman has long hair, it is her glory? For her hair is given to her for a covering. (16) But if anyone is disposed to be contentious—we have no such custom, nor do the churches of God.

THIS PASSAGE IS NOT about hair—short or long! It is about order and orderliness within the Christian community and about Jesus Christ ultimately being the regulator of how we get along. The main assumption for us is that Christ is (at) our head and that we take our directions from him. The rest of it is certainly open to criticism today for a number of compelling reasons.

Remember, Paul is trying to straighten out a mess in Corinth created by individuals and groups who have lost sight of the centrally unifying person of Christ. The bad public relations vibes the Christians are giving to the pagan (secular) public need to be countered. He puts the hammer down by insisting they do things his way; this is no time for a nice freewheeling discussion on what to do.

Paul used culturally accepted practices to keep things orderly in the church. So he goes into this controversial issue about hair. Probably any system will work when your motives and the outcomes are loving, forgiving, and supportive of others. The "hair thing" isn't very compelling now.

So your responsibility as a Christian today is to come up with the best way to keep good order within the group at the same time that you (plural) are sending good vibes out to a world that needs the love, forgiveness, reconciliation, and hope found in Jesus Christ. Use it—hair, clothes, music, whatever—gently. Love and kindness always trump hurting others.

Prayer: Don't let me get stuck in the minutiae of structures when there is good to do. Amen.

49 – Let's Have a Meetin'

*1 Corinthians 11:17–22 — (17) Now in the following instructions
I do not commend you, because when you come together it is not
for the better but for the worse. (18) For, to begin with, when you
come together as a church, I hear that there are divisions among
you; and to some extent I believe it. (19) Indeed, there have to be
factions among you, for only so will it become clear who among
you are genuine. (20) When you come together, it is not really to
eat the Lord's supper. (21) For when the time comes to eat, each of
you goes ahead with your own supper, and one goes hungry and
another becomes drunk. (22) What! Do you not have homes to
eat and drink in? Or do you show contempt for the church of God
and humiliate those who have nothing? What should I say to you?
Should I commend you? In this matter I do not commend you!*

AIN'T IT THE TRUTH? Committee meetings, club meetings, church meetings, dorm meetings. They can be fearsome gatherings, the results of which can be negligible or, in the case of the Corinthians, hurtful. It must have seemed to Paul that the Corinthians could mess up just about every aspect of Christian faith and life. Even when the Lord's Supper was celebrated, they ignored its unifying purpose. The Lord's Supper had a practical purpose: to experience the unity of the body of Christ. That it would bring together all kinds of people whom Christ embraced was revolutionary.

One way to look at this common meal is to unpack the characteristics listed above: it remembers Jesus, who came to establish a new order (the kingdom of God) and died doing just that; it recalls a horrible act committed by a political entity (Rome); it anticipates the return of Christ and the final realization of God's universal community. This sounds political—even subversive. As a continuation of the Jewish celebration of Passover, it has even more political overtones (the Exodus of the Israelites from an oppressive Egyptian Pharaoh).

A true gathering is not only characterized by people being together and by their consideration of each for the other. The Lord's Supper is a revolutionary event. Discernment of this social dimension is a crucial part of living the Christian life well. This central feature of faith for all Christians is a blessed reminder that God has created us to be social in a new, revolutionary fashion.

*Prayer: God, grant me the gift of discernment so that I can know
how to get along with others. Amen.*

211

50 – Discern

1 Corinthians 11:23–34 — (23) For I received from the Lord what I also handed on to you, that the Lord Jesus on the night when he was betrayed took a loaf of bread, (24) and when he had given thanks, he broke it and said, "This is my body that is for you. Do this in remembrance of me." (25) In the same way he took the cup also, after supper, saying, "This cup is the new covenant in my blood. Do this, as often as you drink it, in remembrance of me." (26) For as often as you eat this bread and drink the cup, you proclaim the Lord's death until he comes. (27) Whoever, therefore, eats the bread or drinks the cup of the Lord in an unworthy manner will be answerable for the body and blood of the Lord. (28) Examine yourselves, and only then eat of the bread and drink of the cup. (29) For all who eat and drink without discerning the body, eat and drink judgment against themselves. (30) For this reason many of you are weak and ill, and some have died. (31) But if we judged ourselves, we would not be judged. (32) But when we are judged by the Lord, we are disciplined so that we may not be condemned along with the world. (33) So then, my brothers and sisters, when you come together to eat, wait for one another. (34) If you are hungry, eat at home, so that when you come together, it will not be for your condemnation. About the other things I will give instructions when I come.

JESUS' DEATH ON THE cross is the single, central, paradigmatic, and effective reality for Christians. It turns those who trust in him into new creations who are members of that new reality that is the church or body of Christ. So if we are part of the church, we must live as if we are connected to others in the church—like, if I am an ear that itches, and you are a finger, you scratch me. In other words, the event/celebration of the Lord's Supper is a "put up or shut up" moment.

You (each one of us) need to understand that and participate in the Lord's Supper in positive and knowledgeable ways. Can it be that hard? Discerning the meaning of the Lord's Supper and acting on that discernment is a test case that helps us to be helpful and cooperative with sisters and brothers all the time.

Prayer: Help me to discern the body of Christ. And then behave accordingly! Amen.

51 – Uncommon Good

1 Corinthians 12:1-11 — (1) Now concerning spiritual gifts, brothers and sisters, I do not want you to be uninformed. (2) You know that when you were pagans, you were enticed and led astray to idols that could not speak. (3) Therefore I want you to understand that no one speaking by the Spirit of God ever says "Let Jesus be cursed!" and no one can say "Jesus is Lord" except by the Holy Spirit. (4) Now there are varieties of gifts, but the same Spirit; (5) and there are varieties of services, but the same Lord; (6) and there are varieties of activities, but it is the same God who activates all of them in everyone. (7) To each is given the manifestation of the Spirit for the common good. (8) To one is given through the Spirit the utterance of wisdom, and to another the utterance of knowledge according to the same Spirit, (9) to another faith by the same Spirit, to another gifts of healing by the one Spirit, (10) to another the working of miracles, to another prophecy, to another the discernment of spirits, to another various kinds of tongues, to another the interpretation of tongues. (11) All these are activated by one and the same Spirit, who allots to each one individually just as the Spirit chooses.

YOU ARE A UNIQUE creation necessary to the fulfillment of God's cosmic purpose. You are necessary for the enrichment of others and the completion of the whole of God's work. Unfortunately, the very gifts that make you different and special and interesting can be seen by others as divisive. And that divisiveness can really happen in college. For example, your major differentiates you. So you need to take care not to let the skills you learn create in you a sense of superiority that isolates you from the very people you are preparing to serve. You are to be centered in the Christ who invites diversity but allows no divisiveness.

The poet T. S. Eliot's picture of "the unstilled world [that] still whirled/ About the centre of the silent Word" pictures the world with a center— Christ Jesus, the Word, who alone can hold it all together. At the cross, there is only one world into which we are all called, not on the basis of our own performance but on the basis of Christ. A good task for today might be to identify one way in which your gift(s) contribute to the whole-sum-ness of the church/community and "the common good" of God's new creation.

Prayer: Lord, help me to use my gifts for the common good and let me accept the gifts of others. Amen.

52 – Vive la Différence!

1 Corinthians 12:12-14 — (12) For just as the body is one and has many members, and all the members of the body, though many, are one body, so it is with Christ. (13) For in the one Spirit we were all baptized into one body—Jews or Greeks, slaves or free—and we were all made to drink of one Spirit. (14) Indeed, the body does not consist of one member but of many.

DIVERSITY IS NECESSARY IF the Christian faith is to embrace everyone. God is essentially diverse. Our confession of the Trinity expresses this belief. One of my most satisfactory moments as a college dean was when I could hire new professors who were "different." At one point, we had added teachers who were (respectively) Ugandan, Spanish, Mexican American, and Japanese American—and all of them Christian. This was diversity within a fundamental unity.

We can boast of our ability to "tolerate" others. But toleration implies a sense of superiority on the part of the one being tolerant. Only when there is a basic unifying element can there exist a diversity that can work without tearing apart.

Paul's metaphor of the "body of Christ" to describe the Christian community acknowledges a variety of kinds of differences within the body, where each part is called upon not only to do its part but to have the same care as all of the others for all of the others. Thus the general good is the purpose that each part is to fulfill and in that fulfillment each of us finds our own fulfillment.

Diversity is a fact of college life. If you are a white, male, Christian, American student, every year that you are in college there will be fewer white students, more female students, fewer students with any religion, and more foreign students—a total guarantee of exposure to "difference"! Instead of merely tolerating differences, Scripture calls for hospitality, a virtue that Jesus exhibited all the time. Think about how hospitable Jesus is to welcome you!

Prayer: God, thank you for enabling some of the other members of Christ's body to care for me. Amen.

53 – E Pluribus Unum

1 Corinthians 12:15-26 — (15) If the foot would say, "Because I am not a hand, I do not belong to the body," that would not make it any less a part of the body. (16) And if the ear would say, "Because I am not an eye, I do not belong to the body," that would not make it any less a part of the body. (17) If the whole body were an eye, where would the hearing be? If the whole body were hearing, where would the sense of smell be? (18) But as it is, God arranged the members in the body, each one of them, as he chose. (19) If all were a single member, where would the body be? (20) As it is, there are many members, yet one body. (21) The eye cannot say to the hand, "I have no need of you," nor again the head to the feet, "I have no need of you." (22) On the contrary, the members of the body that seem to be weaker are indispensable, (23) and those members of the body that we think less honorable we clothe with greater honor, and our less respectable members are treated with greater respect; (24) whereas our more respectable members do not need this. But God has so arranged the body, giving the greater honor to the inferior member, (25) that there may be no dissension within the body, but the members may have the same care for one another. (26) If one member suffers, all suffer together with it; if one member is honored, all rejoice together with it.

MY WIFE IS A physical anthropologist who studies skeletons—especially the bones of the hand. She focused her doctoral research on the places on the finger bones where muscles had attached and she found out that those "attachment" locations could tell her a lot about the various actions performed by fingers. So?

The point is that the hand (or ear or eye) is unique, complex, important, and often specially trained. So?

So you will major in a specialty—to prepare for a career, or just because you are interested in it. You will learn skills and new ways of thinking and become a biologist, historian, or architect. On days when studying for your major is a drag, or tiring, or hard, remember your call from God: to love him with all your mind, and to be one helpful and really special part of the "body of Christ."

Prayer: Give me the smarts, discipline, and skills to learn what I need to learn in order to serve others. Amen.

215

54 – Each Has a Job

1 Corinthians 12:27-30 — (27) Now you are the body of Christ and individually members of it. (28) And God has appointed in the church first apostles, second prophets, third teachers; then deeds of power, then gifts of healing, forms of assistance, forms of leadership, various kinds of tongues. (29) Are all apostles? Are all prophets? Are all teachers? Do all work miracles? (30) Do all possess gifts of healing? Do all speak in tongues? Do all interpret?

REMEMBER THAT THE PROBLEM that plagued the Corinthians is the same one that often plagues us—the selfish and sinful uses of our special differences and gifts. Paul has emphasized the unity and harmony that Christ's death on the cross makes possible for Christians. Christ's death on the cross can do that because on the cross there is no place for pride in human achievement. Only now, in the twelfth chapter, does the idea of difference arise. It arises in the context of the "body of Christ"—a metaphor for the church. It is specifically tied to functions that each of us can uniquely contribute to the well-being of all others in the community of believers.

God has appointed, empowered, gifted, and set apart specific persons with the responsibilities for providing specific services to the whole of the rest of the "body." In addition to kings, prophets and the apostles, God has put teachers and even administrators (the Greek means "pilot" or "steersman") as "officers" whose emergence into officials is still governed by the caveats in Ephesians 4:12–13: "to equip the saints for the work of ministry, for building up the body of Christ, until we all attain to the unity of the faith and of the knowledge of the Son of God, to mature manhood, to the measure of the stature of the fullness of Christ" (RSV). And as James 3:1 adds, "we who teach shall be judged with greater strictness." However, it is clear that the "office" is a gift and that it is for the benefit of the whole. Despite the fact that—as a student—you are subservient to those appointed teachers and administrators, there will be a time when you may be appointed to minister to another. That can be a moment of grace for them and fulfillment for you.

Prayer: God, help me to recognize the whole body and to know my place therein. Amen.

55 – Is It Sex or Is It Love?

1 Corinthians 12:31-13:7 — (31) But strive for the greater gifts and I will show you a still more excellent way. (13:1) If I speak in the tongues of mortals and of angels, but do not have love, I am a noisy gong or a clanging cymbal. (2) And if I have prophetic powers, and understand all mysteries and all knowledge, and if I have all faith, so as to remove mountains, but do not have love, I am nothing. (3) If I give away all my possessions, and if I hand over my body so that I may boast, but do not have love, I gain nothing. (4) Love is patient; love is kind; love is not envious or boastful or arrogant (5) or rude. It does not insist on its own way; it is not irritable or resentful; (6) it does not rejoice in wrongdoing, but rejoices in the truth. (7) It bears all things, believes all things, hopes all things, endures all things.

THIS SCRIPTURE PASSAGE IS often read at weddings; that's when two people are convinced that they really love each other and are ready to take the whole deal. Until that point there are a lot of reasons to postpone sex. Assuming that you are wise enough to delay sex until the right time, (marriage being a signal that the time has come), you might ponder the checklist of criteria that can be useful in testing whether you're just messing around sexually or whether the time has come to think about marriage. Here is the list (slightly edited). Check "X" on the items (attitudes, behaviors) that honestly describe your true feelings for the person you think you want to share sex with.

Attitude toward her/him	Never considered it	No	Maybe sometimes
Impatient			
Unkind			
Boastful/arrogant			
Rude			
Insist on my own way			
Irritable/resentful			
Enjoy their mistakes			
Lie			
Suspicious			
Hopeless			
Can't endure			

Prayer: Help me not to cheat on this test. Amen.

56 – Knowledge Has a Limited Shelf Life

I Corinthians 13:8–13 — (8) Love never ends. But as for prophe-
cies, they will come to an end; as for tongues, they will cease; as for
knowledge, it will come to an end. (9) For we know only in part,
and we prophesy only in part; (10) but when the complete comes,
the partial will come to an end. (11) When I was a child, I spoke
like a child, I thought like a child, I reasoned like a child; when
I became an adult, I put an end to childish ways. (12) For now
we see in a mirror, dimly, but then we will see face to face. Now I
know only in part; then I will know fully, even as I have been fully
known. (13) And now faith, hope, and love abide, these three; and
the greatest of these is love.

"Knowledge . . . will come to an end"! This is a claim that should really bother a college student. You work to get knowledge and then what? But you know that the claim is at least partially true. You are a recipient of what Ernest Boyer called the "scholarship of teaching" as teachers pass knowledge and the excitement of discovery on to students. How could that knowledge pass away? As you look back over history there appear many instances of "knowledge" that is no longer true: the earth is flat; lead can change to gold; personality types are recognizable by analyzing bumps on the head; the list is long—and ludicrous. You might well wonder what piece of inherited wisdom that you learned in class today will be abandoned next.

But usually we hope that real knowledge is accumulating and that finally, somehow it will all become ours—a kind of super calculus that will explain all things. Or like the physicists are working on—a single hypothesis that can explain everything that there is. Then, when we will have figured everything out, we will—as the mathematician-physicist Stephen Hawking said—"know the mind of God."

Paul has another idea; knowledge will not ultimately be a factor. What is really important from all we know of religion and science is love and it is "the greatest of these." The usefulness and permanence of love qualifies all else as penultimate at best. Today, to whom can you offer "the greatest of these" and in what form will you deliver it?

Prayer: Thank you for your love that makes all it touches worth-
while. Amen.

57 – The Gift of Gab

I Corinthians 14:1–8 — (1) Pursue love and strive for the spiritual gifts, and especially that you may prophesy. (2) For those who speak in a tongue do not speak to other people but to God; for nobody understands them, since they are speaking mysteries in the Spirit. (3) On the other hand, those who prophesy speak to other people for their upbuilding and encouragement and consolation. (4) Those who speak in a tongue build up themselves, but those who prophesy build up the church. (5) Now I would like all of you to speak in tongues, but even more to prophesy. One who prophesies is greater than one who speaks in tongues, unless someone interprets, so that the church may be built up. (6) Now, brothers and sisters, if I come to you speaking in tongues, how will I benefit you unless I speak to you in some revelation or knowledge or prophecy or teaching? (7) It is the same way with lifeless instruments that produce sound, such as the flute or the harp. If they do not give distinct notes, how will anyone know what is being played? (8) And if the bugle gives an indistinct sound, who will get ready for battle?

"TONGUES," "SPEAKING IN TONGUES," or "glossolalia,"—that's one kind of "speech" that may be spiritual, but it usually makes no sense to anyone but the speaker and God.

"Prophecy," on the other hand, is clear speech . . . but be careful. The nature and purpose of prophecy is not to predict a presumably preprogrammed event, but to speak for—or on behalf of—God. And since God is a God of love, prophecy is to speak lovingly to others with the aim of helping them by means of "upbuilding and encouragement and consolation."

How often have your words—often brilliant, precise, decisive—not been helpful to others? The Corinthians had played with words; they were talented in speech (1:5). The thrust of the Roman and Greek worlds' version of college in Jesus' day was directed toward equipping students with the power of words; rhetoric was the subject of higher education, eloquence and persuasiveness its goal. What students wanted was to learn how to win arguments and thereby to control others and advance themselves. "Tongues" was show-off talk; prophecy was help-the-other-person talk. Like your mom said, "Watch your language!"

Prayer: Jesus, Word of God, help me do what my mother kept telling me to do. Amen.

58 – Start with English

1 Corinthians 14:9–12 — (9) So with yourselves; if in a tongue you utter speech that is not intelligible, how will anyone know what is being said? For you will be speaking into the air. (10) There are doubtless many different kinds of sounds in the world, and nothing is without sound. (11) If then I do not know the meaning of a sound, I will be a foreigner to the speaker and the speaker a foreigner to me. (12) So with yourselves; since you are eager for spiritual gifts, strive to excel in them for building up the church.

"WHY DO I HAVE to take this lousy class?"

Did you ever say that?

Let's move on. Let's change your question to, "Why do I need to take this lousy class?" (Notice the change of "have to" to "need to"? We're overlooking the word "lousy" since that isn't really germane to your question.) You are wondering what the college's motive is in requiring you to take a certain class. What does the college want you to learn in that class? The question is getting better. The quick answer from the college is that you need more basic skills (English, math), or more breadth in your outlook (a class in general education), that it's required in your major (like, you have to know organic chemistry to be a chemistry major).

What about asking your question from a Christian faith point of view? Remember how Jesus said to love God with all your mind (Matt 22:37)? Why might Jesus want you to take that class? If Jesus is indeed at the center of all of creation as you read back in Colossians, learning whatever you might learn in that class would enhance your understanding of the universe that was created "in," "through," and "for" him (Col 1:15–20).

Jesus should be considered as the one behind language, history, physics, every one of the general education classes or classes in your major that teaches you about . . . about . . . whatever it is that the college is having you study.

As a Christian, believing in God who created all there is and in Jesus who holds everything there is together and makes sense of it (Col 1:17), wouldn't you have more reason to learn more about all that stuff than any other student would? Now the question is: "Why am I sitting here arguing instead of focusing on God and studying for that lousy class?"

Prayer: Let me try to get "into you" more than I try to get out of any class. Amen.

59 – Clear Explanations

1 Corinthians 14:13-19 — (13) Therefore, one who speaks in a tongue should pray for the power to interpret. (14) For if I pray in a tongue, my spirit prays but my mind is unproductive. (15) What should I do then? I will pray with the spirit, but I will pray with the mind also; I will sing praise with the spirit, but I will sing praise with the mind also. (16) Otherwise, if you say a blessing with the spirit, how can anyone in the position of an outsider say the "Amen" to your thanksgiving, since the outsider does not know what you are saying? (17) For you may give thanks well enough, but the other person is not built up. (18) I thank God that I speak in tongues more than all of you; (19) nevertheless, in church I would rather speak five words with my mind, in order to instruct others also, than ten thousand words in a tongue.

HAVE YOU SEEN THIS bumper sticker? I saw it recently in a college parking area. It reads: "They can send me to the university but they can't make me think." In this passage, Paul really pushes the envelope: in addition to thinking about your studies, he says to "pray with the mind" and to "sing praise with the mind." Doing all of his "religious" activities with the mind is Paul's preferred mode of action. What gives?

Maybe you have filed "speaking in tongues," "prayer," "hymns," and other Christian expressions under "Emotional Stuff." But the fact is that you are called to be an "academic Christian," one who is skilled in thinking things through in disciplined ways and explaining things to others.

Prayer need not exclude your mind. You shouldn't be "out of your mind" in order to pray or while you pray. Sometimes praying may require thoughtful, mindful engagement. Not that God needs to have things explained to him like he was a freshman. But praying with your mind may help you—the pray-er—gain clarity with regard to what you are asking, saying, praising, or complaining about. And don't ever think that your mind is so pure and esoteric that it doesn't need to be hauled in before God for a regular tune-up.

Like an athlete requires practice, your mind does too. Thinking on the things of your relationship with God is never wasted exercise.

Prayer: Help me to keep thinking more and more clearly about the most important things. Amen.

60 – Grow Up!

1 Corinthians 14:20–25 — (20) Brothers and sisters, do not be children in your thinking; rather, be infants in evil, but in thinking be adults. (21) In the law it is written, "By people of strange tongues and by the lips of foreigners I will speak to this people; yet even then they will not listen to me," says the Lord. (22) Tongues, then, are a sign not for believers but for unbelievers, while prophecy is not for unbelievers but for believers. (23) If, therefore, the whole church comes together and all speak in tongues, and outsiders or unbelievers enter, will they not say that you are out of your mind? (24) But if all prophesy, an unbeliever or outsider who enters is reproved by all and called to account by all. (25) After the secrets of the unbeliever's heart are disclosed, that person will bow down before God and worship him, declaring, "God is really among you."

PAUL IS CONCERNED THAT our Christian faith be intelligible to those within the church for their up-building. Once, in a faculty-wide discussion at our church-related college, a frustrated colleague pleaded, "It would really help if we could quit using the term 'Christian' as a description for what we are trying to do." I knew the experience that she and some others had had—the experience that produced her dis-ease with the project under discussion.

As teenagers, they had been "turned off" by unpleasant experiences in their respective home churches. Those experiences had stunted their Christian growth and in some cases had terminated their Christian faith. Now, their understanding of the faith was one based on their experience as children when they had had the misfortune to have suffered admittedly negative experiences in a particularly narrow Christian community.

They had gone on to grow intellectually and to become college professors. But in their Christian intellects, they were still children, knowing little of the faith either experientially or as a resource for their work with students.

Where are you in your growth as a Christian? No matter your maturity level, today is a good day to mature some more. And if you encounter anyone who demeans your faith, you can be patient with them because their views may not be very mature. Yet your patience with them could be just what they need.

Prayer: Help me every day to mature and speak helpfully to others. Amen.

61 – The Purpose-Driven Meeting

1 Corinthians 14:26-33a — (26) What should be done then, my friends? When you come together, each one has a hymn, a lesson, a revelation, a tongue, or an interpretation. Let all things be done for building up. (27) If anyone speaks in a tongue, let there be only two or at most three, and each in turn; and let one interpret. (28) But if there is no one to interpret, let them be silent in church and speak to themselves and to God. (29) Let two or three prophets speak, and let the others weigh what is said. (30) If a revelation is made to someone else sitting nearby, let the first person be silent. (31) For you can all prophesy one by one, so that all may learn and all be encouraged. (32) And the spirits of prophets are subject to the prophets, (33) for God is a God not of disorder but of peace.

THE REASON FOR YOUR most frequent gatherings as a student is to go to class; there you can learn and tell others—particularly the instructor—what you know. Other popular gatherings are for games (the agony of defeat, the ecstasy of victory) and the big one—commencement.

How often has a gathering of Christians resulted in . . . nothing? Often that is because there is nothing there—no joy, no sadness, no idea, no challenge, no purpose, no plan, and not even a serious question or problem—nothing! Just people gathering because it is routine, or because they feel obligated to be there.

Paul's suggestion for any Christian gathering—Bible study, worship, planning an activity—is that they are to be characterized by a purpose—to share love and edification: "a hymn, a lesson, a revelation, a tongue, or an interpretation." You personally ought to be able to see each "coming together" as an opportunity to be helpful in an informative way.

Coming together has various reasons. But no matter the occasion, you should be able to bring a well prepared "lesson" that can contribute positively to those present and to the task or focus of the meeting. As you look ahead to the gatherings of this day, think of the possible contribution you might make in a class, a social setting, at your job, or in the cafeteria. You have plenty to contribute—if it is only attentive silence or a good question.

Prayer: May my presence always be aimed at there being an edifying lesson. Amen.

62 – Giving and Taking Offense

1 Corinthians 14:33b–40 — (33b) (As in all the churches of the saints, (34) women should be silent in the churches. For they are not permitted to speak, but should be subordinate, as the law also says. (35) If there is anything they desire to know, let them ask their husbands at home. For it is shameful for a woman to speak in church. (36) Or did the word of God originate with you? Or are you the only ones it has reached?) (37) Anyone who claims to be a prophet, or to have spiritual powers, must acknowledge that what I am writing to you is a command of the Lord. (38) Anyone who does not recognize this is not to be recognized. (39) So, my friends, be eager to prophesy, and do not forbid speaking in tongues; (40) but all things should be done decently and in order.

THIS CHAPTER SEEMS TO focus on specific instructions to women—instructions that have caused no little tension within the Christian community, especially lately: Paul tells the Corinthians that women should keep silent in church. Paul's comments about women's behavior have kept many from taking Paul, 1 Corinthians, or even Christianity seriously.

Some people today use this as one of the scriptural supports for putting church and family leadership exclusively in the hands of men. Others ask, "If Jesus Christ is Lord, when did we ever hear him tell women to be quiet in church?" (Answer: Never.) One way to read this is to point out that Paul was asking the church to act like other groups in the culture of that day so non-Christians would not be put off by the freedom women exercised in the Christian fellowship.

We have moved on from Paul's idea of how Christian sisters should act. We know now that even Paul did not fully grasp the idea of Christian freedom in practice even though he did seen to have it in theory (Gal 3:28!). Will this be an occasion for some to discount Paul and the good stuff he teaches? The good order of the group was collapsing, and the goal of mutual up-building threatened, and a positive impact on the surrounding community was jeopardized. You must read and interpret with Jesus at the center, not Paul. Your opportunity today is to prophesy, speaking God's message to those who need to hear it. In the case of 1 Corinthians, the main point has to do with bringing us all together in Christ.

Prayer: God of peace, not confusion: replace my socially invented confusions with the peace of Christ. Amen.

63 – I'm a Witness Too

1 Corinthians 15:1-11 — (1) Now I would remind you, brothers and sisters, of the good news that I proclaimed to you, which you in turn received, in which also you stand, (2) through which also you are being saved, if you hold firmly to the message that I proclaimed to you—unless you have come to believe in vain. (3) For I handed on to you as of first importance what I in turn had received: that Christ died for our sins in accordance with the scriptures, (4) and that he was buried, and that he was raised on the third day in accordance with the scriptures, (5) and that he appeared to Cephas, then to the twelve. (6) Then he appeared to more than five hundred brothers and sisters at one time, most of whom are still alive, though some have died. (7) Then he appeared to James, then to all the apostles. (8) Last of all, as to one untimely born, he appeared also to me. (9) For I am the least of the apostles, unfit to be called an apostle, because I persecuted the church of God. (10) But by the grace of God I am what I am, and his grace toward me has not been in vain. On the contrary, I worked harder than any of them—though it was not I, but the grace of God that is with me. (11) Whether then it was I or they, so we proclaim and so you have come to believe.

AFTER AN HOUR OF lecture it is a good idea for the teacher to recap the main ideas; so with Paul and the Corinthians. After fourteen chapters of detailing their mishandlings of the new life in Christ, Paul summarizes the essentials of the gospel: the new life offered in Jesus Christ's person and action, his death and resurrection. This is not about emulating the behaviors or embodying the ideals of Jesus but about what Jesus already did that changes us. Paul describes himself as the "last . . . least . . . unfit" person imaginable. But transformed by the grace of Christ, Paul was made a part of the people of God and was incorporated into a new narrative.

Then there is a list of witnesses—recipients of this good news. Consider how you—a "theological academic" with a vocation as a college student—might live as the latest in a long line of witnesses. People will ask, as they do for any big event such as Jesus' birth, life, ministry, death and resurrection, "What happened?" What is your answer?

Prayer: Clear my mind and my vision so that I can see the main point: Christ is our salvation. Amen.

64 – Death Stalks the Campus

1 Corinthians 15:12–19 — (12) Now if Christ is proclaimed as raised from the dead, how can some of you say there is no resurrection of the dead? (13) If there is no resurrection of the dead, then Christ has not been raised; (14) and if Christ has not been raised, then our proclamation has been in vain and your faith has been in vain. (15) We are even found to be misrepresenting God, because we testified of God that he raised Christ—whom he did not raise if it is true that the dead are not raised. (16) For if the dead are not raised, then Christ has not been raised. (17) If Christ has not been raised, your faith is futile and you are still in your sins. (18) Then those also who have died in Christ have perished. (19) If for this life only we have hoped in Christ we are of all people most to be pitied.

IT WAS A TRAGEDY when the president of the junior class and 4.0 student died of an alcohol overdose. Her death was mentioned in an earlier meditation (1:18-24, #5); you don't forget that kind of thing.

Denise Carmody (in *Organizing a Christian Mind*) wrote that a truly Christian education would be done in the shadow of death. She wrote, "In any responsible Christian theology of education, the first thing to mark about all the people involved . . . is their mortality, while the second is the presence of God at their end."

The general affirmation of the resurrection is something Christians confess, but when it comes right down to dealing with the possibility of a post-mortem resuscitation of a dead and lifeless corpse then it becomes more difficult to affirm. There can be no general resurrection, no spectacular rearrangement of reality, if there is no specific, concrete, individual resurrection of a particular person.

Jesus was the case in point. If his resurrection cannot be accepted, you can forget any general resurrection and hope of reversal or newness that might follow from it. If Jesus was resurrected, then anything is possible and everything changes. Jesus' resurrection was an unanticipated instance of the hope of resurrection. Your professors may teach you in "the shadow of death," but you need not fear being there as you study because of the assurance that Jesus' resurrection brings.

Prayer: Help me to think of death always in the shadow of Jesus' cross and resurrection. Amen.

65 – Game Changer

1 Corinthians 15:20-34 — (20) But in fact Christ has been raised from the dead, the first fruits of those who have died. (21) For since death came through a human being, the resurrection of the dead has also come through a human being; (22) for as all die in Adam, so all will be made alive in Christ. (23) But each in his own order: Christ the first fruits, then at his coming those who belong to Christ. (24) Then comes the end, when he hands over the kingdom to God the Father, after he has destroyed every ruler and every authority and power. (25) For he must reign until he has put all his enemies under his feet. (26) The last enemy to be destroyed is death. (27) For "God has put all things in subjection under his feet." But when it says, "All things are put in subjection," it is plain that this does not include the one who put all things in subjection under him. (28) When all things are subjected to him, then the Son himself will also be subjected to the one who put all things in subjection under him, so that God may be all in all. (29) Otherwise, what will those people do who receive baptism on behalf of the dead? If the dead are not raised at all, why are people baptized on their behalf? (30) And why are we putting ourselves in danger every hour? (31) I die every day! That is as certain, brothers and sisters, as my boasting of you—a boast that I make in Christ Jesus our Lord. (32) If with merely human hopes I fought with wild animals at Ephesus, what would I have gained by it? If the dead are not raised, "Let us eat and drink, for tomorrow we die." (33) Do not be deceived: "Bad company ruins good morals." (34) Come to a sober and right mind, and sin no more; for some people have no knowledge of God. I say this to your shame.

PAUL CALLS FOR YOU to put complete faith in God and in his bringing Jesus Christ through death and into resurrected life. That is the difference-maker for us Christians. So we don't have to trust ourselves so much. In fact, we would be downright stupid to trust in ourselves as much as we often like to do. This faith stuff isn't about our ability to be right about things; it is about God's ability to be God, do God's stuff, and to let God be God, without our having to understand, defend, and make a good argument for whatever God does. God doesn't depend on us; we depend on him.

Prayer: Lord, stiffen my resolve to believe in and live for the truth of Jesus' resurrection. Amen.

66 – Show Me How

1 Corinthians 15:35–36 — (35) But someone will ask, "How are the dead raised? With what kind of body do they come?" (36) Fool! What you sow does not come to life unless it dies.

WRONG QUESTION! DON'T GET hung up on stuff that's not important. The "someone" who wanted to know "how" the dead rise is sure to be an American. We are keen on knowing how things work. Men discuss motors, guns, and golf; women discuss recipes, clothing, and hairstyles; students discuss . . . well, you know the kinds of things they discuss—like "Will it be on the test?"

Someone in Corinth must have asked about the mechanics of resurrection. This question has intrigued a number of moderns who have attempted to apply the concepts of physics, chemistry, or psychology to Jesus' resurrection in order to, what, make it more plausible? And if it's plausible, then what? To believe in Jesus Christ or in his resurrection on the grounds that something else proves it is to believe that that "something else" is more important than Jesus' resurrection.

Paul's non-answer—which is a metaphor about seeds—is not an explanation. It is an "answer" that neither proves nor explains anything. Paul's goal was not to explain but rather to point to meanings. The questioner is foolish because it isn't the right question. We want to lay things before the judgment seat of our own intellect and find final proofs that satisfy us rather than to put our intellects into the service of God. Instead of explaining the process, Paul emphasizes that the dead are dead. And then they are alive. There is no "how"; there is only God. It might be pretty revolutionary and educational to ask some of the really hard questions in class today.

Prayer: God, help me to ask questions that will find their answers in you. Amen.

67 – Just Chill Out

1 Corinthians 15:37–50 — (37) And as for what you sow, you do not sow the body that is to be, but a bare seed, perhaps of wheat or of some other grain. (38) But God gives it a body as he has chosen, and to each kind of seed its own body. (39) Not all flesh is alike, but there is one flesh for human beings, another for animals, another for birds, and another for fish. (40) There are both heavenly bodies and earthly bodies, but the glory of the heavenly is one thing, and that of the earthly is another. (41) There is one glory of the sun, and another glory of the moon, and another glory of the stars; indeed, star differs from star in glory. (42) So it is with the resurrection of the dead. What is sown is perishable, what is raised is imperishable. (43) It is sown in dishonor, it is raise in glory. It is sown in weakness, it is raised in power. (44) It is sown a physical body, it is raised a spiritual body. If there is a physical body, there is also a spiritual body. (45) Thus it is written, "The first man, Adam, became a living being"; the last Adam became a life-giving spirit. (46) But it is not the spiritual that is first, but the physical, and then the spiritual. (47) The first man was from the earth, a man of dust; the second man is from heaven. (48) As was the man of dust, so are those who are of the dust; and as is the man of heaven, so are those who are of heaven. (49) Just as we have borne the image of the man of dust, we will also bear the image of the man of heaven. (50) What I am saying, brothers and sisters, is this: flesh and blood cannot inherit the kingdom of God, nor does the perishable inherit the imperishable.

WE NEEDN'T TARRY OVER the question of how people are raised from the dead. The important questions have to do with how you face dying and whether you trust God to take care of you as you do face it.

Can't we just leave some mysteries alone? Or, better said, can't we leave them in the hands of the one who is totally in charge of all the things that we can't be in charge of?

Prayer: Lord, let me quietly trust in you for all those things I don't understand and can't control. Amen.

68 – The Real Story: A Mystery

1 Corinthians 15:51–58 — (51) Listen, I will tell you a mystery! We will not all die, but we will all be changed, (52) in a moment, in the twinkling of an eye, at the last trumpet. For the trumpet will sound, and the dead will be raised imperishable, and we will be changed. (53) For this perishable body must put on imperishability, and this mortal body must put on immortality. (54) When this perishable body puts on imperishability, and this mortal body puts on immortality, then the saying that is written will be fulfilled: "Death has been swallowed up in victory." (55) "Where, O death, is your victory? Where, O death, is your sting?" (56) The sting of death is sin, and the power of sin is the law. (57) But thanks be to God, who gives us the victory through our Lord Jesus Christ. (58) Therefore, my beloved, be steadfast, immovable, always excelling in the work of the Lord, because you know that in the Lord your labor is not in vain.

IN THE GOSPEL ACCOUNTS, when Jesus encouraged people not to fear he seemed to be saying that fear was the opposite of belief. If fear and belief are opposites then believers need not fear. The fear we typically associate with dying has been dealt with. We may fear to die for many reasons—it will hurt, it terminates all the good things that life brings us, it seems to be a moment of final judgment.

On that last item—judgment—we know that we aren't good enough to pass muster on any kind of divine judgment. When God checks us out on our life's performance, we all have reason to be apprehensive. Even though you might have been to a few funerals where the deceased seems to have been given a "pass" on the bad stuff they did (or the good stuff they failed to do) you are right to be suspicious of that culturally comfortable funeral practice of getting everyone through the pearly gates and into a good time doing everything they liked to do when still alive.

But Jesus has done his work as God's anointed and provided acceptance and forgiveness for those who give up on trying to gain God's favor by their performance and piety. Maybe the real mystery is why so many folks don't just trust in the mercy of the God who raised Jesus from the dead.

Prayer: Thank you God for swallowing up death with your eternal promise of care. Amen.

69 – Time for Others

1 Corinthians 16:1–14 — (1) Now concerning the collection for the saints: you should follow the directions I gave to the churches of Galatia. (2) On the first day of every week, each of you is to put aside and save whatever extra you earn, so that collections need not be taken when I come. (3) And when I arrive, I will send any whom you approve with letters to take your gift to Jerusalem. (4) If it seems advisable that I should go also, they will accompany me. (5) I will visit you after passing through Macedonia—for I intend to pass through Macedonia—(6) and perhaps I will stay with you or even spend the winter, so that you may send me on my way, wherever I go. (7) I do not want to see you now just in passing, for I hope to spend some time with you, if the Lord permits. (8) But I will stay in Ephesus until Pentecost, (9) for a wide door for effective work has opened to me, and there are many adversaries. (10) If Timothy comes, see that he has nothing to fear among you, for he is doing the work of the Lord just as I am; (11) therefore let no one despise him. Send him on his way in peace, so that he may come to me; for I am expecting him with the brothers. (12) Now concerning our brother Apollos, I strongly urged him to visit you with the other brothers, but he was not at all willing to come now. He will come when he has the opportunity. (13) Keep alert, stand firm in your faith, be courageous, be strong. (14) Let all that you do be done in love.

I LOVED BEING A college teacher—except for the low pay. To support our family of six, I worked weekends as pastor of a small church. You'd think I would have had money on my mind, but I remember well the Sunday I forgot to take the offering; the church treasurer, however, didn't forget and gently chided me after the service.

Despite how distressed Paul has obviously been with the Corinthian church, he did not forget the collection. Here is an example of one faithful person micromanaging several groups of fellow believers, and arranging for gifts to be raised in one place for use by those in another. And get this: the money was being raised in Europe (Corinth, Greece) for churches in Asia (Galatia, in what is today Turkey). Paul definitely had the big picture of the church in mind.

Prayer: Lord, help me organize my thoughts so that there is plenty of room for others in need. Amen.

70 – Time for Friends

1 Corinthians 16:15–24 — (15) Now, brothers and sisters, you know that members of the household of Stephanas were the first converts in Achaia, and they have devoted themselves to the service of the saints; (16) I urge you to put yourselves at the service of such people, and of everyone who works and toils with them. (17) I rejoice at the coming of Stephanas and Fortunatus and Achaicus, because they have made up for your absence; (18) for they refreshed my spirit as well as yours. So give recognition to such persons. (19) The churches of Asia send greetings. Aquila and Prisca, together with the church in their house, greet you warmly in the Lord. (20) All the brothers and sisters send greetings. Greet one another with a holy kiss. (21) I, Paul, write this greeting with my own hand. (22) Let anyone be accursed who has no love for the Lord. Our Lord, come! (23) The grace of the Lord Jesus be with you. (24) My love be with all of you in Christ Jesus.

WE SELDOM SEE TIME as a gift of the Spirit. Paul was busy, founding churches in the face of both Roman and Jewish hostility, keeping in touch with them by mail and personal contacts, macro- and micromanaging a growing constituency of communities around the Mediterranean coast while he supported himself with his own labor. The intensity of Paul's letters, as he attempts to solve large issues in the lives of Christians, suggests an intense individual with no time for the personal and private things in life. Yet his letters betray the existence of an international, cross-cultural and cosmopolitan network of friends whom he enjoyed. Here he reveals concerns tailored to some of those individuals.

How is your personal time used with those entrusted to you: fellow students, roommates, family members, even teachers? Your time and energies are often under such stress and demand that it is easy to overlook the needs of those in your presence. But like the Jesus who suffered (enjoyed?) constant interruptions to his own ministry, Paul constantly brought the needs of individuals to the fore. Are you honored or only annoyed when someone comes to you with a problem? Regardless of your other gifts or abilities, time is something equally given to all and most needed by others. Time is a gift you can try (unsuccessfully) to hoard or share. What would be the most useful way to spend today's gift?

Prayer: Lord Jesus, make me a patient instruments of your love. Amen.

First Peter

Following Jesus into the World

FIRST PETER SEEMS THE perfect letter to anticipate that time when college draws to a close and you face what some people insist is "the real world." It offers hope in Christ as the basis for maintaining and strengthening your faith in the face of a world that can be actively antagonistic. To the extent that the hostility described in the letter comes from social, rather than legal, sources, today's college student is in a situation similar to that of the first recipients of this letter: their faith wasn't illegal; but it was not received well by people among whom they lived—thus the opening greeting "to the exiles of the dispersion."

Because this letter understands Christian discipleship to involve suffering, it may be difficult to wrap your head around that view of the faith. If so, why not just let the suffering and resurrected Jesus Peter writes about wrap his outstretched—on the cross—arms about you with his full gospel message of comfort and assurance.

The letter describes the sustaining power of Jesus in his obedience, suffering, and resurrection. The author recalls that Jesus obeyed the rules and was obedient to the world's powers but nonetheless was tragically mistreated by them. In the Gospel of Matthew, Jesus had described himself as a "stranger" and "in prison" (Matt 25:35–36, 43) and as having "nowhere to lay his head" (Matt 8:20). Peter warns that his readers will encounter the same challenges, knowing that regardless of their good performance (by worldly standards) they may well suffer because of their Christian faith.

In the course of this year, you have moved from a focus on the teachings of Jesus (in Matthew's gospel) to the example of the submissive and obedient Jesus (in 1 Peter). You have moved from discussions about life within the Christian community (self-important and divisive in Corinth, but eager and intellectual in Colossae) to the more personally and communally dangerous life lived on the border between "the world" and the community of Christians described in 1 Peter.

Enjoy the rest of your college experience, confident in the hope and faith that Jesus is sufficient for all of your needs.

1 – Here's a Letter from . . .

1 Peter 1:1 — (1) Peter, an apostle of Jesus Christ, To the exiles of the Dispersion in Pontus, Galatia, Cappadocia, Asia, and Bithynia, . . .

PETER IS PRETTY FAMOUS. He is the most famous of the twelve disciples. He is portrayed in Scripture as their leader. He is famous for walking toward Jesus on water . . . and then sinking when he takes his eyes off of Jesus (Matt 14:28–33). He is famous for wanting to perpetuate that "mountaintop experience" of the transfiguration by building tents for Jesus and Moses and Elijah and wanting to just hang out up there and forget about the problems of the world (Matt 17:1–8). He is famous for telling Jesus that talk about being crucified should be "stuffed" and that Jesus should come up with a better plan (Matt 16:22). He is famous for denying Jesus three times (Matt 26:69–75). The more we hear about this impetuous fisherman who followed Jesus in order to be a fisher of men the more we might be tempted to say, "Famous? Maybe infamous is more like it."

In writing his letter, the author demurs to claim any of these once or future moments of "fame" as the basis of his identity: instead he chooses a much more humble label—"apostle." An apostle is not a title indicating individual importance; rather it is one revealing his relationship to someone more important—the one who has engaged or chosen him to carry a message. In this case, it is Jesus Christ who has selected Peter to be his messenger. We can expect to find a message from Jesus Christ in the letter that follows. Being an "apostle" is important.

You have been baptized—died to sin, raised a new being in Christ—and now you live a new life. Your identity is now based in Jesus. But it's not always easy to keep that new identity from eroding under all sorts of pressures from the surrounding culture.

College can erode. There are temptations that you be like others in one way or another. But it can also be a place to work at exploring, expanding, and securing your identity as a Christ-follower. What might you learn today that can help you in that journey?

Prayer: Help me to "know myself" more clearly as Christ's own beloved. Amen.

2 – Feeling like an Outsider

*1 Peter 1:2a — (2a) . . . who have been chosen and destined by
God the Father and sanctified by the Spirit . . .*

STILL ON THE TOPIC of identity, Peter characterizes his intended readers
in terms of "bad news" and "good news." The bad news is first: the recipients of this letter live in what today is central Turkey; they are "exiles of the
Dispersion." This is a double whammy. By this time in history—about 60 or
70 CE—the Jews had long been "dispersed" or scattered around the known
world. They had been persecuted, cast out of the land given them by God,
and perhaps half of all Jews had lived "dispersed" around the Mediterranean
world for several hundred years.

Many of those Jews had accepted Jesus as the long hoped-for Messiah
foretold in Scripture. So as Christians, those Jews-become-Christians were
a second kind of "exiles" because they were not accepted by the already-
dispersed Jews. Nor could they be fully accepted by the dominant political
system of that day: the Roman government. That government looked with
suspicion and distaste on both Jews and Christians. So the "outsider" feeling these Christians live with has elements of religious exclusion, political
suspicion, and cultural alienation.

But the double whammy of exile/dispersion is trumped by the triple
good news that they are "chosen and destined . . . and sanctified" by God
and the Holy Spirit.

The bad news is a result of the way other people have behaved, believed, and responded. Can you live with that?

The good news is a result of God's decision and action in Jesus Christ.

You may already know how it is to feel "dispersed"—from family and
old friends. You may even feel in "exile"—at school, in the dorm, in certain
classes. The thing is to remember that you are "chosen . . . and destined by
God . . . and sanctified by the Spirit."

*Prayer: Help me to understand that I am never separated from
you. Amen.*

3 – Vocation

1 Peter 1:2b — (2b) . . . to be obedient to Jesus Christ and to be sprinkled with his blood: may grace and peace be yours in abundance.

WE ARE TAKING OUR time getting into this last of our four New Testament texts because this may be the hardest one to deal with. In the first meditation, you thought about your identity (as an "exile"); in the second meditation, you thought about your "location" (exiled in the dispersion and not among friends, but cared for by God). Now you are reminded of your purpose: "to be obedient to Jesus Christ and to be sprinkled with his blood." The key words: obedience and sprinkling.

Sprinkling? Sprinkling with blood? Does not sound good.

No, it doesn't. This is the hard part. It has to do with the suffering (and bleeding and dying) of Jesus. This was a central feature of Jesus' ministry and Peter lets you know that being a Christian, one obedient to Jesus (a Jesus-follower), does not necessarily mean it will be a breeze; instead, it probably means things can be hard.

You are chosen by God for obedience to Jesus. College is a time for exercising your freedom—in a smart, responsible way, of course—to grow and mature intellectually, socially, and as a Christian. One indispensable aspect of that growth has to be obedience. Obedience to the rules of the college is necessary to continue as a member of the college community. Obedience to your professors is necessary if you are to learn and pass your classes, meet the requirements of your major, and receive that degree that certifies you as Bachelor of Arts in music or a Bachelor of Science in chemistry or whatever your major leads you to become.

But—and this is the corollary to Christian obedience—the sufferings of Christ were a result of his doing what God chose him for and chose him to be. You as a disciple of Christ are not guaranteed a free ride on the sufferings of Christ but rather the opportunity to be a disciple of Christ. The theme of this letter—for good or for ill—is that your Christian commitment is to emulate and obey Jesus Christ. And suffering may be included.

Just like college where what you experience as a student gets harder as you mature, being a disciple can get harder as that commitment deepens and matures. And you can do it because God has "chosen . . . destined . . . and sanctified" you.

Prayer: Let me hear your call, O Lord, above the voices that would mislead me. Amen.

4 – Do-Overs Guaranteed

1 Peter 1:3–5 — (3) Blessed be the God and Father of our Lord Jesus Christ! By his great mercy he has given us a new birth into a living hope through the resurrection of Jesus Christ from the dead, (4) and into an inheritance that is imperishable, undefiled, and unfading, kept in heaven for you, (5) who are being protected by the power of God through faith for a salvation ready to be revealed in the last time.

INSTEAD OF BEGINNING WITH a list of "to do's," this letter starts out with comfort and guarantees. Often you are told that you will have to earn your way through life and into God's good graces. In this letter, to encourage Christians in their confrontation with a world that executed Jesus and may irrationally punish them (5:12), the opening focus is on God's gifts of hope and a secure inheritance—all of which is guaranteed in Jesus Christ.

Sometimes college is actually more like the grace of God than you might think. How many times have you blown it in college? A missed answer on a quiz? A blind date gone wrong? A lab assignment you forgot to submit? A falling out with a roommate? An F on a course? Even changing your major?

In some ways, each of these events—and you can probably add your own mistakes to the list—could have been a major error with expensive (in time, money, emotion) consequences. For example, what if you came to college bent on a career as, say, an X. What if you were to speed through college with no mistakes and no deviations, wind up with a job offer across the country working as an X, and then you hated it! What then? None of the alternatives would be good: you could stick with it (unhappy) or quit and leave (expensive).

But college gives you the chance to see if you really want to be an X, or if perhaps Y or Z is more to your liking. Discovering mistakes in college is not as costly as it could be later on. Think of it in terms of taking chances—on classes, professors, friends, new experiences. College—like God—gives you and everyone else opportunities for a "new birth." Think of these gifts that both God and college make available. Think of the great things that can happen to you if you take advantage of them. Here in school, it's no big deal if some of the risks you take fail; and if you succeed, possibilities are there that you can't imagine.

Prayer: Thank you for second chances guaranteed in the resurrection of Jesus. Amen.

5 – No Pain, No Gain

1 Peter 1:6–9 — (6) In this you rejoice, even if now for a little while you have had to suffer various trials, (7) so that the genuineness of your faith—being more precious than gold that, though perishable, is tested by fire—may be found to result in praise and glory and honor when Jesus Christ is revealed. (8) Although you have not seen him, you love him; and even though you do not see him now, you believe in him and rejoice with an indescribable and glorious joy, (9) for you are receiving the outcome of your faith, the salvation of your souls.

DO YOU REMEMBER *SESAME* Street, and how we were taught about near and far? One of the characters would run up close to the camera and shout, "Near!"; then run away, stop, and shout back, "Far!" In this letter, the author makes it clear that there is a now and a then. "Now" is a hard time, characterized by "various trials" and "testing." "When Jesus will be revealed" is a "then" of rejoicing and receiving all the good things God has in store for you. A central theme of this letter is that "now" is not fun, and it is important for you to understand that, why it is the case, and how it can be handled.

In American culture, Christianity is often seen as identical with popular culture so that being a Christian looks pretty easy. In fact, often it is seen as a pathway to social acceptance and overall success. American flags fly in virtually every church. Anyone who dies can be given a church funeral that features public assurances of heavenly bliss for the departed. "Christian" jewelry (crosses especially) and clothing (tee shirts) are popular and commonly worn. The message seems to be that while Christ may have suffered, that suffering was so that you should not need to suffer, but have smooth sailing forevermore.

Peter gives a message that is utterly countercultural. Instead of feeling cozy and comfy in your faith, he promises trials and problems; instead of griping with you about the problems you face, he encourages you to rejoice. He is totally out of tune with twenty-first-century America. And there are good reasons for that, which he wants to share with you.

Prayer: Help me to keep defining "salvation" in your terms, O God. Amen.

6 – Understanding the Future

> *1 Peter 1:10–12 — (10) Concerning this salvation, the prophets who prophesied of the grace that was to be yours made careful search and inquiry, (11) inquiring about the person or time that the Spirit of Christ within them indicated when it testified in advance to the sufferings destined for Christ and the subsequent glory. (12) It was revealed to them that they were serving not themselves but you, in regard to the things that have now been announced to you through those who brought you good news by the Holy Spirit sent from heaven—things into which angels long to look!*

THE OLD TESTAMENT PROPHETS' job was to proclaim and explain God—the nature and character of God and the intention or will of God. It was basically explanatory, not precision forecasting. Among other things, they provided a sort of "job description" for God's Christ, the chosen and anointed one who was hoped for. The prophets wrote about God's intention to offer you grace and glory. But that was not unrelated to Jesus' suffering.

Today there are some folks who proclaim an interesting gospel: Jesus suffered, so I don't have to. Interesting, but what is the logic? First Peter's gospel or message is more consistent if much less fun: Jesus suffered so you (disciples) will too. That's the bad news.

The good news is that—in the long run, finally, fundamentally, when all is said and done, in the total plan of God—the Jesus who was rejected by earthly wisdom, religion, and political decision-making was the recipient of the real power—the power of God—and was raised from the dead to provide us with the assurance of real life in God's own way and own time.

So you are confronted with the easy way (the road to hell is paved with gold!) and the hard way. This is not news, but it is important that you remind yourself of it with some regularity.

> *Prayer: God, thank you for your gifts—of prophets, of Christ, of your purpose for my life. Amen.*

7 – Dressing for the Occasion

1 Peter 1:13-16 — (13) Therefore prepare your minds for action; discipline yourselves; set all your hope on the grace that Jesus Christ will bring you when he is revealed. (14) Like obedient children, do not be conformed to the desires that you formerly had in ignorance. (15) Instead, as he who called you is holy, be holy yourselves in all your conduct; (16) for it is written, "You shall be holy, for I am holy."

"PREPARE YOUR MINDS" IS literally in the original Greek to "wrap up [in clothing] your minds." Instead of conforming your thinking to how you previously lived and thought, the opposite of that is being "holy." So "holy" has to do with mental discipline. You are in the right place to be "holy" in Christ: college!

How about a "holy" club? You laugh? Others might, but consider the Wesley brothers at Oxford University in the late 1720s. A small group of students serious about their studies and their faith committed themselves to a rigorously organized regimen of study (academic and religious), worship, and service in order to fully devote themselves to their calling. The Methodist Church may well have had its roots in their methodical commitment.

The early church was encouraged to keep its vision as it struggled with the world by embracing a change of mind (Rom 12:2). He gave a "fashion" directive recommending the putting on a "suit" of appropriate armor provided by God for the battle (Eph 6:11–17).

What about you in college? You are not only subject to the general culture of America but you are daily assaulted by new, often interesting, often persuasive visions of a world that ought to be and to which you are invited. To deal with that sort of challenge, 1 Peter invites you to take an interesting step: gird up (dress up) the sinews or loins of your mind. He tells us that the battle with "the world" is a battle for hearts and minds and that if you are to win you must get your mind prepared and "dressed" for the challenge.

As you go to classes, meet new people, read new assignments, you are invited to gird up your mind for the work that you will face.

Prayer: Make me strong of mind but tender for the needs of others. Amen.

8 – Does College = Exile?

1 Peter 1:17–21 — (17) If you invoke as Father the one who judges all people impartially according to their deeds, live in reverent fear during the time of your exile. (18) You know that you were ransomed from the futile ways inherited from your ancestors, not with perishable things like silver or gold, (19) but with the precious blood of Christ, like that of a lamb without defect or blemish. (20) He was destined before the foundation of the world, but was revealed at the end of the ages for your sake. (21) Through him you have come to trust in God, who raised him from the dead and gave him glory, so that your faith and hope are set on God.

"DURING THE TIME OF your exile." Sometimes students in college do feel as though they are in "exile"—far from loved ones, having to live under a routine imposed by strangers. You can easily start to feel sorry for yourself. Though you have been "ransomed from the futile ways" of "the world," it can seem like those still living in "the world" are having all the fun.

Reality check! There are now over 50,000,000 people in the world who really are refugees. And there are many more millions displaced inside of their own countries—exiles in every sense but geopolitically. And in the future, millions more may become "climate change refugees." Does it sound "just" that so many be deprived of home, safety, food, clean water, health care?

This reading characterizes God "as Father the one who judges all people impartially according to their deeds." That is a powerful statement: "judges all." All of those millions who suffer are surely included among those for whom God cares, weeps, and intends justice. And "judges all . . . according to their deeds." Anyone responsible for making just regular folks into "exiles" are in trouble. Peter points out that judgment will begin with Christians (4:17). He reminds you to remember "those futile ways inherited from your ancestors"; maybe you can substitute "surrounding secular culture" for "your ancestors." But the takeaway from this Scripture may be that you need to think of the world (that you are studying in college) as a place where millions of people—each with a name, and a face, and a story—are in "exile" and need and hoping to wind up on the right side of judgment. Can you help?

Prayer: Thank you, liberating God, for freeing me from the "futile ways" of the world and to help others. Amen.

9 – Question Authority

1 Peter 1:22-25 — (22) Now that you have purified your souls by your obedience to the truth so that you have genuine mutual love, love one another deeply from the heart. (23) You have been born anew, not of perishable but of imperishable seed, through the living and enduring word of God. (24) For "All flesh is like grass and all its glory like the flower of grass. The grass withers, and the flower falls, (25) but the word of the Lord endures forever." That word is the good news that was announced to you.

PRINTED ON HER TEE shirt was the abrasive command: "Question Authority." That's what she did. And she was an excellent student. The fact that she was an excellent student was a result of the combination of her native intelligence and her propensity to question authority. Her strategy seemed to be one of disobedience to any established rule, tradition, convention, practice, or perceived truths wherever she encountered them. In the classroom she always asked the questions intended to stump the instructor. Outside the classroom she was a thorn in the administration's flesh, agitating for causes, opposing official decisions, and, in general, getting us all to wonder where the truth and the right really lay.

Obedience is not high on the college student's list of virtues. Disobedience is the kind of anti-virtue that tends to be in favor with many students. So when Peter calls you to "obedience to the truth" you may have a knee-jerk reaction. Disobedience to conventional wisdom may not, of course, be such a bad thing. How would we have been able to free slaves, get to the moon, or eliminate polio if someone had not gone against the grain and discovered a new truth, the real truth? So perhaps the real issue is to find out first what the real truth is.

If you can find that really true truth, how solid, unchanging, and attractive might that be? Instead of having to change your politics, your understanding of nutrition, or your spouse every time "truth" changed, you could rely on a reality that did not change? Instead of changing friends, theories, even facts, you could rely on someone who was trustworthy?

Peter assures us that there is such truth—in God's word. That fact provides the basis for your rebirth from a physical being destined for final extinction into an imperishable being. Instead of being subject to your own uncertainties, you are subject only to God's ultimate truth revealed in Christ.

Prayer: Thank you, Lord, for transforming and including me in the imperishable. Amen.

10 – Grow Up Already!

1 Pet 2:1-3 — (1) Rid yourselves, therefore, of all malice, and all guile, insincerity, envy, and all slander. (2) Like newborn infants, long for the pure, spiritual milk, so that by it you may grow into salvation—(3) if indeed you have tasted that the Lord is good.

BABIES CAN BE PRETTY intense. While they don't know much, they do know when they are hungry. And they usually let everyone else know it. When they let out a wail of hunger they don't seem to care where they are, who is there, or any reason that might suggest screaming out at the top of one's lungs is not quite the right etiquette of the moment. "Focused" might be the right word; or "committed"; or "dedicated." Have there been moments like that in your college career? Moments when you were so totally focused that nothing else mattered?

Several times in the New Testament, the writers use the example of infants as models for the Christian life: Hebrews (5:12-14), 1 Corinthians (3:2), Matthew (19:14) and Luke (18:16). Peter encourages you to act like a baby and focus your energies on getting the basic stuff. In our translation, he calls it "the pure, spiritual milk." You know that milk is the basic stuff for babies. The modifier "spiritual" is interesting. In Greek it is *logikos*, a word in which you can recognize "logical" or "reasonable" or "rational." The dictionary tells us that it can mean "spiritual" or "rational." Or both? Why not? If you are to find yourself in the tough predicaments in the world to which Peter alludes, you need a faith that is both spiritually and emotionally powerful on the one hand, and on the other hand is rational, reasonable, and makes some sense. College is an environment in which looking for things that make sense . . . well, makes sense.

Finally, Peter writes that with this "pure, spiritual milk . . . you may grow into salvation." While many in American culture see salvation as something you get immediately after a conversion experience, here it seems to be an end stage after a (long) process of nourishment. If there is the "spiritual milk," then what about spiritual vegetables, spiritual fruit, and spiritual meat? Peter makes it clear throughout that the Christian life is not a one-time decision but is a constant and ongoing following of Jesus throughout all of life. (And what about spiritual dessert?)

Prayer: God of nourishment, continue to feed me so that I may grow into salvation. Amen.

11 – Oxymorons: Jesus Can Do Them Too.

1 Peter 2:4-8 — (4) Come to him, a living stone, though rejected by mortals yet chosen and precious in God's sight, and (5) like living stones, let yourselves be built into a spiritual house, to be a holy priesthood, to offer spiritual sacrifices acceptable to God through Jesus Christ. (6) For it stands in scripture: "See, I am laying in Zion a stone, a cornerstone chosen and precious; and whoever believes in him will not be put to shame." (7) To you then who believe, he is precious; but for those who do not believe, "The stone that the builders rejected has become the very head of the corner," (8) and "A stone that makes them stumble, and a rock that makes them fall." They stumble because they disobey the word, as they were destined to do.

PETER TESTS YOUR ABILITY to hold two contrasting ideas in your head at once: "living" and "stone." Do you remember the pet rock craze? Was bringing a pet rock to college a good idea? Low maintenance, and it did not break school rules? Yes. Cuddly? Afraid not. It was an oxymoron whose time had come and gone. But Jesus as a "living stone"? What is Peter up to?

These christological titles for Jesus are expressions the early Christians came up with to explain how absolutely fabulous Jesus was. As a "stone" Jesus was acknowledged as solid enough to be a foundation upon which Christians could stand. As "living" Jesus would be unique, active, spiritual, and present in your life. Today.

After describing Jesus as a "living stone," Peter moves on to describe Christians with another oxymoron: "spiritual house." This is the second (third?) description of the church or the community of believers. Peter kind of goes wild with his terminology. He wants us to know that you are special. A "house" is a place to live; "spiritual" is the opposite of physical, worldly (sinful?). It would be a great place for people to live . . . because it is built on a "living stone" and it won't shake, crumble, cave in, burn up, or wear out.

Y'all come on now. Set yourself upon Jesus Christ, the "living stone." He can't be rejected easily. He can be cast aside, but you will trip over him on your way out the door. Best to stay in the "spiritual house."

Prayer: Jesus, thanks for being solid as a rock for me. Amen.

12 – Now You're a Group

1 Peter 2:9–12 — (9) But you are a chosen race, a royal priesthood,
a holy nation, God's own people, in order that you may proclaim
the mighty acts of him who called you out of darkness into his
marvelous light. (10) Once you were not a people, but now you are
God's people; once you had not received mercy, but now you have
received mercy. (11) Beloved, I urge you as aliens and exiles to
abstain from the desires of the flesh that wage war against the soul.
(12) Conduct yourselves honorably among the Gentiles, so that,
though they malign you as evildoers, they may see your honorable
deeds and glorify God when he comes to judge.

THESE VERSES OFFER A good summary of 1 Peter. Because you are a
Christian, you may be mistreated wherever you are ("as aliens and exiles"),
but you can "conduct yourselves honorably" wherever you are because God
has embraced you with "light" and "mercy" and the promise of an ultimately
fair judgement of your "conduct."

Often individuals who share the same space (continent, island, zip
code, city block, even dorm space) are not a group, or unity. Sometimes
those individuals are united—by a war, a natural disaster, a political crisis,
even a winning football team. Peter wants his readers to know that despite
the fact that they live in exile in dozens of places and are made to feel
unwelcome almost everywhere they are a people in a special, purposeful,
unbreakable way. Just look at the nouns he uses to name their reality and
notice the adjectival boost he gives to each noun:

Noun	Adjective
race	*chosen*
priesthood	*royal*
nation	*holy*
people	*God's own*
house (see yesterday's reading)	*spiritual*

Peter attends in a unique way to the issues of the identity of his readers.
None of the five nouns describing the followers of Jesus as a group has been
used similarly anywhere else in Scripture. What would your name for the
church be?

Prayer: Thank you for giving me a place in your community—
however it is described. Amen.

13 – Free-Dumb

1 Peter 2:13-17 — (13) For the Lord's sake accept the authority of every human institution, whether of the emperor as supreme, (14) or of governors, as sent by him to punish those who do wrong and to praise those who do right. (15) For it is God's will that by doing right you should silence the ignorance of the foolish. (16) As servants of God, live as free people, yet do not use your freedom as a pretext for evil. (17) Honor everyone. Love the family of believers. Fear God. Honor the emperor.

USE THE RIGHT TOOL for the job.

I haven't worked in a factory or shop for forty years and I don't do a lot of repair work around my home. But I have suffered my share of injuries by using tools incorrectly with often costly results. Among other errors—a screwdriver as substitute for a claw hammer, a penny instead of an electrical fuse, piled boxes as a ladder, and frozen meat (not that it is technically a tool) for a hammer. There are many adjectives that could describe these misguided uses of the wrong tool. "Dumb" would be quite appropriate.

Among the many gifts God has given us is the gift of freedom. It is an astonishingly powerful tool. Humans are the only creatures who have this gift. You get to choose. Others of God's creatures have been programmed to be who they are. That is why you don't expect cats or fish to behave ethically (or unethically). Freedom is the tool you can use to fulfill your essential calling as a human, which is to respond to God the creator—and others—in love.

So here you are—a creature who is essentially free but trapped in the limitations resulting from using freedom in the wrong way. You are now in college where freedom is both highly prized and plentiful. Of course, complete freedom doesn't exist. You are subject to death, to the limitations of time, and space, and gravity. Misuse of the limited freedoms you have is, according to Peter, sin. Your challenge is to use this tool of freedom correctly.

You must not use it against others. Peter suggests a remarkably liberal application: "honor everyone." This is a powerful use of the most powerful tool you have.

Prayer: Keep me thinking clearly despite all of this heady freedom. Amen.

14 – In His Steps

1 Peter 2:18–25 — (18) Slaves, accept the authority of your masters with all deference, not only those who are kind and gentle but also those who are harsh. (19) For it is a credit to you if, being aware of God, you endure pain while suffering unjustly. (20) If you endure when you are beaten for doing wrong, what credit is that? But if you endure when you do right and suffer for it, you have God's approval. (21) For to this you have been called, because Christ also suffered for you, leaving you an example, so that you should follow in his steps. (22) "He committed no sin, and no deceit was found in his mouth." (23) When he was abused, he did not return abuse; when he suffered, he did not threaten; but he entrusted himself to the one who judges justly. (24) He himself bore our sins in his body on the cross, so that, free from sins, we might live for righteousness; by his wounds you have been healed. (25) For you were going astray like sheep, but now you have returned to the shepherd and guardian of your souls.

IN HIS STEPS WAS one of the most popular books ever published. It was written by Charles Sheldon, a minister in Topeka, Kansas, and published in 1896 in the belief that Christians could be persuaded to emulate Jesus. The idea of living like Jesus has been a periodic craze, usually when societies were only going through the motions of being Christian. Francis of Assisi, for instance, (in about 1200) was motivated to do so and founded the Franciscan order. Later, Mennonites sought to live a Jesus-style "simple life." Today perhaps it's "WWJD."

Peter, however, has real suffering in mind when he talks about following in Jesus' steps; those steps led through the gauntlet of religious and political persecution and ended at the cross where a death that seems unjust to us but perfectly legal and justifiable to the majority of people of Jesus' own day. Today, however, there are many who "do right and suffer" anyway. One of Peter's themes is that of unjust suffering—both of Jesus and of others—and another theme is that God both approves your righteous behavior and promises a final judgment that will finally (!) be just because it is the justice of "the one who judges justly."

Prayer: Give me the strength I need to walk in his steps. Amen.

15 – Mutual Consideration

1 Peter 3:1–7 — (1) Wives, in the same way, accept the authority of your husbands, so that, even if some of them do not obey the word, they may be won over without a word by their wives' conduct, (2) when they see the purity and reverence of your lives. (3) Do not adorn yourselves outwardly by braiding your hair, and by wearing gold ornaments or fine clothing; (4) rather, let your adornment be the inner self with the lasting beauty of a gentle and quiet spirit, which is very precious in God's sight. (5) It was in this way long ago that the holy women who hoped in God used to adorn themselves by accepting the authority of their husbands. (6) Thus Sara obeyed Abraham and called him lord. You have become her daughters as long as you do what is good and never let fears alarm you. (7) Husbands, in the same way, show consideration for your wives in your life together, paying honor to the woman as the weaker sex, since they too are also heirs of the gracious gift of life—so that nothing may hinder your prayers.

HIERARCHY IS THE ORDER of the day in higher education: there are freshmen, sophomores, juniors, seniors, graduate students, instructors, assistant professors, associate professors, full professors, department chairs, divisional chairs, deans, provosts, presidents, chancellors, trustees. You are evaluated with an F, D, C, B, or A. (The school I attended graded with the lowest a 7; even 6 was a fail grade; then 5, 4, 3, 2, 1; each number grade was also subdivided: 1+ was .7 and 3- was 3.3; there were 21 possible rankings!)

Economically the college provides its own interesting hierarchy. Presidents usually get the highest salary—except when the football coach does. He—it is, of course, always a man (another evidence of hierarchy)—might receive three or four times as much as the president.

You go to college to rise to the top of this heap and get the perks and the big money. You might succeed. Or you might not. This is a competitive environment.

Christians understand and criticize this hierarchy, but while you are in college you need to submit to almost every hierarchy. But in the process don't abandon yourself to the mystique of hierarchy; don't think "up" is better than "down." Think about it in Christian terms. Where you are in the hierarchy is unimportant; what is important is to maximize your opportunities to "do what is good and never let fears alarm you." In other words, wherever you are in the system, keep cool and do good.

Prayer: Help me to understand submission. Amen.

16 – What Goes with What?

1 Peter 3:8–12 — (8) Finally, all of you, have unity of spirit, sympathy, love for one another, a tender heart, and a humble mind. (9) Do not repay evil for evil or abuse for abuse; but, on the contrary, repay with a blessing. It is for this that you were called—that you might inherit a blessing. (10) For "Those who desire life and desire to see good days, let them keep their tongues from evil and their lips from speaking deceit; (11) let them turn away from evil and do good; let them seek peace and pursue it. (12) For the eyes of the Lord are on the righteous, and his ears are open to their prayer. But the face of the Lord is against those who do evil."

DOES LOVE GO WITH sex? Does restraint go with partying? Does submission go with knowledge? Peter picks up on a theme we have seen elsewhere: the connection between knowledge and love. Sometimes you might hear about someone who loves to learn. They might appear quaint or quirky in this day when you go to school to get your ticket punched for a job—preferably a good (read: well-paid) job.

You usually associate thinking-studying-learning with power and control—from know to know-how with an eye toward that job that you'd like to get. Love, on the other hand, tends to find its association with the irrational, the impetuous, the out of control. Love is blind. You get lovesick. Love points toward others while knowledge for control is all about you.

Another startling reminder here is about unity and sympathy (together-feeling). It all sounds too palsy-walsy, too much togetherness for independent, freethinking, individualistic students on the cusp of a great life.

Religion seems to scandalize people at every corner. In today's reading it comes in the popular assumption that religious people will all think alike—or some such nonsense. You pride yourself on independence of thought. When you look at the options, however, doesn't a lot of your "independence" boil down to pretty narrow choices: watch channel 5 or channel 12; have a Coke or a Pepsi? How often is being "independent" and making "choices" not so much a total breakout as it is another alternative within the narrow range of options we usually face?

There is a theme or thread here: that you be tenderhearted and humble in mind. Don't expect to see a lot of that; but you can be the first in your "neighborhood" to exhibit this scandalous breakout.

Prayer: Keep my mind tough but my heart soft—and keep them connected to each other. Amen.

17 – Don't Run Scared

1 Peter 3:13-17 — (13) Now who will harm you if you are eager to do what is good? (14) But even if you do suffer for doing what is right, you are blessed. Do not fear what they fear, and do not be intimidated, (15) but in your hearts sanctify Christ as Lord. Always be ready to make your defense to anyone who demands from you an accounting for the hope that is in you; (16) yet do it with gentleness and reverence. Keep your conscience clear, so that, when you are maligned, those who abuse you for your good conduct in Christ may be put to shame. (17) For it is better to suffer for doing good, if suffering should be God's will, than to suffer for doing evil.

PETER ENVISIONS YOU AS an exile and stranger likely to suffer in one way or another at the hands of those who feel "at home" but who have some sense of fear or unease about you. What is it about their fear that you need not share? Are there fears that a Christian could legitimately have? Following Jesus—in a life that he, not you, directs—can be a bit scary. And if you take it seriously, it can really spook others. Thus they may fear you and their defense is to intimidate you and perhaps inflict injury. They thought that would work on Jesus, but it didn't.

In the course of setting your path after the model of Jesus, you may not always be certain as to "what would Jesus do" in any given situation. Rather than fret too much (i.e., fear), you might consider Martin Luther's somewhat cavalier response to that dilemma: "Love God, and sin boldly." In other words, commit yourself to Jesus and move ahead trusting in his model and guidance . . . and ultimate forgiveness if you err. If it means suffering for it, so be it.

More likely in your situation, others will want to know what you're up to and why—"demanding an accounting" (in Greek, *logos,* or "word") or a "defense" (in Greek, *apologia,* or "explanation"). Just be prepared to explain your commitment to Jesus any way you want—with examples, Scripture, etc.—and offer it "with gentleness and reverence." You are not "sorry" nor are you looking for an "excuse" for being a Christian. You are simply telling others what has convinced you to trust in Jesus. That can be a terrific witness.

According to Scripture, the only thing to fear is God; and Jesus came and (repeatedly) said: "Fear not."

Prayer: With you I'm fearless; I just need a little support when I get kind of scared. Amen.

18 – To Hell and Back

1 Peter 3:18-22 — (18) For Christ also suffered for sins once for all, the righteous for the unrighteous, in order to bring you to God. He was put to death in the flesh, but made alive in the spirit (19) in which also he went and made a proclamation to the spirits in prison, (20) who in former times did not obey, when God waited patiently in the days of Noah, during the building of the ark, in which a few, that is, eight persons, were saved through water. (21) And baptism, which this prefigured, now saves you—not as a removal of dirt from the body, but as an appeal to God for a good conscience, through the resurrection of Jesus Christ, (22) who has gone into heaven and is at the right hand of God, with angels, authorities, and powers made subject to him.

THIS IS ONE OF those really difficult passages to interpret. In the Apostles' Creed we confess that Jesus died, descended into hell, and then rose. This is the one biblical passage that says anything about the time between Jesus' death and his resurrection. It is connected with Noah and those with him in the ark. They were saved from the flood by floating on water. Peter connects their experience to the church's practice of baptism, which he describes as "an appeal to God for a good conscience."

If you could let Noah go momentarily, perhaps the useful part of this passage is the connection of your baptism to Jesus' resurrection, which is the basis for making your "appeal to God for a good conscience."

Peter summarizes all of the work of Jesus that leads to the possibility that you can be acceptable to God—his suffering, death, trip to "prison" to visit Noah and company, resurrection, and finally his sitting with God and exercising authority over all powers. In baptism you claim the favor made available to us for a good conscience.

Conscience: *con*—with; *science*—knowing. Having a conscience means your knowing about yourself at the same time that others—especially God—know of you. God knows you and because of Jesus' work God accepts you.

Prayer: Lord, help me to live out my baptism. Amen.

19 – Party School Mentality

1 Peter 4:1-6 — (1) Since therefore Christ suffered in the flesh, arm yourselves also with the same intention (for whoever has suffered in the flesh has finished with sin), (2) so as to live for the rest of your earthly life no longer by human desires but by the will of God. (3) You have already spent enough time in doing what the Gentiles like to do, living in licentiousness, passions, drunkenness, revels, carousing and lawless idolatry. (4) They are surprised that you no longer join them in the same excesses of dissipation, and so they blaspheme. (5) But they will have to give an accounting to him who stands ready to judge the living and the dead. (6) For this is the reason the gospel was proclaimed even to the dead, so that, though they had been judged in the flesh as everyone is judged, they might live in the spirit as God does.

IT ALMOST SOUNDS AS though Peter had been to one of those really serious party schools. It also appears that things have not changed a lot in the last 2,000 years when it comes to the futile pursuit of pleasure.

Let's not get suckered into that commonplace of religious thinking that focuses on discrete items of behavior (smoking, drinking). It calls to mind one of the typical Hollywood movie plots in which the antihero who has been a scoundrel all of his (or her) life finally does one good thing. The outcome is that he is now a true hero and the viewer is led to believe that he was always a pretty good guy all along, despite his history of bad acts.

You are not a series of acts; you are fundamentally a person of a particular nature who expresses that nature in specific actions. Anyone who lives a life of "licentiousness, passions, drunkenness, revels, carousing and lawless idolatry" is living out what they want to be. It seems that this kind of life is one seeking enjoyment. Yet you know that the more one seeks pleasure directly, the less likely s/he is to experience it (philosophers and psychologists call that the pleasure paradox, or the paradox of hedonism—that pleasure cannot be acquired by directly pursing happiness). Pleasure comes as a by-product of what might seem at the moment to be not a whole lot of fun.

Peter exhorts you to get on with your life and leave the past behind. It is never too late to find that new fundamental being in Christ.

Prayer: Help me to live so that I might bring joy to others. Amen.

20 – What to Do While Awaiting the End of the World

1 Peter 4:7–11 — (7) The end of all things is near; therefore be serious and discipline yourselves for the sake of your prayers. (8) Above all, maintain constant love for one another, for love covers a multitude of sins. (9) Be hospitable to one another without complaining. (10) Like good stewards of the manifold grace of God, serve one another with whatever gift each of you has received. (11) Whoever speaks must do so as one speaking the very words of God; whoever serves must do so with the strength that God supplies, so that God maybe glorified in all things through Jesus Christ. To him belong the glory and the power forever and ever. Amen.

YOU HAVE ONLY TWO months to live. What will you do? Drop all your classes? (Who needs college if the world is going to end?) Hope for that make-a-wish date with a movie star? Have a double banana split for every meal? Or just keep on with your life as it is going now, with the regular routine? The advice from Peter is to practice hospitality. He suggests your focus be outward, towards others, rather than inward, towards yourself.

Okay. The odds are that you will not die in two months. And who knows when "the end of all things" will happen? So there you are—in your room and the word from Scripture is "be hospitable." With your meager resources, how do you roll out the red carpet of hospitality? What is this hospitality stuff and how do you do it?

In Jesus' day, hospitality was one thing you could offer even if you lacked a lot of this world's things. Travel was hard and dirty, so you gave newcomers a place to sit down, relax, and you washed their feet. The point was to make them feel "at home."

This would be pretty easy if the guests were old friends. How do you show that hospitality to those you do not know? College is a perfect place to rise to such a challenge. Can you offer welcome, warmth, and openness to others so that they do not feel strange with you but instead are treated as old friends in your presence—even if you do not really agree with them on everything? This is not the practice of toleration but rather of a hospitality that takes everyone and every idea seriously. Toleration is blowing it off; hospitality breathes deeply and "covers a multitude of sins."

Prayer: God, always remind me how you have invited me into your kingdom. Amen.

21 – Persistence is Called For

1 Peter 4:12-19 — (12) Beloved, do not be surprised at the fiery ordeal that is taking place among you to test you, as though something strange were happening to you. (13) But rejoice insofar as you are sharing Christ's sufferings, so that you may also be glad and shout for joy when his glory is revealed. (14) If you are reviled for the name of Christ, you are blessed, because the spirit of glory, which is the Spirit of God, is resting on you. (15) But let none of you suffer as a murderer, a thief, a criminal, or even as a mischief maker. (16) Yet if any of you suffers as a Christian, do not consider it a disgrace, but glorify God because you bear this name. (17) For the time has come for judgment to begin with the household of God; if it begins with us, what will be the end for those who do not obey the gospel of God? (18) And "If it is hard for the righteous to be saved, what will become of the ungodly and the sinners?" (19) Therefore, let those suffering in accordance with God's will entrust themselves to a faithful Creator, while continuing to do good.

PETER FINISHES HIS LETTER as he began—recognizing that as a Christian you may have "to suffer various trials" that test your faith (1:6-7); in such a "fiery ordeal" you need to know that you "are sharing Christ's sufferings." But remember that you have the assurance of "a new birth into a living hope through the resurrection of Jesus Christ from the dead."

From the time of the first Christians until now, believers have known that (i) they were "completing what is lacking in Christ's afflictions" (Paul, in Colossians 1:24), and (ii) the end of all things, Christ's return, and the final judgment were soon to happen.

But, you say, "the end ... the return ... the judgment" haven't happened. Yet.

You have the certainty of God's promise "through the resurrection of Jesus Christ from the dead." The timing of "end/return/judgment" is God's just as much as was the raising of Jesus from the grave. Many Christians, instead of trying to calculate the "when" of Christ's return in glory, have spent their energies on being prepared for Christ's return every moment, every "now." For twenty centuries, Peter's letter has been received as God's inspired message of (i) acknowledgement of Christians' suffering, (ii) the promise of ultimate justice in God's court, and (iii) the assurance of an "inheritance that is imperishable."

Prayer: Help me to continue to persist in trust and not insist on my own plans. Amen.

22 – How to Be the Chief Shepherd

1 Peter 5:1–5a — (1) Now as an elder myself and a witness of the sufferings of Christ, as well as one who shares in the glory to be revealed, I exhort the elders among you (2) to tend the flock of God that is in your charge, exercising the oversight, not under compulsion but willingly, as God would have you do it—not for sordid gain but eagerly. (3) Do not lord it over those in your charge, but be examples to the flock. (4) And when the chief shepherd appears, you will win the crown of glory that never fades away. (5) In the same way, you who are younger must accept the authority of the elders.

YOU MAY BE PREPARING for the end of school or just going for that summer job. This passage is about being in charge. It is about leadership. It is about how to exercise responsibility as the boss. Peter's choice of example may not be particularly up-to-date. There are not too many shepherd jobs open. And for the few available, college may not be the best preparation. Peter could have mentioned jobs in the fishing industry. At least he had had experience in both of those areas. But here we are: shepherds.

He puts the whole boss/worker complex into the shepherd/flock metaphor. The workers, the flock, are productive, but prone to going off on their own and not always being cognizant of dangers. In business terms, they are totally out of it when it comes to any SWOT (strengths, weaknesses, opportunities, threats) analysis. So you need a boss (manager, leader) who has the big picture and who cares for all the workers so that they can do their work.

Authority for Peter came from his being "a witness of the sufferings of Christ." Note that he does not refer to the teachings of Jesus or the resurrection of Jesus but to the point of Jesus' life that most influenced—and was most replicated in—his own life: suffering. He had "been there; done that." The trick here is to take the words of Jesus about being a servant as the central and highest task of the disciple and live out that servanthood in everything you do—including being the leader or the boss.

Prayer: If I am ever in charge, clothe me with the wisdom, courage, and love that will help us all. Amen.

23 – What the Well–Dressed Christian Is Wearing

1 Peter 5:5b–11 — (5b) And all of you must clothe yourselves with humility in your dealings with one another, for "God opposes the proud, but gives grace to be humble." (6) Humble yourselves therefore under the mighty hand of God, so that he may exalt you in due time. (7) Cast all your anxiety on him, because he cares for you. (8) Discipline yourselves, keep alert. Like a roaring lion your adversary the devil prowls around, looking for someone to devour. (9) Resist him, steadfast in your faith, for you know that your brothers and sisters in all the world are undergoing the same kinds of suffering. (10) And after you have suffered for a little while, the God of all grace, who has called you to his eternal glory in Christ, will himself restore, support, strengthen, and establish you. (11) To him be the power forever and ever. Amen.

WE USE "DRESS" METAPHORS all the time: put on a happy face; wear your heart on your sleeve. Peter did the same thing: "Clothe yourselves with humility." That choice may seem like a downer. You might think that since he came from a day laborer's background and was a member of a poor and unpopular religion, all he could afford was something drab, like humility. Or maybe he was dressing so as not to call attention to himself.

It certainly does not seem like advice that you would take today. Now you live in freedom and many believe you should be proud of your faith. Wearing crosses (as jewelry) is the thing to do. If you've got it, flaunt it!

Wait. Back to the text. It is not just putting on a facade of humility. The Greek word means something like "wrap yourself around with"—implying a rather complicated outfit. And indeed it is: first, subject yourself to God; second, throw your cares onto him; third, exhibit self-control or self-discipline; then be alert; finally, resist the devil.

Perhaps you have played the game Twister? Players arrange themselves as directed (by a roll of dice or spin of a dial) on large, colored spots on a ground cloth. Place one foot on red; place one foot on green; place one hand on blue; place one hand on yellow. By this time, after following all the instructions, you are bent out of shape. Perhaps putting on all the elements of humility is like Twister—bending you out of shape. But remember God's promise to "restore, support, strengthen, and establish you." It's "dress-up" time!

Prayer: O God, pick me up and dress me for every occasion. Amen.

24 – Strange Bedfellows

1 Peter 5:12–14 — (12) Through Silvanus, whom I consider a faithful brother, I have written this short letter to encourage you and to testify that this is the true grace of God. Stand fast in it. (13) Your sister church in Babylon, chosen together with you, sends you greetings; and so does my son Mark. (14) Greet one another with a kiss of love. Peace to all of you who are in Christ.

At the beginning of the Second Iraq War (2003), a Christian pastor from one of the few Christian churches in Baghdad spoke at a conference held in the US. Those of us at the conference were just beginning to learn about Sunnis and Shiites and other kinds of Muslims, but most of us didn't know anything about Christians in Iraq. As Peter concludes his letter in which he has delivered a sobering picture of what Christians can expect in "the world," you are reminded that there are Christians in places that could be considered pretty bad places, that they are chosen by God just like God chose you, and that they send you greetings, even though you may not receive them or want to hear them.

Most scholars think that Peter's reference to Babylon is not to the area we today know as Baghdad. That would be really prophetic (and spooky!). But no, the reference was probably to the city of Rome. Rome was the big, bad city as far as the Christians of Peter's day were concerned.

Peter offers some really good news here. You are not alone. God chose you, yes, but he also chose others in even the most astonishing places. We are all one in the church, in the body of Christ. Peter describes his church as "your sister church in Babylon, chosen together with you." What a great expression. It describes Christians in such a way that makes it impossible for the world to separate you from others who are chosen. And finally, those Christians send us greetings. How can you send greetings from your church—wherever it is—to other Christians who are suffering trials or ordeals and who would be comforted and inspired by any message or gesture that would "encourage" them? And they might "encourage you." Don't be a Lone Ranger; be a fellow chosen one.

Prayer: God of caring, thank you for Christ who suffered for and with us and for those you send to greet us. Amen.

APPENDIX

Short Verses Tell Big Stories

THE PRECEDING PAGES CONTAIN the complete texts of Colossians, the Gospel According to Matthew, 1 Corinthians, and 1 Peter. You read through the life, death, and resurrection story of Jesus (compliments of Matthew), and read letters addressing urgent issues in the early church. All of these canonical writings have been cherished and found helpful by individual believers and churches ever since. The purpose of the accompanying meditations were to draw you, the student, into conversation with your Christian brothers and sisters in the faith of centuries past, and to see how the blessings of the gospel might inform, enrich, and strengthen you in your vocation as a college student. Why add to that quartet? There are several reasons.

First, to provide an opportunity to see how, with the addition of some information about the whole story behind the biblical book, individual verses (or two or three) can function in the same way as whole books of the New Testament and invite you to share your "story" with the scriptural story and move to a deeper understanding of the faith with practical and helpful outcomes.

Most of us have experienced memorization of verses. That was a good idea, but it did not always serve to fix in our functional memories the larger story of God's creation, humanity's fall, and Jesus Christ's redemptive activities. The following passages are offered with that in mind—each with a meditation as well as some additional comments about the original context/ setting/narrative for the verse(s).

Second, from a practical and calendric point of view, this book was intended to provide a devotion a day for an entire college year. In truth, a "college year" can run from a short 30-some weeks (30 weeks x 7 days=210 days) to a lengthy 36 weeks or more (2 semesters of 16 weeks each plus a January or May term of 4 weeks: 36 weeks x 7 days= 252 days). The four New Testament books relied upon for their text supported a total of 243 readings. Result: we lacked nine readings. This Appendix offers ten more devotions to complete or supplement your school year.

1 – Got Faith?

Mark 9:24 — (24) Immediately the father of the child cried out, "I believe; help my unbelief!"

HAVE YOU EVER HAD this frustration? You believe . . . somewhat . . . but maybe not enough? The whole story in which this confession/plea is located is a miracle story, and it has a happy ending. But . . . .

This man—a father—is desperate. His child had some kind of epileptic condition that threw it into frightful spasms where the child would injure itself. And of course in those days there were no neurologists, no medications, no operations that could help. The situation was a personal catastrophe. The father had probably already tried everything and finally brought the child to Jesus.

But Jesus was gone, up on a mountain "transfiguring" with Moses, Elijah, Peter, James, and John (see Matt 17:1–8; meditation #70). The disciples who remained behind had tried but had been unable to do anything for the child. Upon his return, Jesus wondered what was going on. Once the situation was explained, he told the man that anything is possible to one who believes.

That's where the father's dilemma lies. He does believe. He believes that Jesus had healed some people. He believes that Jesus has a great reputation as a teacher with extraordinary powers. He believes that if he can bring the child to Jesus maybe it can be healed. (It's beginning to get a bit shaky, isn't it?) This is where the rubber really hits the road. This is not about believing Jesus did miracles somewhere, for somebody else. This is about my son and whether Jesus can/will heal him. That is a totally different story. Believe? Yes, some. Enough? Not sure. So right there in the middle of the crowd, with his child's life on the line, he cries out, "Help my unbelief!"

Indeed a happy ending: Jesus helped the man despite his unbelief and helped the child with his illness.

The topic here is one that permeates Scripture and the lives of all Christians. Do we have enough faith? To please God? To guarantee forgiveness? To assure salvation? To get through the next problem? The good news is that Jesus helps our unbelief . . . or in spite of our unbelief.

Prayer: Lord, I believe that I believe, but I'm not always sure about it; help, help, help. Amen.

2 – Truth

John 8:31–32 — (31) Then Jesus said to the Jews who had believed in him, "If you continue in my word, you are truly my disciples; (32) and you will know the truth, and the truth will make you free."

YOU WANT TO KNOW the truth. In relationships. In math problems. In the dates on history quiz. Truth seems important. But it doesn't always seem available. You live in what is being called "postmodern" times, when one of the defining features is that truth is often seen to be relative—you may have yours, but I can have a different one.

One way to look at the narrative the Fourth Gospel tells is to see it as a christological one in which Jesus is portrayed symbolically or metaphorically as bread (bread that nourishes spiritually), as word (of God no less), as a shepherd who is good (as opposed to a hired-by-the-day guy who takes off when danger threatens). So it is not a surprise that the author would point out that truth—the real truth sought by everyone from philosophers to the woman who wants true value at the local market—is not only found in Jesus, but it *is* Jesus.

Are you in that vast truth-seeking majority of humanity? Surely being in college makes the search for truth a daily, even hourly, goal. From the Old Testament book of Proverbs, you have heard that "The fear of the Lord is the beginning of knowledge" (Prov 1:7a). John spells it out a bit differently: "if you continue in my word." Just hang in there, keep focused on Jesus, and the Scripture through which he is revealed to us.

Prayer: Lord Jesus, thank you for being the truth and promising yourself to me. Amen.

3 – –form: Con– or Trans–?

Romans 12:1-2 — (1) I appeal to you therefore, brothers and sisters, by the mercies of God, to present your bodies as a living sacrifice, holy and acceptable to God, which is your spiritual worship. (2) Do not be conformed to this world, but be transformed by the renewing of your minds, so that you may discern what the will of God—what is good and acceptable and perfect.

PRESSURE—FROM YOUR PEERS, YOUR conscience, your parents, TV ads, professors. There is a lot; it comes from everywhere; and you have to decide. It's about clothes, friends, watching TV (or not), music, church, a major, this weekend. Almost all of it is from this world. Much of the time we give in; it's easier. And we go along with what's happening. Problem is, what's happening now is not likely to (i) be terribly satisfying, or (ii) be what's happening in (say) a month or a year from now.

The narrative behind this verse—the basic thrust of Paul's letter to the church in Rome in the middle of the first century CE—is that God sent Jesus to rescue the creation from the big trouble into which his creation had gotten itself. "The world" had made up a whole new plan for living and made a colossal mess of things. Paul spent the first eleven chapters of Romans describing God's redemptive action in Jesus Christ and he now turns to the matter of his readers actually applying the new life available to them. The first thing is to wise up, repent (remember: change the mind), renew your thinking so that it is not conformed to or controlled by "the world."

The interesting thing to note (as a college student) is that the renewal of your mind to discern God's will is not only good for your mind (and probably for your grades in school), but also is worship. Worship God with your mind (we had something like that in 1 Corinthians—sing with the mind, pray with the mind). The goal is to develop truly clear thinking, unaffected and unperverted by "the world," and becoming able to "discern . . . the will of God."

Prayer: Lord, help me to be transformed, not conformed, so I can understand and do what you want for me. Amen.

4 – A New Perspective

2 Corinthians 5:16–19a — (16) From now on, therefore, we regard no one from a human point of view, even though we once knew Christ from a human point of view, we know him no longer in that way. (17) So if anyone is in Christ, there is a new creation: everything old has passed away; see, everything has become new! (18) All this is from God, who reconciled us to himself through Christ, and has given us the ministry of reconciliation; (19a) that is, in Christ God was reconciling the world to himself.

THIS PASSAGE NEEDS TO be walked backwards in order to see how you got to where you are now—a minister of reconciliation, in the same business as Christ. Yes, that's where you are now. Hope you want to stay there.

That ministry is a gift from God via Christ (v. 18a). That seems to be a result of the renewal of everything (v.17d; everything!). For you, all the old stuff is gone (v. 17c). There was a new creation (v. 17b). So, if you are "in Christ" all of the following is part of being "in Christ." Before being "in Christ" you knew him as Jesus (teacher, moralizer, etc. v. 16b) but not as Christ. But now, "in Christ" you have a totally new and different perspective on Jesus Christ.

When Paul talks about having "a human point of view" he probably means something like the set of opinions that most people—especially those who are not believers—have about things; those opinions are easily adopted from parents, peers, the TV you watch. (It's much easier to adopt opinions that are formed by others and held strongly by those around you than it is to get that "mind of Christ" thinking we read about in 1 Corinthians and that is the subject of v. 16 in this portion of Scripture.)

College challenges your perspectives on things. It opens new doors; it even closes some. But nothing and nobody reorganizes your perspectives like Jesus. And when he does it he doesn't just abandon you in case you tumble, but he is there to help you through it, reconcile those new things and move on.

Prayer: Let me see and know you as you truly are, not just the way people say you are. Amen.

5 – Let's (Not) Play Categories!

Galatians 3:28 — (28) There is no longer Jew or Greek, there is no longer slave or free, there is no longer male and female; for all of you are one in Christ Jesus.

YOU ARE EXPANDING YOUR circle. Roommate; suite mates; lab mate; classmates. Boyfriend (girlfriend); then it gets serious; then you get engaged. The circle expands: fiancé's parents, and siblings, and grandparents. In our culture there are categories that will precisely describe most of these new people you encounter in their anticipated relationship to you: in-law, cousin (by marriage), stepchild . . . .

In his book *1493: Uncovering the New World Columbus Created,* Charles C. Mann lists a dizzying set of classifications the new Spanish occupiers used to categorize the offspring of various "racial" couplings. These informal "rules" put people "in their place" and had enormous power to control how everyone would come to value and treat them. Here is a sampling of the categorizing terms: *mulatto, lobo, mestizo, zambo, castizo, morisco, coyote, chamizo, albino, albarazado, barcino, cambujo.* A French effort to do the same in Haiti reportedly had 128 different groupings. These categories implied moral and spiritual worth as well as political and social standing. Establishing the categories facilitated bad treatment and eventually the "castes" themselves justified such behavior on the ground that it was what was due to a person of that particular "mixture" or category.

Such categorization undoubtedly exists where you are—perhaps evident in hazing traditions or other quietly practiced activities. It is probably not openly acknowledged. But you know the unwritten rules of categorization that function on your campus.

The backstory for Paul's letter to the Galatian church had to do with issues that continue to plague Christians today: What is the role that the law—and following, obeying, and performing it—plays in our reconciliation with God (our salvation, our forgiveness, our justification)? Paul spells his answer in multiple ways: It play no role; rules don't help; God doesn't use rules; when we base our lives on rules/laws we only mess up. That is the message. Nor are rules that we make up always helpful. Today's verse is a throwaway line that is truly a bombshell. Those rules that we take for granted to explain and identify other people? Invalid.

Prayer: God thank you for loving me, a (mix of whatever); forgive me for not loving other mixes. Amen.

6 – Walls

Ephesians 2:12–16 — (12) Remember that you were at that time without Christ, being aliens from the commonwealth of Israel, and strangers to the covenants of promise, having no hope and without God in the world. (13) But now in Christ Jesus you who once were far off have been brought near by the blood of Christ. (14) For he is our peace; in his flesh he has made both groups into one and has broken down the dividing wall, that is, the hostility between us. (15) He has abolished the law with its commandments and ordinances, that he might create in himself one new humanity in place of the two, thus making peace, (16) and might reconcile both groups to God in one body through the cross, thus putting to death that hostility through it.

ONE OF THE HISTORIC moments of our time—sorry, this was a bit before your time, but even so you'll "get it"—was the razing of the Berlin Wall. (Google it.) At the end of World War II, the Nazi capital of Germany, Berlin, was almost-simultaneously captured by the US, Great Britain, and Russia and divided up among the Western powers (US, Britain, France) and the Eastern giant, Russia. The Russians built a wall to isolate East Germans from West Germans. Long story, but the short version is that the East Germans hated it, and the wall was finally breached on November 9, 1989. With great joy.

Ephesians is a general letter—it was not originally sent to a specific church—indicating the powerful reconciliation effected by Jesus Christ in his death on the cross. The story behind that seems to be that despite the efforts of institutions (Roman government and military, and Jewish religion and customs) to stifle Jesus' words and works on behalf of the kingdom of God—even killing him—God made clear in Jesus' resurrection that his work was right and the worldly institutions' actions in executing him were wrong. In effect, Jesus smashed and obliterated and demolished the legal and religious laws that the world had employed to separate people from God and each other.

God's intention in Christ was to bring all of his creatures together. Laws and rules weren't doing that. As you study history, politics, and sociology, look carefully at laws—who makes them, who is affected by them, how often they are found to be bad, ineffective, and downright stupid. And notice that Jesus was not a Law Giver, or Law Maker, or Law Checker-Up-er. However, he was a Wall-Buster.

Prayer: Lord, help me to use my freedom to bring your people together. Amen.

7 – Humility

Philippians 2:5–8 — (5) Let the same mind be in you that was in Christ Jesus, (6) who, though he was in the form of God, did not regard equality with God as something to be exploited, (7) but emptied himself, taking the form of a slave, being born in human likeness. And being found in human form, (8) he humbled himself and became obedient to the point of death—even death on a cross.

THIS LOOKS LIKE AN early Christian hymn in praise of Jesus' humility. He expressed that by coming "down" to us humans so that he could then be exalted. Paul apparently used that hymn to give his Philippian readers a prime example of humility—the example found in none other than the Christ of God who started out being God but decided to descend to humankind in order to make it possible for humankind to ultimately ascend to God.

(Incidentally, as you ponder this "emptying" by Christ in his humbling entry into our world, you will have an example of "the mind of Christ" that Paul has exhorted you to have [1 Cor. 2:16, Meditation #10].)

So Christ "emptied himself . . . being born in human likeness." Step one: moving from "equality with God" to being merely human. (Don't be fooled into the Gnostic heresy that Christ was only kidding about being human; Christ, as Jesus, really did die on the cross. But there are a couple more intervening steps in which Christ, now Jesus, "emptied himself" even more.

Step two: rather than just be an ordinary human—like a farmer or a soldier—he became a slave. That would have been humiliating.

Step three: both in doing this "come to earth" thing and in being a slave, Jesus was obedient—to God and to earthly powers (remember the Jesus of 1 Peter?).

Step four: Jesus took the human thing all the way—to death; which can be a humbling experience because there is nothing you can do about it when you are dying.

Step five: "death on a cross"; super humiliating because it "proves" to everyone that you were a criminal and it really exposes you to everyone because you are crucified naked.

In order to do God's will and to fulfill his mission and help us all, Christ Jesus did all this. And it has got to be the most spectacular example of humility ever. And that is the model that Paul recommends!

Prayer: Christ Jesus, thank you for emptying yourself for me; fill me with yourself. Amen.

8 – Testing and Holding

1 Thessalonians 5:21b — (21b) . . . test everything; hold fast to what is good; . . .

THERE IS SO MUCH you have to go through in school—thousands of pages of reading, hundreds of new ideas, dozens of professors. You have to write papers for which you must select the points you want to make and then assemble the particular data or arguments to support those points. Surveying, gathering, selecting, evaluating, eliminating, keeping, organizing, writing. These are things you do, need to practice, need to get good at, if you are to be a successful student.

This isolated verse seems to be a no-brainer in giving scriptural support to college's demands. This piece of advice is found in what scholars believe to be the very earliest written document to be included in the scriptures of the new movement. The narrative in which these words play their original roll is a familiar one: newly converted to Christianity, the Thessalonian church was struggling with implementing their faith and trying to figure out how to deal with the pressures they experienced from a wider skeptical and sometimes hostile community that was not Christian. They seem to have been doing well with these challenges in general, but had expressed concerns about the fate of brothers and sisters who might die before Christ returns and just when that might be. After responding specifically to these concerns with support and encouragement, Paul finishes the letter with a stream of general advice including the advice to be open to "the words of prophets."

It is specifically about prophecy that Paul writes here, urging his readers to listen to prophets and "test everything" they say and then to "hold fast to what is good." Even if you give this a narrow interpretation and apply it only to those who prophesy as Christians today, that would give you a lot to consider, evaluate, and accept (or reject). It seems like good advice, however, to you as a college student, to apply Paul's recommendation to everything you hear, read, discover. And all of this work is to be done in the expectation of the coming of the Lord Jesus Christ who will finally sort it all out.

Prayer: Jesus, Lord and Teacher, be in my soul and heart and mind as I test and am tested in all things. Amen.

9 – Outside the Box

Hebrews 13:12 — (12) Therefore Jesus also suffered outside the city gate in order to sanctify the people by his own blood.

"OUTSIDE OF THE BOX" is a common way to speak of creativity. Outside of town is something else—at least in a biblical setting. That is where the dead were. That is where the toilet was. That is where Jesus was executed. That was unclean.

The story told by the author of Hebrews is an amazing story—brilliant, creative, suggestive. Unlike anything else in the New Testament. The author wanted to tell the story of Jesus in a new way and for a new audience. The new "way" is very Jewish—that Jesus should be viewed as (i) a priest, and (ii) the sacrifice offered by that priest. But there's more. Jesus was not just another priest; he was the perfect priest; so perfect, in fact, that he only needed to make one sacrifice one time and that would take care of everyone's sins forever. And the sacrifice made by the priest Jesus—himself—had much the same character: one sacrifice, perfect forever.

The new audience was one of Greek philosophical bent, who thought in terms of eternal and perfect "forms" (e.g., the good, the true, the beautiful). Our author was hoping to tell Jesus' story as the story of a perfect priest making a perfect sacrifice in an eternal heavenly temple that would be efficacious for all people of all times and available at every moment right now! Wow.

Still, the story of the human Jesus doing his thing outside of the precincts of the city, where there was a lot of bad stuff, shines through in this verse and reminds us that despite the author's intention to frame Jesus' narrative in traditional Jewish religious (priest, offering) and Greek philosophical categories, Jesus broke the mold and made his saving sacrifice outside the city, hence available to all those—perhaps like you?—who, for whatever reasons, at least sometimes, feel themselves outside of . . . the city, the group, the club . . . .

Prayer: Oh Jesus, thank you for coming to get me because I could never have gotten myself to you. Amen.

10 – Go Slow on the Send Key

James 1:19 — (19) You must understand this, my beloved: let everyone be quick to listen, slow to speak, slow to anger.

YOU PROBABLY KNOW PEOPLE who cannot not talk. They are so obvious in their eagerness to get other people to finish talking so that they can speak. And how often are you motivated to speak—perhaps because you are upset or angry? In the day of "social media" how often have you hit the "send" key in the heat of having to "say" something—a joke, an insult, a curse?

College is a great place to learn a bit of caution from James. He writes an utterly practical letter, full of great advice to help Christians get equipped to live their new lives in Christ. He deals with everything from negotiating social situations that consist of rich and poor to controlling that most dangerous of all your body parts—your tongue!

You want to control anger. He suggests that speaking too quickly, especially letting anger that is within you (for whatever reason) get out, can escalate situations. So slow way down on the speaking stuff.

Speed up, "be quick," on the listening part. If the truth were known, you probably have daydreamed through a lecture, hearing the professor drone on about this or that—what was that anyway?—and because you did not "listen," you did not hear, so you do not know. And so you have nothing to say that would make others want to listen to you.

Listening is so important. It is not just a way to get information: Where is the bathroom? What time is it? What is the third law of thermodynamics? What year was *Brown vs. the Board of Education* decided?

If you listen well, you will get to know other people—some you don't yet know—some you already know, but could know better: that special friend; the author of a favorite book; a total stranger; your dad.

College is a great place to practice this skill—a skill that will come in handy every day. Practicing this enhanced mode of listening (and watching) may even make you more "saintly." At least you will be behaving much like those saints pictured in ancient icons: they have small mouths but very large eyes and ears.

Prayer: Help me be a better listener, to hear the information, to know the speaker, and to be quick about it. Amen.

9 781498 219730